THE COMMON LAW LIBRARY

# GATLEY

## ON

## LIBEL

D1610617

## AND

## SLANDER

First Supplement
to the
Eleventh Edition

Up-to-date until September 2010

**SWEET & MAXWELL**     THOMSON REUTERS

Published in 2010 by Thomson Reuters (Legal) Limited
(Registered in England & Wales, Company No.1679046.
Registered Office and address for service: 100 Avenue Road, London, NW3 3PF)
Trading as Sweet & Maxwell

Typeset by Interactive Sciences Ltd, Gloucester

Printed and bound in Great Britain by Ashford Colour Press, Gosport.

For further information on our products and services, visit:
www.sweetandmaxwell.co.uk

No natural forests were destroyed to make this product. Only farmed timber was used and
replanted.

**A CIP catalogue record for this book is available from the British Library**

| | |
|---|---|
| ISBN Main Work | 978–1–84703–492–2 |
| ISBN Supplement | 978–0–41404–217–9 |

©
Thomson Reuters (Legal) Limited
2010

# JOINT EDITORS

RICHARD PARKES, Q.C., M.A. (CANTAB),
*A Circuit Judge, Bencher of Gray's Inn*

W.V.H. ROGERS, M.A. (CANTAB),
*Senior Fellow at the University of Nottingham,
Barrister of Gray's Inn*

# CONTRIBUTING EDITORS

GODWIN BUSUTTIL, M.A., M.PHIL. (CANTAB),
*Barrister of Lincoln's Inn*

ADAM SPEKER, B.A.
*Barrister of Middle Temple*

CLIVE WALKER, LL.B. (LEEDS), PH.D. (MANCHESTER)
*Professor of Criminal Justice Studies at the
University of Leeds, Solicitor*

# HOW TO USE THIS SUPPLEMENT

This is the First Supplement to the Eleventh Edition of *Gatley on Libel and Slander* and has been compiled according to the structure of the main volume.

At the beginning of each chapter of this Supplement the mini table of contents from the main volume has been included.
Where a heading in this table of contents has been marked with a square pointer (■), this indicates that there is material that is new to the work in the Supplement to which the reader should refer.

Within each chapter, updating information is referenced to the relevant paragraph in the main volume. New paragraphs which have been introduced in this Supplement have been identified as, e.g. 25.19A. This enables references contained within these paragraphs to be identified in the tables included in this Supplement.

# PREFACE

A preface might seem supererogatory for a supplement, but there are two matters which prompt us to write a few words.

This is the first *Gatley* publication since 1998 which has not been guided by Patrick Milmo. We have all missed his counsel, always wise, always charming but also firm, and we should record that he, more than any other, was responsible for pulling the 9th edition into shape after the book had lain untouched for 17 years.

These are interesting times. Some might think that a supplement to a professional book should contain only the "law as it is". But the last year or so has seen a fierce, if not always illuminating, debate (campaign might be a better word, since a common assumption seems to be that the United States model is the only one possible in the modern world) on the shape and role of defamation law. So even though Lord Lester's Defamation Bill is now unlikely to progress because of a government promise of further action in the quite near future, we have included it because it provides a useful focus on these issues.

The primary responsibility for the various parts has been as follows: Godwin Busuttil, Chs 31 to 33; Richard Parkes, Chs 26, 27 and 34 to 37; Horton Rogers, Chs 1 to 23; Adam Speker, Chs 28 to 30 and 38; Clive Walker, Chs 24 and 25 (criminal libel disappeared rather suddenly in the Coroners and Justice Act 2009). David Hirst has updated the damages awards at Appendix 3.

**Richard Parkes**                                      **Horton Rogers**
Winchester                                                    Leeds

October 2010

# TABLE OF CASES

# TABLE OF STATUTES

# TABLE OF STATUTORY INSTRUMENTS

# TABLE OF NATIONAL (NON UK) LEGISLATION

*References in bold indicate where legislation is reproduced in full*

# TABLE OF CIVIL PROCEDURE RULES

# TABLE OF PRACTICE DIRECTIONS

# TABLE OF EUROPEAN AND INTERNATIONAL CONVENTIONS AND TREATIES

# TABLE OF EUROPEAN DIRECTIVES

# INTRODUCTION

## Section 1. Introductory

*Ireland.* The Irish Defamation Bill was passed as the Defamation Act 2009 and **1.4** came into force on January 1, 2010 (Defamation Act 2009 (Commencement) Order, SI 2009/517). In general the provisions are very similar to those of the Bill set out in the Main Work. Various of the provisions are referred to later in this Supplement but the Act may be summarised as follows.

1. Libel and slander are merged into a tort of defamation, which continues to be actionable per se (s.6).
2. There is only one cause of action for the publication of a defamatory statement even if it contains more than one defamatory imputation (e.g. a true innuendo) (s.9).
3. There is a statutory provision on "class libel" which is thought to represent the current Irish and English common law (s.10).
4. There is a single publication rule in cases of multiple publication unless the court orders otherwise in the interests of justice (s.11). But in any event the limitation period of one year (up to two years if the court so directs) runs from the first publication (s.38).
5. The right of corporations to sue is put on a statutory basis and the right exists whether or not the corporation has incurred or is likely to incur financial loss as a result of the publication (s.12).
6. There is provision for rulings on meaning and on whether a meaning is capable of being defamatory (s.14).
7. Justification is renamed truth (s.16).
8. Absolute privilege applies to a statement which would have been regarded as absolutely privileged under the law in force immediately before the commencement of the Act (s.17(1)). Without prejudice to the generality of that, there is a list of twenty three occasions of absolute privilege in s.17(2), e.g. statements made in the Oireachtas, in the course of judicial proceedings, in fair and accurate reports of public court proceedings or in the proceedings and reports of certain tribunals and inquiries.
9. Qualified privilege applies to a statement which would have been regarded as having been made on an occasion of qualified privilege under the law (other than the Defamation Act 1961) in force immediately before

[1]

the commencement of the Act (s.18(1)). Without prejudice to the generality of that, s.18(2) puts the classical *"Toogood v Spyring*/duty and interest" (see Main Work, Ch.14) privilege in statutory form; and s.18(3) and (4) and Sch.1 provide the statutory "reporting" privileges equivalent to those found in Sch.1 of the English Defamation Act 1996 (with the same distinction between statements privileged simpliciter and those privileged subject to explanation or contradiction). Qualified privilege is defeated by malice (s.19). The Act does not contain the provisions which were found in the Bill and which would have replaced malice with a statutory definition of the circumstances in which the protection of privilege was lost.

10. Fair comment is renamed honest opinion. It is for the defendant to show that he held the opinion or, where he is not the author, that he believed the author held it (s.18). For the purpose of distinguishing between allegations of fact and opinion the matters to which the court is to have regard are to include (a) the extent to which the statement is capable of being proved, (b) the extent to which the statement was made in circumstances in which it was likely to have been reasonably understood as a statement of opinion rather than a statement consisting of an allegation of fact; and (c) the words used in the statement and the extent to which the statement was subject to a qualification or a disclaimer or was accompanied by cautionary words (s.21).

11. There is an offer of amends procedure broadly similar to the English one (ss.22 and 23) but the burden on the claimant of defeating the defence if the offer is not accepted is rather less onerous (see Main Work, para.19.6) since the defence is not available if the defendant "knew or ought reasonably to have known" that the statement referred to the plaintiff and was false and defamatory of him (s.23(2)).

12. There is a *"Reynolds* type" defence but not under the label of qualified privilege (s.26).

> "[It is] a defence (to be known, and in this section referred to, as 'the defence of fair and reasonable publication') to a defamation action for the defendant to prove that the statement in respect of which the action was brought was published—
>
>> (*a*) in good faith, and
>> (*b*) in the course of, or for the purposes of, the discussion of a subject of public importance, the discussion of which was for the public benefit, and
>> (*c*) in all the circumstances of the case, it was fair and reasonable to publish the statement."

Some of the relevant specified factors are similar to those in *Reynolds* (s.26(2)). However, the provision in the Bill requiring the defendant to believe the statement to be true (which would have prevented its use in "reportage") was removed.

13. There is provision for a defence of innocent publication, which is broadly similar to the provisions of s.1 of the English Act of 1996 (though rather briefer).

14. There is provision for a declaration of falsity (s.28—note that it is specifically provided that the applicant is not required to prove that the statement is false), payment into court (s.29) and the making of an order requiring the defendant to publish a correction (s.30).
15. There are provisions on the factors to be taken into account in assessing damages (s.31) which reflect the previous general law and s.32 deals with aggravated and exemplary (punitive) damages (the latter being in principle available wherever the defendant knew the statement was untrue or he was reckless).
16. There is provision for summary disposal (s.34).
17. Criminal libel is abolished (s.35).
18. The Act does not affect the operation of the general law in relation to defamation except to the extent that it provides otherwise (either expressly or by necessary implication) (s.3(2)). Hence for example the question of what is defamatory is a matter for the common law.
19. There is to be a review of the operation of the Act not less than five years after its passing (i.e. commencing by July 23, 2014) (s.5(1)).

For the adoption in Canada of a defence of responsible communication on matters of public interest see para.15.23, below.

*The European Convention on Human Rights.* The fact that art.8 of the Conven- **1.5** tion encompasses the protection of reputation as well as privacy is having an impact (so far uncertain) on the English law of defamation: see e.g. para.14.3, below. However, the judgment of the ECtHR in *Karakó v Hungary* (2009), App. no.39311/05 does not, perhaps, clarify this area. Like many ECtHR cases it concerned what we would in the past have called criminal libel but this time the applicant's complaint was that the state had failed to press criminal proceedings to protect his reputation. Since the applicant was a politician, what he complained of was an election flyer criticising his voting record and he had declined to take the civil proceedings which were open to him, this was hardly promising raw material for a grand affirmation of reputation as an art.8 right and it is not surprising that there was held to be no violation. However, what the majority of the court said was this:

"20. In regard to cases in which a violation of the rights guaranteed in Article 8 is asserted and the alleged interference with those rights originates in an expression, the Court points out that the protection granted by the State should be understood as one taking into consideration its obligations under Article 10 of the Convention. It is the latter provision which has been specifically designed by the drafters of the Convention to provide guidance concerning freedom of speech—also a core issue in the present application.

21. In addressing this problem, the Court reiterates that 'private life' includes personal identity (*Von Hannover v. Germany*, no. 59320/00, § 50, ECHR 2004–VI). The Court further observes that the Convention, as interpreted in the *Von Hannover* judgment regarding the individual's image, extends the protection of private life to the protection of personal integrity. This approach itself results from a broad interpretation of Article 8 to encompass notions of personal integrity and the free development of the personality.

22. Concerning the question whether or not the notion of 'private life' should be extended to include reputation as well, the Court notes that the references to personal integrity in the *Von Hannover* judgment reflect a clear distinction, ubiquitous in the private and constitutional law of several Member States, between personal integrity and reputation, the two being protected in different legal ways. In the legislation of several Member States, reputation has traditionally been protected by the law of defamation as a matter related primarily to financial interests or social status.

23. For the Court, personal integrity rights falling within the ambit of Article 8 are unrelated to the external evaluation of the individual, whereas in matters of reputation, that evaluation is decisive: one may lose the esteem of society—perhaps rightly so—but not one's integrity, which remains inalienable. In the Court's case-law, reputation has only been deemed to be an independent right sporadically (see *Petrina v. Romania*, no. 78060/01, 14 October 2008, and *Armonienė v. Lithuania*, no. 36919/02, 25 November 2008) and mostly when the factual allegations were of such a seriously offensive nature that their publication had an inevitable direct effect on the applicant's private life. However, in the instant case, the applicant has not shown that the publication in question, allegedly affecting his reputation, constituted such a serious interference with his private life as to undermine his personal integrity. The Court therefore concludes that it was the applicant's reputation alone which was at stake in the context of an expression made to his alleged detriment.

24. The Court reiterates that paragraph 2 of Article 10 recognises that freedom of speech may be restricted in order to protect reputation (see paragraph 16 above). In other words, the Convention itself announces that restrictions on freedom of expression are to be determined within the framework of Article 10 enshrining freedom of speech.

25. The Court is therefore satisfied that the inherent logic of Article 10, that is to say, the special rule contained in its second paragraph, precludes the possibility of conflict with Article 8. In the Court's view, the expression 'the rights of others' in the latter provision encompasses the right to personal integrity and serves as a ground for limitation of freedom of expression in so far as the interference designed to protect private life is proportionate.

26. It follows that, notwithstanding the fact that the applicant claims a violation of Article 8 of the Convention, the Court has to determine whether the principles inherent to Article 10 were properly applied by the Hungarian authorities."

The nature of the case law of the court and the fact-sensitive nature of freedom of expression cases makes it difficult to attempt too close an analysis of this, but to an English lawyer the distinction drawn between reputation and integrity presents some difficulties. Indeed the word "integrity" does not appear to be being used in what is probably its primary English usage, namely honesty or uprightness. Thus one might say of a prominent political "fixer" that he was someone of little integrity. That would prima facie be defamatory (though no doubt it might also be fair comment). Rather the sense seems to be of "being whole, unimpaired, unviolated", the sense in which we use the word when we speak of "bodily integrity". That of course fits very well in the original, primary context of art.8, namely privacy, which has nothing to do with honesty (see also para.22.3, below). If this is correct the implication may be that art.8 is only engaged where there is an attack on reputation which is very serious. Judge Joceine agreed with the result but in his partly concurring opinion said:

"4. With regard to paragraphs 22 and 23 of the present judgment and especially the question (see paragraph 22), as to whether the notion of 'private life' should be extended to include reputation as well, I think that such a question is unnecessary, because the jurisprudence of the Court has been clearly developed on this point. In the said *Pfeifer v. Austria* case the Court stated: 'It has already been accepted in the Convention organs' case-law that a person's right to protection of his or her reputation is encompassed by Article 8 as being part of the right to respect for private life'.

In another case, *Chauvy and Others v. France* (no. 64915/01, § 70, ECHR 2004-VI), concerning a complaint under Article 10, the Court found that a person's reputation, which was affected by the publication of a book, was protected by Article 8 as part of the right to respect for private life and had to be balanced against the right to freedom of expression. This approach was followed in *Abeberry v. France* ((dec.), no. 58729/00, 21 September 2004) and *Leempoel & S.A. ED. Ciné Revue v. Belgium* (no. 64772/01, § 67, 9 November 2006). I agree that the right to the protection of a person's reputation and honour, as such, was left open in *Gunnarsson v. Iceland* ((dec.), no. 4591/04, 20 October 2005). However, in the *Pfeifer case* (§ 35), the Court came to the conclusion that *a person's reputation*, even if that person is criticised in the context of a public debate, forms *part of his or her personal identity and psychological integrity* and therefore also falls within the scope of his or her 'private life', and Article 8 therefore applies.

5. The same approach was followed in the more recent judgment of *Petrina v. Romania* (no. 78060/01, judgment of 14 October 2008, §§ 28–29), to which the majority make no reference, but where the Court confirmed that a person's reputation is protected by Article 8 of the Convention as an integral part of his or her private life.

Therefore, I think that the question in paragraph 22 of the present judgment is not needed for the reasons explained above. Furthermore, I cannot agree with the majority's position in paragraph 23 that a person's reputation has been deemed to be an independent right only sporadically, or mostly when the factual allegations were of a serious nature. In my opinion, it is clear from the jurisprudence of the Court which I have cited above that a person's reputation falls within the scope of 'private life' and attracts the protection of Article 8, not only sporadically but whenever it is justified according to the circumstances of the concrete case."

From an English point of view the most important point is that the case was interpreted by the Supreme Court in *Guardian News and Media Ltd, Re* [2010] UKSC 1; [2010] 2 W.L.R. 325. This case concerned not defamation but an application by newspapers for the discharge of anonymity orders which had been made in connection with directions made against certain persons under the Terrorism (United Nations Measures) Order 2006, SI 2006/257. However, one of those persons supported the continuation of the anonymity orders on the ground that the disclosure of his name would injure his reputation when he would have no opportunity to defend it because he had not been charged with any criminal offence. Although the orders were all discharged on the ground that in the circumstances the public interest in full reporting of matters of public concern outweighed the art.8 rights of the persons subject to the directions, the SC rejected the newspapers' argument that *Karakó* meant that reputation did not fall within the scope of art.8. Delivering the judgment of the court, Lord Rodger said:

"39. As the European Court's judgment in *Karakó* itself shows, in *Petrina v Romania* (application no 78060/01), 14 October 2008, the court had confirmed, at para 19, that the right to protection of reputation is a right which, as an element of private life, falls within the scope of article 8 ('le droit à la protection de la réputation est un droit qui relève, en tant qu'élément de la vie privée, de l'article 8 de la Convention'). The court had gone on, at para 29, to survey its previous case law, ending up with the statement in *Pfeifer v Austria* (2007) 48 EHRR 175, 183, para 35, that 'a person's reputation, even if that person is criticised in the context of a public debate, forms part of his or her personal identity and psychological integrity . . . '.

40. In *Karakó* the European Court did not depart from that earlier jurisprudence. Rather, it accepted, at para 23, that some attacks on a person's reputation could be of such a seriously offensive nature as to have an inevitable direct effect on the victim's private life. But the court took the view that, on the facts, the applicant had not shown that the publication in question had constituted such a serious interference with his private life as to undermine his personal integrity. That being so, the applicant's reputation alone was at stake in the context of the expression which was said to have damaged it.

41. Contrary to what [counsel] suggested, however, this conclusion did not mean that the court was proceeding on the basis that the applicant's claim in respect of his reputation did not fall within the scope of article 8. That would have been inconsistent with the court's previous case law and would also have made nonsense of the reasoning in paras 24–29 of the judgment. In particular, in paras 24 and 25 the court is concerned with the inter-relationship of articles 8 and 10 in the circumstances. The outcome of that discussion (para 26) is that, even though the applicant is founding on article 8, the court must consider whether the Hungarian authorities properly applied the principles inherent in article 10. The court concludes that they did (para 27). Putting the two strands together, the court goes on to find, in para 28, that the applicant's claim that his reputation as a politician has been harmed is not sustainable under article 8 and that a limitation of his opponent's right to freedom of expression under article 10 would have been disproportionate. That leads, finally, to the conclusion that there has been no violation of article 8.

42. In short, in *Karakó* the European Court was concerned with the application of articles 8 and 10 in a situation where, in the court's view, the applicant had not shown that the attack on his reputation had so seriously interfered with his private life as to undermine his personal integrity. In fact, the court does not mention any specific effects on the applicant's private life. In the present case, however, as already set out at para 21 above, M does explain how he anticipates that his private life would be affected if his identity were revealed. Admittedly, he appears at one point to single out the alleged damage to his reputation. Nevertheless, the Court is really being invited to consider the impact of publication of his name on his reputation as a member of the community in which he lives and the effect that this would have on his relationship with other members of that community. In that situation the alleged effect on his reputation should be regarded as one of the reasons why, he contends, a report that identified him would seriously affect his private life. On that basis the report would engage article 8(1)."

Only a few days before *Karakó*, the ECtHR gave a judgment arising from a particularly serious case of defamation (an imputation of suspicion of double murder) in *A v Norway* (2009) App. no.28070/06 (para.15.4, below). The applicability of art.8 was undisputed but the court said that it saw no reason to hold otherwise. Overall, therefore, it is very difficult to support the statement in para.180 of the explanatory notes to Lord Lester's Defamation Bill (see para.11.12, below) that

"it is unclear from the current case law of the European Court of Human Rights whether the scope of Article 8 includes the protection of reputation as a positive right".

Section 2. Defamation and the Law of Torts

**Trial and remedies.** In Scotland as in England defamation is outside the    **1.11**
general provision for legal aid. In *DW(AP), Petitioner* [2009] CSOH 151 the
Outer House considered the provision for exceptional cases (now the Civil Legal
Aid for Defamation and Verbal Injury Proceedings Direction 2008, which is
similar to the English Exceptional Funding criteria). See further para.26.2,
below.

**Freedom of expression, the media and defamation.** *Lord Lester's Defama-*    **1.12**
*tion Bill.* In May 2010 Lord Lester introduced a Defamation Bill (Defamation
Bill (HL) 2010–11). During the Second Reading on July 9, 2010 the Government
intimated that there would be consultation which it was hoped would lead to a
Government draft Bill in the next session. There is therefore no prospect of the
current Bill becoming law but it would not be surprising, especially in view of
the shortness of the proposed time scale, if the Government draft reflected many
provisions of it. Accordingly its text is reproduced here and it is referred to at
various points below. In the period before the introduction of the Bill there were
a number of reports with some degree of official status which initiated discussion
and/or made proposals on a number of aspects of defamation, some of which are
reflected in the Bill.

- The Ministry of Justice in September 2009 published a consultation paper
  on the multiple publication rule and the internet and provisionally concluded
  in March 2010 that there should be a single publication rule instead.
- After a consultation paper on conditional fee success payments in defamation cases the Ministry of Justice concluded that these should be limited to
  10 per cent. However, this proposal did not go through and the issue has
  now been subsumed in the general consideration of Lord Justice Jackson's
  *Review of Civil Litigation Costs* (2009).
- In February 2010 the House of Commons Culture, Media and Sport Committee produced its report, *Press Standards, Privacy and Libel* (Second
  Report of Session 2009–10 HC 362–1). This considered, among other
  things, the *Reynolds* defence, corporations, fair comment and multiple
  publication.
- A Libel Working Group appointed by the Justice Secretary reported in
  March 2010 on *Reynolds*, multiple publication, "libel tourism" and proce-
  dural issues.

The Defamation Bill
HL Bill 3 55/1

**Defamation Bill [HL]**

CONTENTS

*Defences*

1 Responsible publication on matters of public interest
2 Honest opinion
3 Establishing a defence of honest opinion

*Defences*

## 1 Responsible publication on matters of public interest

(1) Any defendant in an action for defamation has a defence if the defendant shows that—

(a) the words or matters complained of were published for the purposes of, or otherwise in connection with, the discussion of a matter of public interest; and

(b) the defendant acted responsibly in making the publication.

(2) Subsection (1) applies irrespective of whether the publication contains statements of fact or inferences or opinions.

(3) The court when deciding for the purposes of subsection (1)(b) whether the defendant has acted responsibly must have regard to all the circumstances of the case.

(4) Those circumstances may include (among other things)—

    (a) the nature of the publication and its context;

    (b) the nature and seriousness of anything alleged about the claimant;

    (c) what information the defendant had before publication;

    (d) what steps (if any) were taken by the defendant to verify what was published;

    (e) if appropriate, whether the defendant gave the claimant an opportunity to comment before publication;

    (f) whether there were factors supporting urgent publication;

    (g) the extent of the defendant's compliance with any relevant code of conduct or other relevant guidelines; or

    (h) whether subsection (5) applies.

(5) Where a publication reports accurately and impartially on a pre-existing matter (for example, that there is a dispute between two parties), a defendant may be regarded as acting responsibly to the extent that the court is satisfied that it is in the public interest for the existence of that matter, and anything reported in connection with it, to be the subject of a report or series of reports.

(6) In determining for the purposes of subsection (5) whether publication is in the public interest, the court may disregard any question as to the truth of anything reported in connection with a pre-existing matter.

## 2 Honest opinion

In an action for defamation, the defence known before the commencement of this section as the defence of fair comment is, after commencement, to be known as the defence of honest opinion.

## 3 Establishing a defence of honest opinion

(1) A defendant has a defence of honest opinion in an action for defamation if the defendant shows that Conditions 1 to 4 are satisfied (subject to subsections (7) and (8)).

(2) Condition 1 is that the words or matters complained of relate to a matter of public interest.

(3) Condition 2 is that, in the circumstances in which the words or matters are published, an ordinary person would reasonably consider those words or matters to be an opinion.

(4) Condition 3 is that, at the time of publication, there existed—

    (a) one or more facts;

    (b) any material that falls within section 1 (responsible publication on matters of public interest);

    (c) any material that falls within section 6, 7 or 8 (statutory privilege); or

    (d) any material that is otherwise protected by privilege.

(5) Condition 4 is that an honest person could form the opinion on the basis of the facts or material shown by the defendant in satisfying Condition 3.

(6) In relation to the facts or material relied on by the defendant as providing a basis for the opinion, no account is to be taken of—

   (a) anything that the defendant does not show, provided that the defendant shows that Condition 4 is satisfied on the basis of what is shown;

   (b) whether the defendant first learned of the facts or material before or after publication; or

   (c) whether the facts or material were or were not included (by reference or otherwise) in the publication.

(7) There is no defence of honest opinion if the claimant shows that the defendant did not in fact hold the opinion.

(8) Where the defendant was not the author ("A") of the words or matters complained of, there is no defence of honest opinion if the claimant shows that—

   (a) the defendant knew that A did not in fact hold the opinion; or

   (b) the defendant had reason to believe that A did not in fact hold the opinion and published without determining whether or not A did hold it.

## 4 Truth

In an action for defamation, the defence known before the commencement of this section as the defence of justification is, after commencement, to be known as the defence of truth.

## 5 Establishing a defence of truth

(1) A defendant has a defence of truth in an action for defamation if the words or matters complained of are substantially true.

(2) For these purposes, the defendant may show either that—

   (a) the meaning (or meanings) alleged by the claimant are substantially true; or

   (b) the words or matters complained of have a less serious meaning (or meanings) and each such meaning is substantially true.

(3) A defence of justification does not fail only because a particular meaning alleged by the claimant is not shown as being substantially true, if that meaning would not materially injure the claimant's reputation having regard to the truth of what the defendant has shown to be substantially true.

(4) Where—

   (a) the words or matters complained of make two or more distinct allegations; and

   (b) the truth of every allegation is not shown;

a defence of justification does not fail only because of paragraph (b) if anything not shown to be true does not materially injure the claimant's reputation having regard to the truth of the remaining allegations.

*Statutory privilege*

## 6 Reports of court proceedings protected by absolute privilege

(1) A fair and accurate report of proceedings in public before a court to which this section applies, if published contemporaneously with the proceedings, is absolutely privileged.

(2) A report of proceedings which by an order of the court, or as a consequence of any statutory provision, is required to be postponed is to be treated as published contemporaneously if it is published as soon as practicable after publication is permitted.

(3) This section applies to—

  (a) any court in the United Kingdom;
  (b) the European Court of Justice or any court attached to that court;
  (c) the European Court of Human Rights;
  (d) any international criminal tribunal established by the Security Council of the United Nations or by an international agreement to which the United Kingdom is a party;
  (e) any court established under the law of a country or territory outside the United Kingdom;
  (f) the Inter-American Court of Human Rights;
  (g) the African Court of Human and People's Rights;
  (h) the International Court of Justice; and
  (i) any other judicial or arbitral tribunal deciding matters in dispute between States.

In paragraph (a) "court" includes any tribunal or body exercising the judicial power of the State.

## 7 Reports etc of certain Parliamentary matters protected by absolute privilege

(1) The following are absolutely privileged—

  (a) a fair and accurate report of proceedings in Parliament;
  (b) a fair and accurate report of anything published by or on the authority of Parliament; and
  (c) a fair and accurate copy of, extract from or summary of anything published by or on the authority of Parliament.

(2) The court must stay any proceedings where the defendant shows that—

  (a) the proceedings relate to the publication of anything that falls within paragraph (a), (b) or (c) of subsection (1); or
  (b) the proceedings seek to prevent or postpone the making of any such publication.

(3) This section also has effect in relation to the Welsh Assembly and the Northern Ireland Assembly (and any reference to Parliament is to be read as a reference to the Assembly in question).

**8 Other reports etc protected by qualified privilege**

(1) The publication of any report or other statement mentioned in Schedule 1 to this Act is privileged unless the publication is shown to be made with malice, subject as follows.

(2) In an action for defamation in respect of the publication of a report or other statement mentioned in Part 2 of Schedule 1, there is no defence under this section if the claimant shows that the defendant—

(a) was requested by the claimant to publish in a suitable manner a reasonable letter or statement by way of explanation or contradiction; and

(b) refused or neglected to do so without sufficient cause.

(3) For this purpose "in a suitable manner" means in the same manner as the publication complained of or in a manner that is adequate and reasonable in the circumstances.

(4) This section does not apply to the publication to the public, or a section of the public, of matter which is not of public concern and the publication of which is not for the public benefit.

(5) Nothing in this section is to be construed—

(a) as protecting the publication of matter the publication of which is prohibited by law; or

(b) as limiting or abridging any privilege subsisting apart from this section.

*Publication*

**9 Responsibility for publication**

(1) Any defendant in an action for defamation has a defence if the defendant shows that the defendant's only involvement in the publication of the words or matters complained of—

(a) is as a facilitator; or

(b) is as a broadcaster of a live programme in circumstances in which it was not reasonably foreseeable that those words or matters would be published.

(2) Any defendant in an action for defamation, apart from a primary publisher, has a defence unless the claimant shows that—

(a) the notice requirements specified in subsection (3) have been complied with;

(b) the notice period specified in subsection (4) has expired; and

(c) the words or matters complained of have not been removed from the publication.

(3) The notice requirements are that the substance of the claimant's complaint must be communicated in writing to the defendant, specifying—

(a) the words or matters complained of and the person (or persons) to whom they relate;
(b) the publication that contains those words or matters;
(c) why the claimant considers the words or matters to be defamatory;
(d) the details of any matters relied on in the publication which the claimant considers to be untrue; and
(e) why the claimant considers the words or matters to be harmful in the circumstances in which they were published.

(4) The notice period is—

(a) the period of 14 days starting with the date of receipt by the defendant of all the information required by subsection (3); or
(b) such other period as the court may specify (whether of its own motion or on an application by any party to the action).

(5) Employees or agents of a primary publisher, or other person who publishes the words or matters complained of, are in the same position as their principal to the extent that they are responsible for the content of what is published or the decision to publish it.

(6) In this section—
"facilitator" means a person who is concerned only with the transmission or storage of the content of the publication and has no other influence or control over it; and
"primary publisher" means an author, an editor or a person who exercises effective control of an author or editor.

(7) For the purposes of the definition of "primary publisher" in subsection (6)—
"author" means—

(a) a person who originates the words or matters complained of; but
(b) does not include a person who does not intend that they be published; and

"editor", in relation to a publication, means a person with editorial or equivalent responsibility for the content of the publication or the decision to publish it.

(8) This section does not apply to any cause of action which arose before the section came into force.

## 10 Multiple publications

(1) In any case to which subsection (2) applies—

(a) the first occasion on which the publication is made available to the public generally (or to any section of the public) is to be regarded for all purposes as the date of publication of each subsequent publication; and
(b) in an action for defamation based on any publication to which this section applies, the cause of action is to be treated as having accrued on that date.

(2) This subsection applies to any publication (such as a book, newspaper, periodical or material in an archive) which—

(a) is published by the same person on multiple occasions; and

(b) on each occasion, has the same, or substantially the same, content.

(3) Subsection (2) does not apply where a subsequent publication is made in a materially different manner, but this is without prejudice to that publication itself constituting a first publication for the purposes of subsection (1).

*Cause of action*

### 11 Action for defamation brought by body corporate

A body corporate which seeks to pursue an action for defamation must show that the publication of the words or matters complained of has caused, or is likely to cause, substantial financial loss to the body corporate.

### 12 Striking out where claimant suffers no substantial harm

(1) The court must strike out an action for defamation unless the claimant shows that—

(a) the publication of the words or matters complained of has caused substantial harm to the claimant's reputation; or

(b) it is likely that such harm will be caused to the claimant's reputation by the publication.

(2) Subsection (1) does not apply if, in exceptional circumstances, the court is satisfied that it would be in the interests of justice not to strike out the action.

(3) In determining whether a claimant's reputation is or may be substantially harmed, the court must have regard to all the circumstances of the case.

(4) An order under subsection (1) may be made by the court of its own motion or on an application by any party to the action.

(5) Subsection (1) does not limit any power to strike out proceedings which is exercisable apart from this section.

### 13 Harmful event in cases of publication outside the jurisdiction

(1) This section applies in an action for defamation where the court is satisfied that the words or matters complained of have also been published outside the jurisdiction (including publication outside the jurisdiction of any words or matters that differ only in ways not affecting their substance).

(2) No harmful event is to be regarded as having occurred in relation to the claimant unless the publication in the jurisdiction can reasonably be regarded as having caused substantial harm to the claimant's reputation having regard to the extent of publication elsewhere.

*Trial by jury*

### 14 Reversal of presumption of trial by a jury in defamation proceedings

In section 69(1)(b) of the Senior Courts Act 1981 (trial by jury) omit the words "libel, slander".

## 15 Determining an application for trial by a jury

(1) If the court is satisfied that it is in the interests of justice to do so, it may order trial by jury of such matter or matters arising in an action for defamation as are specified in the order.

(2) An order under subsection (1) may be made on an application by any party to the action and the court determining the application must have regard to all the circumstances of the case.

(3) Those circumstances may include (among other things)—

    (a) whether there is a public interest in the subject matter of the action or anything arising in connection with it;

    (b) the identity of any of the parties to the action;

    (c) any office or other position held by any party to the action;

    (d) whether it is in the interests of justice that the verdict of a jury or a reasoned judgment be obtained on any matter arising in the action;

    (e) the extent to which early resolution of any matter (for example, as to the meaning of the words complained of) is likely to facilitate settlement of the action, improve active case management or assist in achieving a just and equitable outcome; and

    (f) whether the trial is likely to require the prolonged examination of documents or accounts or any scientific or local investigation which cannot conveniently be made with a jury.

(4) An application must be made in accordance with such procedure as may be prescribed by rules of court.

*Evidence concerning proceedings in Parliament*

## 16 Evidence concerning proceedings in Parliament

(1) In this section "the relevant protection", in relation to the proceedings of either House of Parliament, means the protection of any enactment or rule of law which prevents proceedings in Parliament being impeached or questioned in any court or place out of Parliament.

(2) The Speaker of either House of Parliament may, in accordance with Standing Orders of that House, by notice in writing waive the application of the relevant protection to such proceedings in an action for defamation as are specified in that notice.

(3) Where the relevant protection is waived in relation to any proceedings in an action for defamation—

    (a) that protection is not to apply to prevent evidence being given, questions being asked or statements, submissions, comments or findings being made in those proceedings; and

    (b) none of those things is to be regarded as infringing the privilege of either House of Parliament.

(4) Nothing in this section affects any enactment or rule of law so far as it protects a person from legal liability for words spoken or things done in the course of, or for the purposes of or incidental to, any proceedings in Parliament.

(5) Without prejudice to the generality of subsection (4), that subsection applies to—

    (a) the giving of evidence before either House or a committee;

    (b) the presentation or submission of a document to either House or a committee;

    (c) the preparation of a document for the purposes of or incidental to the transacting of any such business;

    (d) the formulation, making or publication of a document, including a report, by or pursuant to an order of either House or a committee; and

    (e) any communication with the Parliamentary Commissioner for Standards or any person having functions in connection with the registration of members' interests. In this subsection "a committee" means a committee of either House or a joint committee of both Houses of Parliament.

*Miscellaneous and supplementary*

**17 Interpretation**

(1) In this Act—

"the 1996 Act" means the Defamation Act 1996;

"archive" includes any collection of sound recordings, images or other information however stored (including by electronic means);

"author" has the meaning given in section 9;

"publication" and "publish", in relation to a statement, have the meaning they have for the purposes of the law of defamation generally but "primary publisher" is specially defined for the purposes of section 9;

"statement" means words, pictures, visual images, gestures or any other method of signifying meaning;

"statutory provision" means—

    (a) a provision contained in an Act or in subordinate legislation within the meaning of the Interpretation Act 1978;

    (b) a provision contained in an Act of the Scottish Parliament or in an instrument made under such an Act; or

    (c) a statutory provision within the meaning of the Interpretation Act (Northern Ireland) 1954.

(2) In this Act any reference to—

    (a) a defendant in an action for defamation includes any person against whom a counterclaim for defamation is brought; and

    (b) an action for defamation is to be construed accordingly.

**18 Minor and consequential provision**

Schedule 2 contains minor and consequential amendments.

**19 Repeals**

Schedule 3 contains repeals.

**20 Extent**

(1) This Act extends to England, Wales and Northern Ireland.
(2) An amendment or repeal contained in this Act has the same extent as the enactment to which it relates.
(3) Subsection (2) does not apply to any amendment or repeal of an enactment which extends to Scotland.

**21 Commencement**

(1) The following provisions of this Act come into force on the day this Act is passed—

  (a) section 20;
  (b) this section; and
  (c) section 22.

(2) The other provisions of this Act come into force on such day as may be appointed by order of the Secretary of State; and different days may be appointed for different purposes.
(3) Any such order is to be made by statutory instrument.

**22 Short title**

This Act may be cited as the Defamation Act 2010.

SCHEDULES

SCHEDULE 1 Section 8

QUALIFIED PRIVILEGE

PART 1

*Statements having qualified privilege without explanation or contradiction*

  1 A fair and accurate report of proceedings in public of a legislature anywhere in the world.
  2 A fair and accurate report of—

  (a) proceedings in public before a court anywhere in the world;
  (b) any statements or submissions which, for the purposes of any such proceedings, are made by, or on behalf of, any of the parties.

  3 A fair and accurate report of proceedings in public of a person appointed to hold a public inquiry by a government or legislature anywhere in the world.
  4 A fair and accurate report of proceedings in public anywhere in the world of an international organisation or an international conference.
  5 A fair and accurate copy of or extract from any register or other document required by law to be open to public inspection.
  6 A notice or advertisement published by or on the authority of a court, or of a judge or officer of a court, anywhere in the world.
  7 A fair and accurate copy of, extract from or summary of matter published by or on the authority of a government or legislature anywhere in the world.

8 A fair and accurate copy of, extract from or summary of matter published anywhere in the world by an international organisation or an international conference.

PART 2

*Statements privileged subject to explanation or contradiction*

9 (1) A fair and accurate copy of, extract from or summary of, a notice or other matter issued for the information of the public by or on behalf of—

(a) a legislature in the United Kingdom or another member State;
(b) a legislature in any other country or territory;
(c) the government of the United Kingdom or another member State;
(d) the government of any other country or territory;
(e) the European Parliament;
(f) the European Commission;
(g) an authority anywhere in the world which performs governmental functions;
(h) an international organisation or international conference.

(2) In this paragraph "governmental functions" includes—

(a) police functions; and
(b) functions performed by a public authority within the meaning of section 6 of the Human Rights Act 1998.

10 A fair and accurate copy of, extract from or summary of a document made available by—

(a) a court in the United Kingdom or another member State;
(b) a court in any other country or territory;
(c) any court attached to a court falling within sub-paragraph (a) or (b);
(d) a judge or officer of any court falling within any of sub-paragraphs (a) to (c).

11 A fair and accurate copy of, extract from or summary of material in an archive where—

(a) the material has been publicly available online for a period of at least 12 months starting with the date of first publication by or on behalf of the archive; and
(b) in the course of that period, no challenge has been made, whether in the courts or otherwise, which indicates that the material is considered to be defamatory.

12 (1) A fair and accurate report of proceedings at any public meeting or sitting in the United Kingdom of—

(a) a local authority or local authority committee;
(b) in the case of a local authority which are operating executive arrangements, the executive of that authority or a committee of that executive;

(c) a justice or justices of the peace acting otherwise than as a court exercising judicial authority;

(d) a commission, tribunal, committee or person appointed for the purposes of any inquiry by any statutory provision, by Her Majesty or by a Minister of the Crown, a member of the Scottish Executive, the Welsh Ministers or the Counsel General to the Welsh Assembly Government, or a Northern Ireland Department;

(e) a person appointed by a local authority to hold a local inquiry in pursuance of any statutory provision;

(f) any other tribunal, board, committee or body constituted by or under, and exercising functions under, any statutory provision.

(2) In the case of a local authority which are operating executive arrangements, a fair and accurate record of any decision made by any member of the executive where that record is required to be made and available for public inspection by virtue of section 22 of the Local Government Act 2000 or of any provision in regulations made under that section.

(3) In sub-paragraphs (1)(a) and (b) and (2)—
"local authority" means—

(a) in relation to England and Wales, a principal council within the meaning of the Local Government Act 1972, any body falling within any paragraph of section 100J(1) of that Act or an authority or body to which the Public Bodies (Admission to Meetings) Act 1960 applies;

(b) in relation to Scotland, a council constituted under section 2 of the Local Government etc. (Scotland) Act 1994 or an authority or body to which the Public Bodies (Admission to Meetings) Act 1960 applies;

(c) in relation to Northern Ireland, any authority or body to which sections 23 to 27 of the Local Government Act (Northern Ireland) 1972 apply; and

"local authority committee" means any committee of a local authority or of local authorities, and includes—

(a) any committee or sub-committee in relation to which sections 100A to 100D of the Local Government Act 1972 apply by virtue of section 100E of that Act (whether or not also by virtue of section 100J of that Act); and

(b) any committee or sub-committee in relation to which sections 50A to 50D of the Local Government (Scotland) Act 1973 apply by virtue of section 50E of that Act.

(4) In sub-paragraphs (1) and (2) "executive" and "executive arrangements" have the same meaning as in Part 2 of the Local Government Act 2000.

(5) A fair and accurate report of any corresponding proceedings in—

(a) any of the Channel Islands or the Isle of Man;

(b) another member State; or

(c) any other country or territory.

13 (1) A fair and accurate report of proceedings at any public meeting held in the United Kingdom, in another member State or in any other country or territory.

(2) In this paragraph a "public meeting" means a meeting bona fide and lawfully held for a lawful purpose and for the furtherance or discussion of a matter of public concern, whether admission to the meeting is general or restricted.

14 A fair and accurate report of proceedings at a press conference given—

(a) by or on behalf of any body, officer or other person falling within this Schedule or designated under it; and

(b) in respect of published material to which qualified privilege applies by virtue of section 8.

15 (1) A fair and accurate report of proceedings at a general meeting of a UK public company or an overseas company.

(2) A fair and accurate copy of, extract from or summary of any document circulated to members of a UK public company or of an overseas company—

(a) by or with the authority of the board of directors of the company;

(b) by the auditors of the company; or

(c) by any member of the company in pursuance of a right conferred by any statutory provision.

(3) A fair and accurate copy of, extract from or summary of any document circulated to members of a UK public company or of an overseas company, which relates to the appointment, resignation, retirement or dismissal of directors of the company.

(4) In this paragraph—
"overseas company" means—

(a) a company incorporated outside the United Kingdom; and

(b) any other body corporate formed under the law of another member State or any other country or territory; and

"UK public company" means—

(a) a public company within the meaning of section 4(2) of the Companies Act 2006 or Article 12(3) of the Companies (Northern Ireland) Order 1986 (S.I. 1986/1032 (N.I. 6)); or

(b) a body corporate incorporated by or registered under any other statutory provision, or by Royal Charter, or formed in pursuance of letters patent.

(5) A fair and accurate report of proceedings at any corresponding meeting of, or copy of or extract from any corresponding document circulated to members of, a public company formed under the law of—

(a) any of the Channel Islands or the Isle of Man;

(b) another member State; or

(c) any other country or territory.

16 A fair and accurate report of any finding or decision of any of the following descriptions of association, formed in the United Kingdom, another member State or any other country or territory, or of any committee or governing body of such an association—

(a) an association formed for the purpose of promoting or encouraging the exercise of or interest in any art, science, religion or learning, and empowered by its constitution to exercise control over or adjudicate on matters of interest or concern to the association, or the actions or conduct of any person subject to such control or adjudication;

(b) an association formed for the purpose of promoting or safeguarding the interests of any trade, business, industry or profession, or of the persons carrying on or engaged in any trade, business, industry or profession, and empowered by its constitution to exercise control over or adjudicate upon matters connected with that trade, business, industry or profession, or the actions or conduct of those persons;

(c) an association formed for the purpose of promoting or safeguarding the interests of a game, sport or pastime to the playing or exercise of which members of the public are invited or admitted, and empowered by its constitution to exercise control over or adjudicate upon persons connected with or taking part in the game, sport or pastime;

(d) an association formed for the purpose of promoting charitable objects or other objects beneficial to the community and empowered by its constitution to exercise control over or to adjudicate on matters of interest or concern to the association, or the actions or conduct of any person subject to such control or adjudication.

17 (1) A fair and accurate report of, copy of, extract from or summary of, any adjudication, report, statement or notice issued by a body, officer or other person designated for the purposes of this paragraph—

(a) for England and Wales or Northern Ireland, by order of the Lord Chancellor; and

(b) for Scotland, by order of the Secretary of State.

(2) An order under this paragraph is to be made by statutory instrument which is subject to annulment in pursuance of a resolution of either House of Parliament.

PART 3

*Supplementary provisions*

18 (1) In this Schedule—
"court" includes—

(a) the European Court of Justice (or any court attached to that court) and the Court of Auditors of the European Communities;

(b) the European Court of Human Rights;

(c) any international criminal tribunal established by the Security Council of the United Nations or by an international agreement to which the United Kingdom is a party;

(d) the International Court of Justice and any other judicial or arbitral tribunal deciding matters in dispute between States; and

(e) any tribunal or body exercising the judicial power of the State;

"international conference" means a conference attended by representatives of two or more governments;

"international organisation" means an organisation of which two or more governments are members, and includes any committee or other subordinate body of such an organisation; and

"legislature" includes a local legislature.

(2) References in this Schedule to the United Kingdom or another member State include any European dependent territory of the United Kingdom or other member State.

(3) In paragraphs 1, 3 and 7 "legislature" includes the European Parliament.

19 (1) Provision may be made by order identifying—

(a) for the purposes of paragraph 12, the corresponding proceedings referred to in sub-paragraph (5);

(b) for the purposes of paragraph 15, the corresponding meetings and documents referred to in sub-paragraph (5).

(2) An order under this paragraph may be made—

(a) for England and Wales or Northern Ireland, by the Lord Chancellor; and

(b) for Scotland, by the Secretary of State.

(3) An order under this paragraph is to be made by statutory instrument which is subject to annulment in pursuance of a resolution of either House of Parliament.

SCHEDULE 2 Section 18

MINOR AND CONSEQUENTIAL AMENDMENTS

*Parliamentary Papers Act 1840*

1 The Parliamentary Papers Act 1840 ceases to have effect.

*Defamation Act 1952*

2 The Defamation Act 1952 is amended in accordance with paragraphs 3 to 5.

3 Omit section 5 (justification).

4 Omit section 6 (fair comment).

5 Omit section 9(1) (extension of certain defences to broadcasting).

*Rehabilitation of Offenders Act 1974*

6 In section 8(6) of the Rehabilitation of Offenders Act 1974 (defamation actions: reports of court proceedings), for "section 14 of the Defamation Act 1996" substitute "section 6 of the Defamation Act 2010".

*Rehabilitation of Offenders (Northern Ireland) Order 1978 (S.I. 1978/1908 (N.I.27))*

7 In Article 9(6) of the Rehabilitation of Offenders (Northern Ireland) Order 1978 (defamation actions: reports of court proceedings), for "section 14 of the Defamation Act 1996" substitute "section 6 of the Defamation Act 2010".

*Limitation Act 1980*

8 For section 4A of the Limitation Act 1980 (time limit for actions for defamation or malicious falsehood) substitute—

**"4A Time limit for actions for defamation or malicious false hood**

(1) The time limit under section 2 of this Act shall not apply to an action for—

(a) libel or slander, or

(b) slander of title, slander of goods or other malicious falsehood,

but no such action shall be brought after the expiration of one year from the date on which the cause of action accrued.

(2) In any case to which section 10 of the Defamation Act 2010 (multiple publications) applies, the date on which a cause of action in libel or slander shall be treated as having accrued is the date of first publication referred to in that section.".

9 For section 32A of the Limitation Act 1980 (discretionary exclusion of time limit for actions for defamation or malicious falsehood) substitute—

**"32A Discretionary exclusion of time limit for actions for defamation or malicious falsehood**

(1) If it appears to the court that it would be in the interests of justice to allow an action to proceed notwithstanding that the period of limitation has expired, the court may direct that section 4A(1) shall not apply to the action or shall not apply to any specified cause of action to which the action relates.

(2) In acting under this section the court shall have regard to all the circumstances of the case and in particular to—

(a) the length of, and the reasons for, any delay in bringing the action;

(b) where the reason or one of the reasons for delay was that all or any of the facts relevant to the cause of action did not become known to the claimant until after the end of the period mentioned in section 4A(1)—

(i) the date on which any such facts did become known to the claimant, and

(ii) the extent to which the claimant acted promptly and reasonably once the claimant knew whether or not the facts in question might be capable of giving rise to an action;

(c) the extent to which, having regard to the delay, relevant evidence is likely—

(i) to be unavailable, or

(ii) to be less cogent than if the action had been brought within the period mentioned in section 4A(1); and

(d) in relation only to an action that falls within section 4A(2)—

(i) any material change of circumstances since the date of first publication, and

(ii) whether the defendant, has without sufficient cause, refused or neglected to comply with any reasonable request by the claimant to remove or correct any inaccuracy in the publication or to publish in a suitable manner a reasonable letter or statement by way of explanation or contradiction.

(3) In the case of an action for slander of title, slander of goods or other malicious falsehood brought by a personal representative—

(a) the references in subsection (2) to the claimant shall be construed as including the deceased person to whom the cause of action accrued and any previous personal representative of that person; and

(b) nothing in section 28(3) of this Act shall be construed as affecting the court's discretion under this section.

(4) In this section "the court" means the court in which the action has been brought.".

*Limitation (Northern Ireland) Order 1989 (S.I. 1989/1339 (N.I.11))*

10 The Limitation (Northern Ireland) Order 1989 is amended in accordance with paragraphs 11 and 12.

11 In article 6 (time limit: certain actions founded on tort) after paragraph (2) insert—

"(2A) In any case to which section 10 of the Defamation Act 2010 (multiple publications) applies, the date on which a cause of action in libel or slander shall be treated as having accrued is the date of first publication referred to in that section.".

12 In article 51 (court's power to override time limit: actions for defamation or malicious falsehood), at the end of paragraph (2)(c) insert "and (d) in relation only to an action that falls within article 6(2A)—

(i) any material change of circumstances since the date of first publication, and

(ii) whether the defendant, has without sufficient cause, refused or neglected to comply with any reasonable request by the claimant to remove or correct any inaccuracy in the publication or to publish in a suitable manner a reasonable letter or statement by way of explanation or contradiction.".

*Defamation Act 1996*

13 In the Defamation Act 1996, omit the following provisions—

    (a) section 1 (responsibility for publication);
    (b) section 13 (evidence concerning proceedings in Parliament);
    (c) section 14 (reports of court proceedings absolutely privileged);
    (d) section 15 (reports etc protected by qualified privilege);
    (e) Schedule 1 (qualified privilege).

**Libel as a crime.** The crime of defamatory libel in England, Wales and **1.13** Northern Ireland was abolished by s.73(b) of the Coroners and Justice Act 2009, which came into force on January 12, 2010 (s.182(2)(a)). Consequential amendments are made to, inter alia, the Libel Act 1843, the Newspaper Libel and Registration Act 1881, the Law of Libel Amendment Act 1888, the Defamation Act 1952, the Theatres Act 1968, the Broadcasting Act 1990, the Defamation Act 1996 and the Legal Deposit Libraries Act 2003; and the Libel Act 1792 is repealed (Sch.23, Pt.2). The crime was also abolished in Ireland by s.35 of the Defamation Act 2009.

SECTION 2. DEFAMATION AND THE LAW OF TORTS

*Verbal torts and interests. Note 217.* In *Ballard v Multiplex Ltd* [2008] **1.20** NSWSC 1019 the principle that damages in conspiracy do not cover loss of reputation was applied.

CHAPTER 2

# DEFAMATORY IMPUTATIONS

**2.1**　The various "definitions" of what is defamatory were reviewed by Tugendhat J. in *Thornton v Telegraph Media Group Ltd* [2010] EWHC 1414 (QB); [2010] E.M.L.R. 25 at [27]–[35]. He suggested as a possible ordering of defamation cases the following:

> "[33] . . . i) There are two main varieties of each of the torts of libel and slander: (A) personal defamation, where there are imputations as to the character or attributes of an individual and (B) business or professional defamation, where the imputation is as to an attribute of an individual, a corporation, a trade union, a charity, or similar body, and that imputation is as to the way the profession or business is conducted. These varieties are not mutually exclusive: the same words may carry both varieties of imputation. By contrast, if the imputation is as to the product of the business or profession, then it will be the tort of malicious falsehood, not defamation, to which the claimant must look for any remedy.
>
> ii) Personal defamation comes in a number of sub-varieties including: a) Imputations as to what is 'illegal, mischievous, or sinful' in Pollock CB's phrase . . . This would perhaps now be expressed as what is illegal, or unethical or immoral, or socially harmful, but will now cover imputations which are less serious than that . . . ; b) Imputations as to something which is not voluntary, or the result of the claimant's conscious act or choice, but rather a misfortune for which no direct moral responsibility can be placed upon the claimant (such as disease . . . ); c) Imputations which ridicule the claimant . . . .
>
> iii) Business or professional defamation also comes in a number of sub-varieties . . . : a) Imputations upon a person, firm or other body who provides goods or services that the goods or services are below a required standard in some respect which is likely to cause adverse consequences to the customer, patient or client. In these cases there may be only a limited role for the opinion or attitude of right-thinking members of society, because the required standard will usually be one that is set by the professional body or a regulatory authority; b) Imputations upon a person, firm or body which may deter other people from providing any financial support that may be needed, or from accepting employment, or otherwise dealing with them. In these cases there may be more of a role for the opinion or attitude of right-thinking members of society.
>
> [34] In addition to these varieties, there is a distinction between sub-varieties of business defamation in which: (a) The action is brought by an individual, where damage may include injury to feelings, and (b) The action is brought by a corporation, where damage cannot include injury to feelings."

16

The learned judge also considered that there was

"a further reason why cases of business defamation require separate consideration, whether or not there is a separate tort of 'business defamation'. What is at stake in a defamation reflecting on a person's character is now likely to be recognised as engaging that person's rights under Art 8. On the other hand, if an alleged defamation engages only a person's professional attributes, then what is at stake is less likely to engage their rights under Art 8, but may engage only their commercial or property rights (which are Convention rights, if at all, under Art 1 of the First Protocol) . . . However, neither party advanced submissions to me on the basis of Art 8. So it is not necessary to consider that aspect of the matter further" (at [38]).

See further on "business" cases para.2.26, below.

The question whether any distinction is to be drawn between statements damaging to professional or business reputation and others was considered by the High Court of Australia in *Radio 2UE Sydney Pty Ltd v Chesterton* [2009] HCA 16. The imputations relevant to the appeal were that the plaintiff (a) was a bombastic, beer-bellied buffoon, (b) was not to be taken seriously as a journalist and (c) had been fired by Radio 2UE. In her direction the trial judge had drawn a distinction between these imputations and others which said "something personal" about the plaintiff ((a) seems not to have been regarded as falling into that category). With regard to the "personal" imputations the jury were directed to ask whether they "would be regarded by ordinary right-thinking members of the community as defamatory, as damaging to his reputation"; but with regard to the imputations involved in the appeal the direction was that they were "concerned with [the plaintiff's] reputation in his profession as a journalist and in that respect you ask yourselves whether the imputations, if conveyed, damaged him in that respect, that is in the practice of his profession as a journalist." The jury found for the plaintiff in respect of all imputations. The High Court dismissed the defendants' appeal. The joint judgment of French C.J. and Gummow, Kiefel and Bell JJ. is based upon the following propositions. (1) The test for defamation in Australia is whether the words are likely to lead an ordinary reasonable person to think the less of the plaintiff; this is essentially the test stated by Lord Atkin in *Sim v Stretch*. (2) This test does not necessarily imply the application of any judgment of a moral or ethical nature.

(3)

"The concept of 'reputation' in the law of defamation comprehends all aspects of a person's standing in the community . . . In principle therefore the general test for defamation should apply to an imputation concerning any aspect of a person's reputation. A conclusion as to whether injury to reputation has occurred is the answer to the question posed by the general test, whether it be stated as whether a person's standing in the community, or the estimation in which people hold that person, has been lowered or simply whether the imputation is likely to cause people to think the less of a plaintiff. An imputation which defames a person in their professional or business reputation does not have a different effect. It will cause people to think the less of that person in that aspect of their reputation. For any imputation to be actionable, whether it reflects upon a person's character or their business or professional reputation, the test must be satisfied" (at [36]).

(4) It is not therefore correct to say that general community standards are irrelevant to imputations about a person's conduct in a business as opposed to

imputations about "character". Moral or ethical standards about honesty or fidelity may of course be relevant to certain imputations about business conduct but this:

> "does not suggest a true dichotomy as between imputations of that kind and those as to character, with different standards applying to each. Rather it confirms as practicable the general test as applying in all cases involving all aspects of reputation. In such cases the ordinary reasonable person may be expected to draw upon such community standards as may be relevant, in order to answer the question whether there has been injury to that reputation. In keeping with that test it may be said such standards are those by which a person's standing in the community, the esteem in which others hold them, is lowered.
>
> The focus upon moral or ethical standards, in discussions about standards of the community, no doubt reflects the fact that they are the standards most often identified as relevant in actions for defamation. There are obviously other standards, for example as to the behaviour expected of persons within the community, which may not involve a sense of wrongdoing. In some cases injury to reputation may appear so obvious that a standard, which may unconsciously be applied, is not identified. And in some cases such a conclusion may be possible without the need to identify a standard. It may be obvious that people will be thought the less of simply because of what is said about them.
>
> The imputations in *Gacic v John Fairfax* [[2006] NSWCA 175; (2006) 66 NSWLR 675] were considered to fall within this latter category. Another example may be the attribution of authorship of a work of very inferior quality, which may be taken to affect an established author's high reputation, without more. Whether a social standard applies to an imputation of a person's lack of competence to carry out a profession or business may not be so clear, particularly where it is also conveyed that the person held themselves out as competent and for reward. It is not necessary to determine such questions; in each case the plaintiff will have been defamed because he or she has suffered a loss of reputation. The applicability of the general test towards that conclusion cannot be denied because a general community standard does not apply in a particular case. The test does not depend for its exercise upon the existence of standards" (at [46]–[48]).

Taken as a whole the judge's direction would clearly have conveyed to the jury that their task was to assess the injury to the plaintiff's reputation of all the imputations and that they were to do this from the point of view of "ordinary, reasonable, decent members of the community". Heydon J., agreeing, pointed out that the direction as a whole was replete with references to the ordinary, reasonable member of the community. On this basis, the

> "only angle from which . . . the direction could be criticised is that just before the passage containing the impugned [passage], the trial judge said of the five non-business imputations:
>
>> '[T]hey are imputations of something personal about [the respondent's] personal reputation. If you decide that any of those imputations have been conveyed by the broadcast, then you ask whether that imputation would be regarded by ordinary right-thinking members of the community as defamatory, as damaging to his reputation.'

The appellant argued in effect that the express reference to the test for the non-business imputations at that point, coupled with the trial judge's failure to repeat it in the immediately following sentence containing the impugned passage, was an exclusion of its applicability to the business imputations. That submission must fail, on the ground that there are so many other passages conforming to what is being assumed to be the correct approach that the jury cannot have misunderstood the point made by the trial judge in them" (at [72]).

As Heydon J. said, a

"summing up is a structured and solemn piece of prose. When considering prose of that kind, to find out the meaning of particular words forming part of a sentence, it is normal not to examine the words in isolation, as though they were recorded on a fragment of papyrus or were part of an edict of Asoka on a broken pillar. Rather it is desirable to ascertain the meaning of the sentence as a whole" (at [71]).

SECTION 1. WHAT IS DEFAMATORY

See generally *Thornton v Telegraph Media Group Ltd* [2010] EWHC 1414 (QB); [2010] E.M.L.R. 25 para.2.1, above.

**Words causing others to shun or avoid one.** In considering the difficult 2.6 relationship between defamation and misuse of private information in *Terry (formerly LNS) v Persons Unknown* [2010] EWHC 119 (QB); [2010] E.M.L.R. 16 (as to which see paras 22.10 and 27.21A, below) Tugendhat J. suggested that there "are cases where the information would in the past have been said to be defamatory even though it related to matters which were involuntary, e.g. disease. There was always a difficulty in fitting such cases into defamation, but it was done because of the absence of any alternative cause of action"—the implication being that such cases should now be "located" in misuse of private information (subject, no doubt, for the lower courts, to precedent). The difficulty with this is that the hurt felt by a person who is falsely said to have been raped or to have been suffering from mental disorder is surely different from (and some might say, greater than) that suffered by a person who has been truly revealed to have suffered such misfortunes. In *Thornton v Telegraph Media Group Ltd* [2010] EWHC 1414 (QB); [2010] E.M.L.R. 25 at [35] the same judge said that claims in this category "are now likely to be brought under misuse of private information, although that will not necessarily or always be the case".

While not denying that an imputation of mental disorder was capable of being defamatory the NSWCA held in *Mallik v McGeown* [2008] NSWCA 230 that it was open to the jury to conclude that contemporary community attitudes in twenty-first century Australia were such that ordinary reasonable readers would not think less of a person for being described as demented.

**Words lowering a person in the estimation of others.** In *Ecclestone v* 2.7 *Telegraph Media Group Ltd* [2009] EWHC 2779 (QB) the defendants published a story that the claimant, a fashion designer, had said "I am not a veggie and I don't have much time for people like the McCartneys and Annie Lennox [well-known promoters of vegetarianism]". Sharp J. struck out the claim as being incapable of bearing any defamatory meaning. It was impossible to say that the public generally would think less of the claimant because of the view she was said to have expressed on vegetarianism or because it might be regarded as dismissive or disrespectful of the persons referred to. As long ago as *Sim v Stretch* Lord Atkin had remarked that "the protection [of reputation] is undermined when exhibitions of bad manners or discourtesy are placed on the same level as attacks on character and are treated as actionable wrongs." It was not a case where the view expressed would generally have been regarded as outrageous, nor was there any implication of hypocrisy or of the opinion being expressed in an abusive fashion. This view that there is a minimum threshold of seriousness would have been applied in *Thornton v Telegraph Media Group Ltd* [2010] EWHC 1414 (QB); [2010] E.M.L.R. 25 had it been necessary to do so but it was not necessary because the imputation did not even pass the initial threshold of imputing anything remotely discreditable.

2.8      **Relative reputations, comparisons.** Statements denigrating the claimant's abilities will almost always be made in the context of some reference, express or implied, to facts about his performance, thus attracting fair comment. In *Dee v Telegraph Media Group Ltd* [2010] EWHC 924 (QB); [2010] E.M.L.R. 20, however, the assertion that the claimant was the world's worst tennis player was regarded as inseparable from and "parasitic" upon his match record. No sensible reader could really think that "the suggestion that the Claimant was 'the world's worst . . . professional' was a free standing and objectively verifiable allegation independent of his record of losses in the 54 matches played all around the world" (at [38]). Hence there was a defence of justification and it was unnecessary to consider fair comment. See further, para.2.26, below.

In *Beckinsale v Express Newspapers Ltd*, July 9, 2009 the defendants agreed to pay damages in settlement where their story gave the impression that an actress's career was in decline.

SECTION 2. STANDARD OF OPINION

2.10     **The community as a whole.** See *Thornton v Telegraph Media Group Ltd* [2010] EWHC 1414 (QB); [2010] E.M.L.R. 25, paras 2.1, above and 2.26, below.

2.13     **Meaning and imputations in these cases.** *Note 152.* See also *Radio 2UE Sydney Pty Ltd v Chesterton* [2008] NSWCA 66 at [10]; *Radio 2UE Sydney Pty Ltd v Chesterton* [2009] HCA 16 at [31]; *JWH Group Pty Ltd v Buckeridge (No 3)* [2009] WASC 271 at [78].

2.14     **Anti-social views.** In *Williams v MGN Ltd* [2009] EWHC 3150 (QB) Eady J. held that on the basis of the cases cited in the text the imputation that the claimant was a "grass" was incapable of being defamatory.

2.16     **State of public opinion.** For some more examples of changes in public attitudes see *Trad v Harbour Radio Pty Ltd* [2009] NSWSC 750 at [14]. See also *Momo v Wakeri*, Case No.78 of 2009 (Papua New Guinea, via *http://www.paclii.org* [Accessed September 22, 2010]).

2.17     **State of the law.** *Disrespectful behaviour.* See *Ecclestone v Telegraph Media Group Ltd* [2009] EWHC 2779 (QB), para.2.7, above. Behaviour legal but perceived as improper. See *Lait v Evening Standard* [2010] EWHC 642 (QB), para.2.34, below.

In *Bradbury v Westpac Banking Corp* [2008] NZHC 111 at [149] it is suggested that in a fiscal context the

> "words 'evasion' and 'avoidance' carry much the same meaning for a lay person. The latter does not suggest impropriety in the income tax context. While the word 'evasion' carries a connotation of improper conduct to somebody familiar with income tax law, ordinary people are not aware of this nuance."

SECTION 3. INSTANCES OF DEFAMATORY IMPUTATIONS

(a) *General*

**Instances of defamatory words.** *Note 165.* See also *Levi v Bates* [2009]   **2.19**
EWHC 1495 (QB).

**Sexual conduct.** Even in the world of show business in the twenty-first   **2.20**
century one should not discount the hurt that a false allegation of adultery or
sexual disloyalty may cause: *Bowman v MGN Ltd* [2010] EWHC 895 (QB) at
[14].

(b) *Credit*

**Cheques and bills.** *Last sentence.* On the *Aktas* case (fn.286) and privilege see   **2.25**
para.14.43, below.

In *Bumiputra-Commerce Bank Bhd v Top-A Plastic Sdn Bhd* [2008] 5 M.L.J.
534 the Malaysia CA upheld a decision that the notations "frozen account" and
"refer to drawer" on cheques were defamatory.

(c) *Reputation in Business, Trade or Profession*

**Reputation in business, trade or profession.** Two English cases have given   **2.26**
detailed consideration of this area (see also para.2.1, above). In *Dee v Telegraph
Media Group Ltd* [2010] EWHC 924 (QB); [2010] E.M.L.R. 20 the defendants
gave the claimant's match record and on that basis described him as the "world's
worst tennis pro". While there was no doubt that in some cases an imputation of
lack of professional skill could be defamatory, Sharp J. had reservations about
translating that proposition to the world of sport. In the case of professional
people like architects or solicitors want of competence had clear potential
consequences for people who took advantage of their services but that could
hardly be said of a professional tennis player. "Losing in sport is . . . an occupa-
tional hazard. Shaky hands for a surgeon, or endangering the lives of your dental
patients through an unproven anaesthetic cannot be so characterised" (at [49]).
Such a statement about a sportsman seemed more likely to be a "value judgment". Nevertheless, although the matter had not been clearly pleaded in that
way, Sharp J. was prepared to accept that the nub of the complaint was that the
claimant had been held up to ridicule. However, the match record being proved

(in the meaning contended for by the defendants) and the "world's worst" imputation being inseparable from that, it was held that the defence of justification was bound to succeed and the defendants obtained summary judgment. Note Sharp J.'s view on other possible meanings:

> "I have no trouble in concluding that the words complained of when read in their context . . . are capable of bearing *a* meaning defamatory of the Claimant: for example, that he lacks insight into his own lack of talent, and unreasonably persists in pursuing a career to which he is not suited; or—as it was put in the letter of claim but not in the Particulars of Claim—that he unreasonably and unrealistically persists in a career as a professional tennis player which is an expensive waste of money and doomed to failure. That meaning says something about him and his character; and people might think the less of him, if that is what the words complained of did mean. But this is not the meaning of which the Claimant complains" (at [38]).

In *Thornton v Telegraph Media Group Ltd* [2010] EWHC 1414 (QB); [2010] E.M.L.R. 25 the defendants' review of the claimant's book accused her of the practice of "copy approval" in interviews, something of which journalists disapproved. Tugendhat J. held that this could not be a "personal" libel because there was no plea that it suggested anything like hypocrisy and it imputed nothing disreputable by the standards of ordinary people, whatever journalists might think. Nor could it be a business or professional libel. The position of a writer was comparable to that of a sportsman (see *Dee*, above): writers are free to write to different standards for different readerships and it could not be defamatory of the claimant to say that she did not apply the standards accepted by journalists. "There is no consequence for prospective readers of Dr Thornton's Book which corresponds to the consequences that may be suffered by a patient from the shaky hand or unproven anaesthetic technique of a dental surgeon" (at [103]). Of course the "effect upon others" point cannot be the end of the argument in all cases. To say of an historian (or, indeed, a journalist) that he is slipshod in checking his sources is plainly defamatory but that is because it imputes that he ignores the standards of his particular branch of the "writing" profession.

In any event in *Thornton* the allegation failed to meet the required standard of seriousness: see para.2.7, above.

**2.28**    **Imputation of unfitness in office.** *Note 313.* See also *Hlophe v Constitutional Court of South Africa* [2009] ZASCA 36 (allegation of improper interference with proceedings).

**2.31**    *The Clergy. Blake v Associated Newspapers* (fn.339) was followed in *Baba Jeet Singh Ji Maharaj v Eastern Media Group* [2010] EWHC 1294 (QB) (Sikh doctrines).

**2.33**    *Politics.* In *Lait v Evening Standard* [2010] EWHC 642 (QB) Eady J. said:

> [8] "In the light of all that has taken place over the past 12 months, it is in my judgment unreal to suggest that readers would not think the worse of a member of Parliament who had taken advantage of (or 'milked') the expenses system simply because he or she had stayed within the letter of the law or of the rules. Everybody knows that some members of Parliament have been forced to 'pay back' sums of money, either by party leaders or by media pressure, even though the payments had originally been made in accordance

with the prevailing rules. That is because they are perceived now as having behaved disreputably . . .

[11] Most readers will know, therefore, that much of that conduct was lawful and recognised as being within the system. So why, asks [counsel], would anyone think the worse of the Claimant? That is all well and good, but the fact remains that the article uses the words 'forced' and 'emerged', which are capable in my judgment of suggesting something to her discredit. She had to be forced to 'pay back' sums of money to which, at least morally, she is now thought not to have been entitled. She had initially tried to avoid doing the right thing and, what is more, it did not 'emerge' for some unspecified time. This introduces connotations of concealment and being underhanded."

See also *Miller v Associated Newspapers Ltd* [2010] EWHC 700 (QB) at [18]; and *Fierravianti-Wells v Nationwide News Pty Ltd* [2010] NSWSC 648 ("rorting").

*Note 404. A-S* case on appeal, sub nom. *Al-Shennag v Statewide Roads Ltd*    **2.36** [2008] NSWCA 300.

**Incompetence and want of judgment.** It has been said that too much should    **2.38** not be read into Lord Esher's example of the wine merchant. In fact Lord Esher spoke of the animadversion on the wine as imputing that the merchant's judgement was bad. But merchants "may choose to deal in . . . different products directed to different markets. Not all shoppers want vintage wine. Some merchants may choose to sell poorer quality wine, because if they did not, many of their customers would buy less wine, or no wine at all. Even a wine lover may be happy to drink vintage champagne on one day, and some other sparkling wine (at a fraction of the price) on another. The same supermarket may be proud to sell wines of both types, displaying them within an arm's length of each other on the same stacks": *Thornton v Telegraph Media Group Ltd* [2010] EWHC 1414 (QB); [2010] E.M.L.R. 25 at [42].

*Lack of credentials.* In *Ayan v Islamic Coordinating Council of Victoria Pty Ltd* [2009] VSC 119 a statement that the claimant wrongly claimed to have authority to supply Halal certificates was held defamatory.

"To say of a person that they claim an authority they do not have and therefore those who require their services should not deal with them is both to lower that person in the estimation of right thinking members of the community and to cause that person to be shunned or avoided. In this case, the sting of the libel is that the plaintiff requires the authority of [the relevant body] in order to perform the services he has been performing and he has wrongly claimed that he has this authority, when in fact he does not possess any such authority" (at [24]).

# CHAPTER 3

# THE FORM AND MEANING OF THE DEFAMATORY STATEMENT

SECTION 2. THE DISTINCTION BETWEEN LIBEL AND SLANDER

**3.6**    **The consequences of the distinction.** *Ireland*. The Irish Defamation Act 2009 provides:

> "6.—(1) The tort of libel and the tort of slander—
>
> (*a*)  shall cease to be so described, and
> (*b*)  shall, instead, be collectively described, and are referred to in this Act, as the 'tort of defamation' . . .
>
> (5) The tort of defamation is actionable without proof of special damage."

**3.9**    **Broadcasting: statute.** Criminal libel was abolished by s.73(b) of the Coroners and Justice Act 2009.

SECTION 3. INTERPRETATION

**3.13**    **The general approach.** *Strained interpretations*. In *McJannett v Armstrong* [2009] WASC 3 the description of the plaintiff as a "renegade unionist" was capable of bearing the meaning that he had deserted the union cause but not that he had engaged in illegal activity.

*Note 143*. Reference to *Lowe v Associated Newspapers*. See also *Johnson v MGN Ltd* [2009] EWHC 1481 (QB) though this time the opacity worked in the claimant's favour.

*Television programmes*. See *Bond v BBC* [2009] EWHC 539 (QB), para.3.29, below.

**3.15**    **Reasonable understanding.** In holding in *Ajinomoto Sweeteners Europe SAS v Asda Stores Ltd* [2009] EWHC 1717 (QB); [2010] Q.B. 204 that the single meaning rule applied to malicious falsehood as much as to defamation (but see below) Tugendhat J. at [29] expressed the view that

> "the reason for the rule in defamation is to protect freedom of expression on the one hand, and the right to reputation on the other hand, striking a balance between the two.

The rule is a control mechanism. . . . An alternative to the single meaning rule would be, as suggested by Jacob J [in the *Vodafone* case], that the statement was false to a substantial number of people. That test would not, of course, apply when the statement was made only to one, or a few people, as is sometimes the case. In such a case the alternative to the single meaning rule might in effect have to be whatever meaning happens to be attributed to the statement by the person to whom it is made. Either of these alternatives would strike a balance more favourable to protection of reputation, and less to freedom of expression, than the existing rule. They would allow more successful claims in defamation"

(at [31]). The decision was reversed by the CA, which held that the single meaning rule did not apply to malicious falsehood: [2010] EWCA Civ 609. See para.21.5, below. Sedley L.J. said at [32] that in the libel context what was

"a pragmatic practice became elevated into a rule of law and has remained in place without any enduring rationale. It is frequently otiose, as counsel's own experience testifies, because in the great majority of defamation cases the choice between libel and no libel, by the time the case goes to a verdict, is an either-or choice."

Referring to Tugendhat J.'s views below, Rimer L.J. said at [43]:

"If the single meaning rule does achieve a fair balance in defamation law between the parties' competing interests, that would appear to be the result of luck rather than judgment; and how the measure of such claimed fairness might be assessed may anyway be questionable. The application of the rule can also be said to carry with it the potential for swinging the balance unfairly against one party of the other, resulting in no compensation in cases when fairness might suggest that some should be due, or in over-compensation in others."

X has a neighbour dispute with C. X seeks the assistance of D, the landlord of X and C. After taking some steps D writes to X and the letter contains the words "let me know if [C] is abusive etc." This comes to C's attention. The CA held that on any view this could not be read as an assertion that C was, or was likely to be, abusive but Sedley L.J. referred to the air of unreality in judging the statement by the standards of the hypothetical reasonable reader when X was the only recipient: *Freeguard v Martlet Homes Ltd* [2008] EWCA Civ 1577 at [6]. It seems likely that an alternative approach leading to the same result might have been to strike out on the basis that the claim was not worth the candle, para.6.2, below.

**The innuendo: extrinsic facts.** For a marginal case see *Trkulja v Yahoo Inc* **3.20** [2010] VSC 215.

**Knowledge of extrinsic facts: (1) relied on by claimant.** For a case where the **3.21** pleader was impaled on a logical dilemma see *Trkulja v Google Inc Llc* [2010] VSC 226.

**More than one meaning possible.** In *Horlick v Associated Newspapers Ltd* **3.23** [2010] EWHC 1544 (QB) Eady J. said at [9]:

"It is sometimes said that the reasonable reader does not, and should not, select one bad meaning where other non-defamatory meanings are available. That is not to be confused, on the other hand, with the untenable proposition that the reasonable reader should be taken as always selecting the least defamatory of the available meanings. It is a question of how the particular article, put in its context, strikes the reader. If he or she thinks that the message conveyed by the article is defamatory, and towards the more serious end of the scale, there would be no reason to opt for an alternative possible meaning just because it is less serious."

The fact that A is said to have conferred on B a benefit which was (or is reasonably to be suspected of being) contrary to some rules governing A's behaviour, does not necessarily impute impropriety (or reasonable suspicion of it) to B: *Miller v Associated Newspapers Ltd* [2010] EWHC 700 (QB). It is necessary to focus on the facts of the case.

> "Whether a particular article imputes anything to the discredit of a person who receives favours will inevitably depend, not only on the wording of the article in question, but also upon the status of the protagonists relative to one another and the nature of the relationship between them" (at [11]).

**3.24**    **Mere conjectures or strained meanings.** In *Clarke (t/a Elumina Iberica UK) v Bain* [2008] EWHC 2636 (QB) it was held that an allegation of breach of a commercial contract could not, without more, impute dishonesty.

> "Breaches of a distribution agreement and non-payment of goods sold and delivered can in principle be accompanied by dishonesty, but that is neither necessary nor common. Other explanations are much more likely. Only a person who was unduly suspicious and determined to select a bad meaning where a lesser meaning was available could understand that an allegation of dishonesty was being made" (at [12]).

**3.27**    **"Levels" of defamatory meanings.** While it may be true that a defendant may not respond with a plea of justification based on "suspicion" where the only legitimate meaning of his words is "guilt" (see text to fnn.295–298) yet one must bear in mind that the claimant does not have unfettered control of the imputations to be determined (see Main Work, para.11.14). See *West Australian Newspapers Ltd v Elliott* [2008] WASCA 172.

On damages in "suspicion" cases see *Greig v WIN Television NSW Pty Ltd* [2009] NSWSC 632.

A defendant who has to justify an allegation of reasonable grounds to suspect has a lower burden than showing reasonable grounds to *believe*, for facts which can reasonably ground a suspicion may be quite insufficient reasonably to ground a belief: *Sands v Channel Seven Adelaide Pty Ltd* [2009] SASC 215 at [140]. The appeal was dismissed, [2010] SASC 202 but at [120] it is said that the categorisation into three levels "even if rigidly applied in the United Kingdom, has not been so embraced by the Australian courts". See also *West Australian Newspapers Ltd v Elliott*, above at [70].

*Note 284.* See also *Marke v Ewart* [2009] VSC 544 (publication went further than simply reporting that plaintiff under investigation).

**3.29**    **Context and circumstances of publication.** *Television programme.* In *Bond v BBC* [2009] EWHC 539 (QB) at [9] Eady J. said:

"It is important to acknowledge that assessing the meaning(s) of an hour long television programme is to a large extent a matter of impression. Yet it is also necessary to remember that the test is objective, so that one must always have in mind how the reasonable viewer would interpret it. Nonetheless, it is recognised in the authorities that the judge can take into account his or her own subjective reaction as part of the process. Beyond that, one must not be over-analytical, in the sense of subjecting the text to a leisurely or legalistic breakdown: ordinary viewers will not have had that opportunity. The overall flavour of a programme may contribute to an interpretation which would not necessarily be found when subjecting the text to piecemeal analysis. There is a risk that such an exercise will focus on the trees and miss the wood."

**Publication must be taken as a whole.** *First sentence.* See *Monks v Warwick* **3.30**
*DC* [2009] EWHC 959 (QB).

The problems raised by multiple, successive publications on the same matter on the internet are illustrated by *Budu v BBC* [2010] EWHC 616 (QB). Action was brought on three pieces in the BBC archive from a number of years before. The first plainly stated that the subject of it, who had had a job offer withdrawn after vetting, was an illegal immigrant but it did not name the claimant. The second and third pieces did name him but largely gave his side of the story, which was that he was legally here but without indefinite leave to remain (though it was subsequently granted to him). In practical terms the only way in which a searcher could come across the first piece was by reading the second and/or the third and following the hyperlink therein to the first. The claimant had not pleaded that persons who knew the facts and could identify him from the first piece had read it and it was not arguable that the matter was so notorious that a jury could infer that there must be a reader or readers who happened across the first article, and happened to know it referred to him. Sharp J. held that if anyone had indeed read the first piece it had to be seen through the prism of the second and third and, taken as a whole, the material could do no more than suggest at worst that there were questions over the claimant's immigration status.

**Meaning collected from other parts of same publication or from other** **3.32**
**publications.** There is a review of this issue in the context of newspapers in *Dee v Telegraph Media Group Ltd* [2010] EWHC 924 (QB); [2010] E.M.L.R. 20. Sharp J. held that the issue is whether the two pieces are sufficiently closely connected to be regarded as a single publication (Lord Bridge in *Charleston* at [70]), that there is no particular presumption about continuation pages and separate items and that the issue may be determined on a Part 24 application. On the facts the front page article drew attention to the "full story" inside and it was not arguable that they could be separated for the purposes of determining meaning.

The question of how far it is necessary to take account of hyperlinked internet pages was further considered in *Kermode v Fairfax Media Publications Pty Ltd* [2009] NSWSC 1263. Distinguishing *Beran v John Fairfax* (fn.343) McCallum J. said at [28] that the

"nature of Internet browsing is such that it is difficult to say what path of links might be followed on any site, regardless of any cross-referencing between the items in question. Some readers might work their way meticulously through every link. Some might download the precise combination contended for by the defendants in the present case, but that is plainly not the only reasonable view as to what constitutes the publication."

See also *Ali v Associated Newspapers Ltd* [2010] EWHC 100 (QB); *Islam Expo Ltd v Spectator (1828) Ltd* [2010] EWHC 2011 (QB); and *Crookes v Newton* [2009] BCCA 392.

**3.34** **Context and circumstances: spoken words and words published in jest.** In *John v Guardian News and Media Ltd* [2008] EWHC 3066 (QB) the words were not reasonably capable of the defamatory meanings complained of because it was obvious to the reasonable reader that they were an attempt at humour by "putting words in the claimant's mouth". The defendants were a serious newspaper and would not be taken to be making serious accusations of misconduct in this way.

**3.35** **Vulgar abuse.** *Context.* See also *Noorani v Calver* [2009] EWHC 561 (QB).

CHAPTER 4

# SLANDERS ACTIONABLE PER SE

SECTION 2. CRIMINAL OFFENCES

**Charge need not be specific.** See also *Noorani v Calver* [2009] EWHC 561   **4.7**
(QB) (terrorist).

# PUBLICATION

SECTION 1. GENERAL PRINCIPLES

**6.1**    **General principles: publication.** The "law of defamation has loaded the word '*publish*' with a gloss which would seem bizarre to all but the cognoscenti": *Tom & Bill Waterhouse Pty Ltd v Racing New South Wales* [2008] NSWSC 1013 at [26] (there is an entertaining gloss on this at [25]; the case concerned an offence of publishing a race field under the Racing Administration Act 1998 (NSW)).

Proof of communication to another may not be necessary in other legal contexts: *R v Sheppard* [2010] EWCA Crim 65. Is communication to a *human being* necessary in defamation? In certain circumstances there may be communication between automated systems which leads to consequences adverse to the claimant, e.g. where a credit application is rejected by the provider's computer because of default information sent by the system of a credit information provider. In *Dale v Veda Advantage Information Services and Solutions Ltd* [2009] FCA 305 it was conceded by the claimants that the report must be read by a human being. However, it has been held that there may be liability for fraud where false information is given to a machine which processes information so as to grant or deny a benefit: *Renault UK Ltd v Fleetpro Technical Services* [2007] EWHC 2541 (QB).

**6.2**    **General principles: limited publication.** Abuse of process has been called in aid in some cases involving a purely English publication (see also para.9.1, below). Although there are statements that the jurisdiction is exceptional and rarely exercised, reliance on it seems to be becoming quite frequent and in *Thornton v Telegraph Media Group Ltd* [2010] EWHC 1414 (QB); [2010] E.M.L.R. 25 at [62] Tugendhat J. said that "each of the three judges who are currently hearing most of the defamation cases are applying the principle of *Jameel v Dow Jones* with some frequency, and in a number of different, but related, contexts in defamation actions". In *Noorani v Calver* [2009] EWHC 561 (QB) the contention that *Jameel* should be applied was said to be unanswerable where the defendant was said to have stated orally to the claimant's wife and daughter that the claimant was an Islamic terrorist. *Lonzim Plc v Sprague* [2009]

EWHC 2838 (QB) was a claim for a slander published to about half a dozen persons at a company meeting. If the words were defamatory at all they were at the "trivial or innocuous end" of defamatory meaning and the costs of proceedings would be wholly disproportionate to any damages awarded. In *Sanders v Percy* [2009] EWHC 1870 (QB), a slander case, the claim was struck out in so far as it concerned publication to the claimant's solicitor of statements concerning the claimant's resemblance (or lack of it) to Ali G; but not in so far as it concerned benefit fraud. The facts that the accusation was serious and that the defendant was a court officer pointed towards allowing the claim to proceed. There was some analogy with the alternative ground under CPR 24.2 for allowing an action to proceed even if it has no real prospect of success: that there is nevertheless a "compelling reason why the case should be disposed of at a trial". For another slander case (with a more detailed analysis than most) involving among other things a contention that the claimant had an improper collateral purpose in bringing the proceedings, see *Bridle v Williams*, March 17, 2010, Case no.HQ09X02688. In *Lonzim* there was also a claim for libel in the online edition of a South African publication, the *Financial Mail*. Whether this had been read by anyone within the jurisdiction was speculative but at best the publication here was minimal and again the claim was an abuse of process. Contrast *Haji-Ioannou v Dixon* [2009] EWHC 178 (QB) and [2009] EWCA Civ 694 (only limited publication complained of but charge against prominent businessman capable of being read as one of dishonesty); *Underhill v Corser* [2010] EWHC 1195 (QB) (430 publications privileged; judge refused to strike out the claim in respect of 13 non-privileged publications; the charge was of dishonesty and the aim of the proceedings was vindication, which could not necessarily be achieved with regard to the privileged communications; the "fact that a claimant may not be able to pay the costs of a case if he loses is not of itself a reason why he should be denied access to justice" (at [143])); and *Hughes v Alan Dick & Co Ltd* [2008] EWHC 2695 (QB) (serious slander with limited publication).

However, where a claim is brought against a journal based abroad the issue of abuse of process and whether there is a real and substantial tort here cannot "depend upon a numbers game, with the court fixing an arbitrary minimum according to the facts of the case": *Mardas v New York Times Co* [2008] EWHC 3135 (QB); [2009] E.M.L.R. 8 at [15]. Further, where there is limited publication it may be necessary to consider the defendant's response. If D accuses C of being a charlatan and puts in a defence of justification it may be justifiable to allow the claimant to meet that: *Mardas* at [18]. See further on abuse of process, para. 32.44, below.

*Lord Lester's Defamation Bill.* See para.1.12, above. Cl.12 would require the claimant to overcome an initial hurdle of showing that the publication has caused or is likely to cause substantial harm to his reputation or face striking out ("must strike out"), whereas under the current abuse of process principle (which appears to be preserved by cl.12(5)) the ball is in the defendant's court. This would presumably add some expense to the preparation of all cases since the claimant will have to be prepared to meet the point even if the defendant is unlikely to raise it. Nothing in the Bill appears directly to address the question of the expense of libel proceedings, which is widely perceived to be a major problem. Given the presence of cl.12(2) it would not seem that the Bill would provide any clearer principle than the present law of abuse of process.

**6.3**    **General principles: multiple publication.** *Loutchansky v Times Newspapers* (fn.40) found its way to the European Court of Human Rights in *Times Newspapers Ltd v UK (Nos. 1 and 2)* [2009] E.M.L.R. 14 (March 10, 2009, Apps 3002/03 and 23676/03). The court held that the rule that a separate internet publication gave rise to a new cause of action did not infringe art.10 of the Convention. The court agreed that newspaper internet archives made a substantial contribution

> "to preserving and making available news and information. Such archives constitute an important source for education and historical research, particularly as they are readily accessible to the public and are generally free. The Court therefore considers that, while the primary function of the press in a democracy is to act as a 'public watchdog', it has a valuable secondary role in maintaining and making available to the public archives containing news which has previously been reported. However, the margin of appreciation afforded to States in striking the balance between the competing rights is likely to be greater where news archives of past events, rather than news reporting of current affairs, are concerned. In particular, the duty of the press to act in accordance with the principles of responsible journalism by ensuring the accuracy of historical, rather than perishable, information published is likely to be more stringent in the absence of any urgency in publishing the material" (at [45]).

However, the CA had said that the attachment of a qualification to the archive warning against treating it as the truth would normally remove the sting from the publication, this had now been done in the case, the action in respect of the internet publication had been brought within 15 months of that in respect of the paper edition and it was not therefore a case in which the defendants had been affected in their ability to defend the claim by the passage of time. On qualifying previously published Internet material see also *Flood v Times Newspapers Ltd* [2010] EWCA Civ 804; [2010] E.M.L.R. 26, para.15.12, below.

Irish law is now very defendant-friendly in this area. Where a statement is published to two or more persons, *whether contemporaneously or not*, there is only one cause of action, though where the interests of justice so require the court may give leave to bring more than one action (s.11). However, the limitation period is one year (or in the court's discretion up to two years when the interests of justice so require) and the cause of action accrues when the matter is first published (in the case of the internet when it first becomes generally available): para.19.13, below.

*Lord Lester's Defamation Bill.* See para.1.12, above. Cl.10 would make a radical change in the law by introducing a single publication rule. The language is perhaps not the happiest since the word "publication" appears to be used twice in cl.10(1)(a) in the popular sense of the thing which contains the defamatory matter. However, the intention is clear enough. Once the material has been made available to the public (or a section thereof) generally, any subsequent publication of it by the same person in a manner which is not materially different is to be regarded as made at the same time as the first. This would be particularly significant for material on the internet (see the definition of "archive" in cl.17(1)). This appears to be mitigated by the new version of s.32A of the

Limitation Act 1980 found in Sch.2, para.9, which would allow the court to "disapply" the limitation period not only on account of ignorance of the libel but also where there has been a material change in the circumstances since the first publication (e.g. the definitive clearing of a person originally under suspicion?) and the defendant has failed to comply with a reasonable request to correct or qualify. It is not entirely clear why it is thought necessary to have both limbs of cl.10(1). If (b) stood alone it would be the equivalent of the Irish Act (see above) but (a) also provides that the date of the initial publication is to be regarded "for all purposes" as the date of later publications. What might the purposes other than limitation be?

**Joint and several liability.** It is not consistent with the principles governing joint liability                                              **6.5**

> "to contend that a person suffers actionable damage on account of the conduct of one of the joint tortfeasors who participated in the publication, and separate actionable damage in respect of the participation by another joint tortfeasor. Once liability as a joint tortfeasor is established, each of the joint tortfeasors is liable for the whole of the damage": *Bracks v Smyth-Kirk* [2008] NSWSC 930 at [52]. On appeal, [2009] NSWCA 401.

SECTION 2. PUBLICATION

**Acts amounting to publication.** *Byrne v Deane* (fn.61) was distinguished in *Underhill v Corser* [2010] EWHC 1195 (QB). The treasurer and member of the management board of a charitable society did not publish when he was aware that an editorial would appear but took no action and gave no further thought to the matter. In *Byrne v Deane* the defendants were proprietors and had power to remove the offending notice.                                              **6.6**

The issue in *Crookes v Newton* [2009] BCCA 392 was whether the defendant had published defamatory material in web pages to which his page contained hyperlinks. The court held that the mere fact that the link was provided did not amount to publication since it could be equivalent to a mere bibliographical footnote, though there might be added circumstances of encouragement which might make the link equivalent to publication. The court differed on the application of this to the facts. See also para.6.34, below.

*Ireland.* The Irish Defamation Act 2009 provides:

> "6— ... (2) The tort of defamation consists of the publication, by any means, of a defamatory statement concerning a person to one or more than one person (other than the first-mentioned person), and 'defamation' shall be construed accordingly."

**Husband and wife.** *Note 64.* See also *Noorani v Calver*, para.6.2, above.                                              **6.7**

**Communication to claimant's agent.** There is American (and some Canadian) authority extending the scope of non-publication further than to the situation of the agent of a company (e.g. communication to a lawyer representing the claimant). See *Grimmer v Carleton Road Industries Asscn* [2009] NSSC 169.                                              **6.8**

[43]

**6.9      Communications within organisation.** *Note 77.* See also *Tom & Bill Water-house Pty Ltd v Racing New South Wales* [2008] NSWSC 1013 at [55].

**6.10      Publication at common law: intention and foresight.** *Ireland.* The Irish Defamation Act 2009 provides:

> "6— . . . (4) There shall be no publication for the purposes of the tort of defamation if the defamatory statement concerned is published to the person to whom it relates and to a person other than the person to whom it relates in circumstances where—
>
> (*a*) it was not intended that the statement would be published to the second-mentioned person, and
> (*b*) it was not reasonably foreseeable that publication of the statement to the first-mentioned person would result in its being published to the second-mentioned person."

Presumably it is not intended that there should be publication where there is no intention to publish to anyone at all, as where the defendant believes he is alone and is talking to himself.

**6.14      Proof of publication.** *Internet publications.* In *Brady v Norman* [2008] EWHC 2481 (QB) there was evidence of the numbers of persons who had accessed the website on which the statement appeared, but the issue was whether it could be inferred that these included persons who had no community of interest with the defendant for the purposes of privilege (there being evidence of non-interested publishees in the case of the hard copy). It was held that it could not.

> "Such [uninterested] people might have done so, and they might not. Without some evidence to justify the inference (for instance, evidence that the ASLEF site and the information contained in it provide an attractive resource for transport enthusiasts generally, rather than simply for members and staff) it seems to me to be no more than pure speculation to infer that an 'outsider' would have read the words complained of" (at [26]).

See also *Carrie v Tolkien* [2009] EWHC 29 (QB); [2009] E.M.L.R. 9, para.19.10, below.

The denial in *Al-Amoudi v Brisard* (fn.114) that there is any presumption of publication to substantial numbers of persons on the internet is regarded as the law of South Australia in *Sands v Channel Seven Adelaide Pty Ltd* [2009] SASC 215 at [390] (appeal dismissed [2010] SASC 202).

SECTION 3. PARTICULAR PUBLISHERS AND DISTRIBUTORS

**6.18      Internet service providers and other carriers: common law.** For the American Speech Act of 2010 see para.26.31, below. The availability of easily accessible material on the internet more or less in perpetuity magnifies the potential insidious effect of defamation: see Tugendhat J.'s remarks in *Clarke (t/a Elumina Iberica UK) v Bain* [2008] EWHC 2636 (QB) at [55] and in *Flood v Times Newspapers Ltd* [2009] EWHC 2375; [2010] E.M.L.R. 8 at [233] (reversed on appeal, [2010] EWCA Civ 804; [2010] E.M.L.R. 26 but without affecting this point). In *Budu v BBC* [2010] EWHC 616 (QB) the claimant contended that his future employment was at risk from potential employers doing searches on him but on the facts Sharp J. held that this had not been made out.

The liability of the operator of an automated internet search engine was considered in *Metropolitan International Schools Ltd v Designtechnica Corp* [2009] EWHC 1765; [2009] E.M.L.R. 27. Following the line he had taken in *Bunt v Tilley* (fn.139) Eady J. held that the operator did not at common law publish words in the "snippets" generated by the search engine.

> "It is fundamentally important to have in mind that the [operator] has no role to play in formulating the search terms. Accordingly, it could not prevent the snippet appearing in response to the user's request unless it has taken some positive step in advance. There being no input from the [operator], therefore, on the scenario I have so far posited, it cannot be characterised as a publisher at common law. It has not authorised or caused the snippet to appear on the user's screen in any meaningful sense. It has merely, by the provision of its search service, played the role of a facilitator" (at [51]).

It might be that the compiler of a complex manual library catalogue who included snippets from the books in the catalogue "published" that material but in that case he would at least have taken a conscious decision to include the material. That left open the situation after the operator had been informed that its engine was throwing up the offending material. Here

> "it is not possible to draw a complete analogy with a website host. One cannot merely press a button to ensure that the offending words will never reappear on a Google search snippet: there is no control over the search terms typed in by future users. If the words are thrown up in response to a future search, it would by no means follow that the [operator] has authorised or acquiesced in that process" (at [55]).

It was possible for an operator to block particular URLs notified to it and on the facts some steps of this sort had been taken; but the evidence showed that that this would have a limited effect and was easily evaded by the originator of the material moving it. If the operator were required to attempt to block particular words or phrases that would be easily evaded by changes in terminology and would have the effect of depriving the user of access to large numbers of innocent sites. As counsel for the operator put it, "it is practically impossible, and certainly disproportionate, to expect the [operator] to embark on a wild goose chase in order to determine where the words complained of, or some of them, might from time to time 'pop up' on the Web" (at [62]). Eady J. accepted at [64] that there might be "room for debate as to what further blocking steps it would be open for [the defendants] to take, or how effective they might be," but that did not alter his conclusion that there was no common law publication on the facts.

The reverse situation was one of the issues in *Budu v BBC* [2010] EWHC 616 (QB)—an attempt to make the originator of material liable for the publication of a search engine "snippet" (for facts see para.3.30, above). The material in the defendants' web archive, taken as a whole, could bear no worse a meaning than that there were questions about the claimant's immigration status, but the Google snippet, which had simply automatically extracted a few words from one of the pieces in the archive, might give the impression that the claimant was a security risk. Sharp J. held that the defendants could not be liable for the snippet. They could not be liable under ordinary principles for republication since the snippet did not "republish" the archive material, it gave a distorted view of it. It was of course argued that on such facts a claimant is left without remedy against anyone: not against the originator because what he said has been distorted; and not against the search engine operator because under *Metropolitan* the operator has not published what the web crawler robot has produced. To take an extreme (and perhaps unrealistic) case, a newspaper archive might contain the following: "C's conviction and sentence of 10 years for rape were quashed by the Court of Appeal yesterday. The Lord Chief Justice said that C had been the victim of a wicked conspiracy and a terrible miscarriage of justice". Suppose then the robot produces "C, conviction, 10 years, rape: *http://www . . . ".* That would certainly not be a fair and accurate report of judicial proceedings but if there is no publication at all we never get to that defence. One possibility "might be to regard the underlying article as necessary context, or actually as part of the same publication . . . , so that the snippet could not then be read in isolation from the underlying article to which it provides a direct link" (at [76]), perhaps on the basis that "those who use . . . search engines are well aware that such a snippet is merely a fragment of a larger whole (the underlying publication); by analogy, a tiny extract torn at random from a page to which no human publisher has attached any particular significance" (at [75]). That might, however, be small comfort to C, who would no doubt prefer the thing was removed. No doubt it is possible for the operator without too much difficulty to modify a particular, identified hyperlink but the claimant faces the further problem that there are many search engines about. On hyperlinks see *Crookes v Newton* [2009] BCCA 392, para.6.6, above.

**6.22**     **Publisher.** The applicability of s.1 of the 1996 Act to an internet search engine was considered in *Metropolitan International Schools Ltd v Designtechnica Corp*, above. It was not suggested that the operator of the search engine was liable for the material on the sites to which the engine directed users—the claim was brought only in respect of the "snippets" generated (sometimes with an automatic editing process) from the material through which the engine searched. Eady J. thought it would be difficult to say that the operator was not a publisher in the sense of s.1 but it was unnecessary to decide this since it did not publish at common law.

**6.27**     **Relationship of the Defamation Act 1996 and the common law.** This issue was fully considered in *Metropolitan International Schools Ltd v Designtechnica Corp*, above. Having referred to the difficulties presented by the view of Lord Denning M.R. in *Goldsmith v Sperrings* (fn.225), Eady J. said that he was:

> "prepared to find that the defence was not actually abolished in 1996 (albeit no doubt effectively superseded) . . . In the event, however, it makes very little difference . . . It would almost certainly not be available to a defendant who has had it drawn to his attention that the words are defamatory or, at least, arguably so. To that extent, the common law defence is much more closely in line with the statutory defence introduced in s.1 of the 1996 Act" (at [70].

*Lord Lester's Defamation Bill.* See para.1.12, above. Cl.9 would repeal s.1 of the 1996 Act (though it would not restrict the European-based defences below). There would be three categories of publisher: primary publishers, that is to say, authors, editors and persons who exercise effective control of authors or editors; persons who are not primary publishers (the word "secondary" is not used); and, as a sub-group of the second category, persons who are "facilitators" (or live broadcasters). In the first category authors and editors are defined in substantially the same way as under s.1 of the 1996 Act and presumably the person having control of them will usually be the equivalent of the "commercial publishers" treated in the same way as them under that section. These defendants would bear full responsibility as now. Non-primary publishers would have a defence unless the claimant could show that they had received the requisite notice specifying the defamatory material under cl.9(3) and had failed within 14 days (or such other period as the court may specify) to remove the matter complained of from the publication. This defence is clearly set in the context of internet publication: a newspaper which has put copies on the streets cannot remove the material (though it is sometimes possible to call in copies of a book) and if no publication has yet taken place but the person aggrieved is seeking removal the defendant does not need a defence. The reasonable care and lack of knowledge of the defamatory nature of the publication which figure in s.1 of the 1996 Act find no place here because the focus is different, liability is based on failure to remove the material on complaint, though it is not perhaps obvious why a non-primary publisher who knows or suspects that the material is defamatory but hopes he will get away with it, should escape liability. The fact that the court may specify a period longer than 14 days for removal clearly contemplates that it is involved because an action is on foot and if the publisher requires more time to investigate or take technical steps it may presumably specify a longer period even if the fixed period of 14 days has expired.

Perhaps the greatest problem of cl.9 is that it is not clear how the line will be drawn between non-primary publishers subject to this "notice" defence and mere facilitators, who have an unqualified defence. A facilitator is a person who is concerned only with the transmission or storage of the material and who has no other influence or control over it. Again there is a problem of the "internet focus". A printer, for example, has the statutory defence under s.1 of the 1996 Act if he has taken reasonable care etc. He certainly has no involvement in the formulation of the content of the material but it seems hardly natural to say that his only involvement is in the "transmission or storage" of the material. If the printer is not a mere facilitator, however, the above procedure is simply inapt to cover his situation because he has no capacity to remove the material and he would have lost his existing s.1 defence. A bookseller or library might in a sense be said to be involved in transmission or storage but such a person does take active steps to make the material available and so is presumably intended not to be a facilitator: there would be something bizarre in the bookseller's being able to continue to sell copies of a work which was admitted to be defamatory—and sales would no doubt be boosted by that fact. It might seem obvious that an internet service provider is a mere facilitator (except in so far as it generates its own material) but if that were so in all situations it would mean that the protection from liability would extend considerably further than that under the Electronic Commerce (EC Directive) Regulations (Main Work, para.6.28 and below). Under those the "host" is liable in damages if he fails expeditiously to remove the material on notice of it, but under cl.9 a facilitator is completely immune. The defamed person cannot even claim an injunction. This would seem to take the freedom of expression of a person who has no interest in communicating anything at all except the thoughts of others for remuneration a very long way. No doubt a service provider who plays a purely passive transmission role (for example transmitting an email) is a facilitator, though in that case the provision is hardly necessary since it does not publish at common law anyway (see para.16.18, Main Work and above). It is thought that the host of defamatory internet material does more than merely transmit or store in this sense: when its server responds to the external request for the material it is surely analogous to the bookseller delivering the requested book to the customer. In the internet context it must be borne in mind that the originator of the material is quite likely to be a "man of straw".

**6.28**    **The Electronic Commerce (E.C. Directive) Regulations 2002.** *"For remuneration".* The Regulations apply only where the service is provided "for remuneration". If that phrase stood alone Eady J. in *Metropolitan International Schools Ltd v Designtechnica Corp* [2009] EWHC 1765; [2009] E.M.L.R. 27 thought that it would imply that the recipient was directly paying for it, but that "on balance" Recital 18 of the Directive indicated that services financed by advertising were covered: at [84].

*Search engines.* A number of European countries have enacted further legislation specifically protecting the operators of search engines and this is reviewed in *Metropolitan International Schools Ltd v Designtechnica Corp*, above, at [97]–[111]. There are some difficulties in classifying such an operator for the purposes of the three categories in the Regulations but Eady J. did not consider it necessary to decide the issue since he had held that the defendants were not publishers at common law (see above).

**6.31**    **Hosting.** Reg.19 is directed at the storage by the defendant of information provided by others who receive the service, not information generated by the defendant. However, sources of information may be combined, as where a newspaper website contains an article and a "Have your say about this" section directed at readers. In *Kaschke v Gray* [2010] EWHC 690 (QB) it was held that

> "when considering in a particular case whether a defendant is entitled to the immunity conferred by Regulation 19 (subject to satisfying the extra conditions) the question to be asked is whether the information society service provided by the defendant in respect of the information containing the defamatory words which would otherwise give rise to liability consists only of and is limited to storage of that information. If the answer to that question is that it does consist only of storage of the information, Regulation 19 immunity is potentially available even if it would not be available in respect of other information also stored by the defendant in respect of which the service provided by the defendant goes beyond mere storage" (at [75]).

See also *Karim v Newsquest Media Group Ltd* [2009] EWHC 3205 (QB) and *Mulvaney v Sporting Exchange Ltd (t/a Betfair)* [2009] IEHC 33. It is not, however, obvious that in cases of this type the defendant is supplying an information society service for remuneration. The focus of the reg.19 immunity is upon the particular hosted information of which complaint is made so that if with regard to that the defendant exercises an editorial function the immunity may be lost. In *Kaschke* the Master had found against the defendant on his Part 24 application based on s.1 of the Defamation Act 1996 and there was no appeal against that.

Reg.19 (in its original form as art.14 of the Directive) was visited by the ECJ in *Google France SARL v Louis Vuitton Malletier SA* (C 236/08). The context was a reference from the French courts in a trademark infringement dispute. The court said that

> "Article 14 of Directive . . . must be interpreted as meaning that the rule laid down therein applies to an internet referencing service provider in the case where that service provider has not played an active role of such a kind as to give it knowledge of, or control over, the data stored. If it has not played such a role, that service provider cannot be held liable for the data which it has stored at the request of an advertiser, unless, having obtained knowledge of the unlawful nature of those data or of that advertiser's activities, it failed to act expeditiously to remove or to disable access to the data concerned" (at [114]).

The case involved not "natural" searches determined by Google algorithms (see para.6.18, above) but a service called Adwords, under which "Google processes the data entered by advertisers and the resulting display of the ads is made under conditions which Google controls. Thus, Google determines the order of display according to, inter alia, the remuneration paid by the advertisers" (at [115]). It would be for the national court to determine whether the terms of Google's arrangements with advertisers prevented the situation falling within the scope of the test stated at [114].

### Section 4. Republication and Repetition

#### (a) *Liability of republisher*

**General principles.** *Lord Lester's Defamation Bill.* See para.1.12, above. If A **6.32** publishes a libel and D later repeats the substance of it, the publication by D would not fall within cl.10 so that the publication by D would be a separate one and time would run against D from the moment when it actually took place, not when A first published. But suppose A authorised or intended the republication by D so that at common law A would be treated as republishing? Does the second publication by A fall within cl.10 (it is assumed that the second publication is "in the same manner" as the first, e.g. on the internet)?

**Publication by reference.** In *Ali v Associated Newspapers Ltd* [2010] EWHC **6.34** 100 (QB) Eady J. at [28] said:

> "One point that was briefly addressed in the course of submissions was that of the hyperlink [in the claimant's blog to a newspaper interview]. It was said that it is so far undecided in the authorities whether, as a matter of generality, any material to which

attention is drawn in a blog by this means should be taken to be incorporated as part of the blog itself. I suspect that a general rule of thumb is unlikely to be adopted. Much will depend on the circumstances of the particular case."

See also *Islam Expo Ltd v Spectator (1828) Ltd* [2010] EWHC 2011 (QB).

*Note 267.* See also *Peters v TV New Zealand*, December 20, 2007, CIV 2004-404-003311, applying *Buchanan v Jennings*.

### (b) *Liability of the original publisher*

**6.36**    **General principle.** Some doubt has been cast on the proposition that the claimant has a choice between suing on the further publication as a separate cause of action or treating the further publication as increasing the damage flowing from the first. In *Baturina v Times Newspapers Ltd* [2010] EWHC 696 (QB); [2010] E.M.L.R. 18 the publication in the English edition of the newspaper did not give rise to any cause of action because it had not been pleaded that there were any identified readers within the jurisdiction who would have had the necessary knowledge to make it defamatory in an innuendo sense and it was not a case where the facts might be sufficiently widely known to enable the claimant to rely on a presumption or inference that some readers will have known them. However, there were further claims in respect of (1) copies of the newspaper distributed in Russia (2) publications in Russia by third parties which replicated the defendants' words or some of them (3) publications in Russia by third parties which put a gloss on the defendants' words by making a direct allegation of illegality on the part of the claimant and (4) internet publications of the newspaper here and in Russia, which might have been accessed by persons with the requisite knowledge to understand the allegations in a defamatory sense. In the case of category (1) the claimant might have been able to establish at trial the relevant knowledge on the part of some readers in Russia and it was not right to strike out that part of the claim. Category (4) was governed by the current general approach that there is no rebuttable presumption that material placed on a generally accessible website has been published to a substantial number of persons (whether within the jurisdiction or elsewhere). The defendants were not liable for publications in category (3) because the independent allegation of wrongdoing broke the chain of causation. Category (2) was to some extent analogous with category (1) provided it was established (as was in fact admitted) that it was foreseeable that the story would be republished in Russia. However, the claimant was seeking to rely on both bases of liability, i.e. that she had a separate cause of action in respect of the category (2) publications in Russia and that the damage flowing from those publications stemmed from the initial publication in England. With regard to the second basis of recovery Eady J. said:

[51] "[Counsel] raises a fundamental point of principle in relation to how the law now appears to treat claims for additional damage where the later publications have not been sued upon as giving rise to a separate cause of action. He referred, in particular, to the words of Bingham LJ (as he then was) in *Slipper*, which was concerned with damage flowing from the reviews of the television programme. At p.296G–H, his Lordship accepted that the plaintiff could not found a cause of action on the film reviews as

amounting to publication or republication of the libel by the BBC. Nevertheless, he went on to acknowledge the legitimacy of a claim in respect of the damage caused by those reviews *as part of the damage alleged to flow from the libellous publication itself.*

[52] [Counsel] queries the juridical basis of the proposition that a claimant can recover damages flowing from a publication in respect of which he could not establish primary liability on the part of the defendant. It is difficult to reconcile these two propositions as a matter of causation . . .

[53] It may be, as [counsel] suggests, that what the Court of Appeal in *Slipper* was recognising implicitly was that it would have been open to the plaintiff to sue on any of the reviews, as distinct causes of action, in so far as they simply republished the words of the libel itself. (That would correspond to [category 2 above] . . . in the present case.) He cited particular passages in the judgments of Stocker LJ, at pp.295G–296E and Slade LJ, at pp.300F–H and 302D–303A. The latter made reference to the BBC being in a position reasonably to foresee that newspaper reviews would repeat the defamatory sting. It seems as though the analysis should be in terms of foreseeability and *novus actus interveniens*. If this were not so, submits [counsel], all a claimant would ever need to do in respect of 'republications' would be to claim damages by way of aggravation. There would never be any need to go through the disciplines of establishing a separate cause of action in its own right."

*Note 283.* See also *Habib v Radio 2UE Sydney Pty Ltd* [2009] NSWCA 231 and *Bracks v Smyth-Kirk* [2009] NSWCA 401.

**Alteration of defamatory matter.** See *Budu v BBC* [2010] EWHC 616 (QB),   **6.38** para.6.18, above (garbled version of original in search engine snippet).

CHAPTER 7

# IDENTITY OF THE PERSON DEFAMED

SECTION 1. REFERENCE TO THE CLAIMANT

**7.2** **Claimant need not be referred to by name.** *Note 27.* See also *Universal Communications Network Inc (t/a New Tang Dynasty) v Chinese Media Group (Aust) Pty Ltd* [2008] NSWCA 1.

**7.3** **Statement capable of referring to the claimant.** *Note 32.* See *Club La Costa (UK) Plc v Gebhard* [2008] EWHC 2552 (QB) at [37].

*Ireland.* The Irish Defamation Act 2009 provides:

"6— . . . (3) A defamatory statement concerns a person if it could reasonably be understood as referring to him or her."

SECTION 3. CLAIMANT MEMBER OF A CLASS

**7.9** **Words referring to a class.** *Ireland.* The Irish Defamation Act 2009 provides:

"10.—Where a person publishes a defamatory statement concerning a class of persons, a member of that class shall have a cause of action under this Act against that person if—

(a) by reason of the number of persons who are members of that class, or
(b) by virtue of the circumstances in which the statement is published,

the statement could reasonably be understood to refer, in particular, to the member concerned."

# PARTIES: WHO MAY SUE AND BE SUED

SECTION 7. DECEASED PERSONS AND REPRESENTATIVES

### (a) *Right to sue*

**Defamation of person who subsequently dies.** *Ireland.* By the Irish Defama-  **8.12**
tion Act 2009, s.39(2), amending s.7 of the Civil Liability Act 1961, a cause of
action for defamation vested in a person immediately before his death survives
for the benefit of his estate but the damages "shall not include general damages,
punitive damages or aggravated damages".

### (b) *Liability*

**General rule.** *Ireland.* There is a matching Irish provision in s.39(3) for the  **8.13**
case where the defamer dies, i.e. a subsisting cause of action survives against his
estate but there are no general, punitive or aggravated damages.

SECTION 9. CORPORATIONS AND GOVERNMENTAL BODIES

(a) *Right to sue*

**8.16    Trading corporations.** The ECtHR again stated in *Kulis v Poland* (2009), App. no.27209/03 that a company has the right to take proceedings for defamation. On the facts (which would plainly have amounted to fair comment in English law) the imposition of liability on the applicants was disproportionate.

*Lord Lester's Defamation Bill.* See para.1.12, above. Cl.11 would require a body corporate to show that the publication has caused, or is likely to cause, substantial financial loss to it. Although under the present law a corporation does not have to prove actual financial loss flowing from the libel, the libel must have a *tendency* to injure it in the way of its business (see Main Work) and as is pointed out in fn.83 the NZCA regarded the very similar s.6 of the New Zealand Act as restating the common law (though the word "substantial" does not appear in that). So the impact of cl.11 might depend on what sort of evidence would be necessary to establish likelihood of substantial financial loss. If I say that C Ltd knowingly sells products which are bad for consumers' health that clearly "tends" to cause it financial loss. Would C be required to produce evidence of the actual reaction in the potential market?

*Note 85.* On the relationship between defamation and injurious falsehood under the Australian legislation see *Beechwood Homes (NSW) Pty Ltd v Camenzuli* [2010] NSWSC 521.

**8.17    Defamatory statements against company's officers.** In *David Regan & Co Pty Ltd v West Australian Newspapers Ltd* [2007] WASCA 14 the publication was alleged to mean that the plaintiff company had employed a real estate agent who was guilty of dishonesty. The CA held that this was capable of being defamatory of the company. Pullin JA held that it was not decisive that the plaintiff might not be "at fault"—it would plainly have been defamatory to allege that the plaintiff was insolvent; and Buss JA said that it was

"reasonably arguable that an imputation that a small corporation (such as the first appellant), which carries on business as a real estate agent in a small country town, employs an agent who has been found guilty of acting dishonestly or deceptively, constitutes a reflection upon the business reputation of the corporation" (at [35]).

*Note 101.* See also *Tiscali UK Ltd v British Telecommunications Plc* [2008] EWHC 2927 (QB).

**8.20    Governmental bodies.** *Ireland.* The Irish Defamation Act 2009 provides:

"12.—The provisions of this Act apply to a body corporate as they apply to a natural person, and a body corporate may bring a defamation action under this Act in respect of a statement concerning it that it claims is defamatory whether or not it has incurred or is likely to incur financial loss as a result of the publication of that statement."

There therefore appears to be no equivalent of the English rule that a governmental body (being a corporation) may not sue for defamation.

SECTION 11. FIRMS

(a) *Right to sue*

**Generally.** *Note 164.* Right of action in partnership does not preclude claim by    **8.25**
individual partner. See also *Ayan v Islamic Coordinating Council of Victoria Pty
Ltd* [2009] VSC 119.

SECTION 12. UNINCORPORATED ASSOCIATIONS

**Generally.** In *North London Central Mosque Trust v Policy Exchange* [2009]    **8.28**
EWHC 3311 (QB) an unincorporated charitable trust was not a legal entity and
was incapable of having a reputation for the purposes of the law of libel. Sedley
L.J. gave permission to appeal against refusal of an application to substitute the
trustees as claimants on behalf of the trust (rather than as having been collectively defamed as individuals): [2010] EWCA Civ 526.

CHAPTER 9

# REMEDIES

SECTION 1. COMPENSATORY (GENERAL) DAMAGES

**9.1**  **Damages the primary remedy: vindication and other remedies.** See the remarks of Young J.A. on declarations in *Bracks v Smyth-Kirk* [2009] NSWCA 401; and of Tugendhat J. on the impact of privilege on vindication in *Underhill v Corser* [2010] EWHC 1195 (QB).

In *Clift v Slough BC* [2009] EWHC 1550 (QB); [2009] 4 All E.R. 756 (see para.14.3, below) where the defendants had run defences of justification and qualified privilege and it had been held that the latter did not apply to all the publications, the jury were required to return a special verdict on justification and malice. They found that the imputations were not justified but that there was no malice, awarding damages for the non-privileged publications.

Abuse of process has been considered above (para.6.2) in connexion with limited publication. However, it is not possible to confine the jurisdiction to that situation, since the underlying ideas that there is no "real and substantial tort and that "the game is not worth the candle" cannot be confined to limited publication cases. Thus in *Williams v MGN Ltd* [2009] EWHC 3150 (QB), where the allegation was that the claimant was a henchman of a notorious gun criminal the claim was struck out as an abuse of process "because having regard to the Claimant's background and serious criminal convictions . . . it would be inappropriate to regard the article . . . and its references to him as constituting a 'real and substantial tort'". In *Kaschke v Osler* [2010] EWHC 1075 (QB) the accusation was of youthful political folly many years before and the claim was statute-barred (see also *Kaschke v Gray* [2010] EWHC 1907 (QB)). It is plainly not the law that there is an abuse of process simply because the costs involved in establishing a contested claim will exceed any damages likely to be awarded, otherwise many claims attracting damages in five or even six figures would constitute an abuse (the same must apply a fortiori to claims based on misuse of private information, where damages are generally substantially lower than for libel). However, it may be necessary to consider whether the claimant has achieved his aim in some other way than by pursuing an action for damages. In *Hays Plc v Hartley* [2010] EWHC 1068 (QB) A, B and C, former employees of the claimant, made serious accusations against it to persons including the defendant; he passed them on to a journalist and they found their way to the *Sunday*

*Mirror*, which published them. The claimants sued A, B and C but this claim was settled without payment of damages or costs along with employment tribunal proceedings which A, B and C were pursuing against the claimants. This settlement included a public statement in which it was accepted that there was no basis for the charges against the claimants. The claimants did not sue the *Sunday Mirror* but did sue the defendant, alleging publication to the *Sunday Mirror* and relying on the republication in the newspaper on damages. The claimants had no prospect of recovering their substantial costs against the defendant even if they won, but wished to avoid the likely liability for his costs if they discontinued. Tugendhat J. struck out the claim:

> "In my judgment the significant facts are that the Claimant is a corporation, that the Defendant is a professional intermediary and not the originator of the words complained of, that the action is brought on the publication to a single individual, the Journalist, that the republication gave proper coverage to the Claimant's case (so any damages would be likely to be modest) and that the Claimant has received vindication both from the originators of the words (in the form of the Public Statement) and from MGN (in the form of the republication on their website of the Public Statement). That damages would on any view be modest is accepted . . . In so far as the damages may have value as money they are not worth pursuing. If the Claimant pursued this action to trial and won, there is little prospect that it would be able to enforce any award that it might have. The defendant would be unable to pay any significant part of the damages and costs that might be awarded against him. Damages in defamation actions have an additional value: they are symbolic. They mark the seriousness of the defamation and are a part of the vindication. But in the present case, the sum itself could not be so high as to add any value in terms of vindication to the Public Statement" (at [59]).

See also *Budu v BBC* [2010] EWHC 616 (QB) and see further para.32.44, below.

*Ireland.* The Irish Defamation Act 2009 contains two non-damages restorative remedies. First, by s.28 a person who claims to be the subject of a defamatory statement may apply to the Circuit Court for a declaratory order that the statement is false and defamatory. The court is to make an order to that effect if the statement satisfies those conditions, the respondent has no defence and the respondent has failed to make, at the applicant's request, an apology, correction or retraction. The applicant is not required to prove that the statement was false. No damages may be awarded on such an application, nor may the applicant bring any other proceedings in respect of any cause of action arising out of the statement. Secondly, by s.30 the court may, on the application of a successful plaintiff in a defamation action, make an order directing the defendant to publish a correction of the statement in such a manner as will ensure (unless the plaintiff otherwise requests) "that it is communicated to all or substantially all of those persons to whom the defamatory statement was published". Such an order may also be made in a Circuit Court application for a declaratory order under s.28.

**General damages compensatory.** In *Andrews v Aylott* [2010] EWHC 597 **9.2** (QB) (not a defamation case) Tugendhat J. at [38] seems to have accepted the submission that libel damages include compensation to the successful Claimant for the inconvenience, anxiety and distress of having to resort to and pursue proceedings. The same judge in *Clarke (t/a Elumina Iberica UK) v Bain* [2008] EWHC 2636 (QB) at [55] said:

> "Defamation actions are not primarily about recovering money damages, but about vindication of a Claimant's reputation. If a successful libel Claimant recovers, say, £30,000, that figure does not represent the measure of his success. In many cases, after paying his irrecoverable costs, he will be out of pocket if he recovers that amount as damages. That does not mean the litigation is not worthwhile. A Claimant wrongly accused of some serious fault, such as malpractice or dishonesty in business, may well suffer very large unquantifiable loss if he does not recover his reputation. The value of the verdict in his favour is expected to consist substantially in the future loss that it is hoped will be avoided by the vindication. Where, as here, the publication complained of is on an internet news service, a verdict in his favour may provide him with a means of persuading the publishers of an archive to edit it."

Lord Hoffmann, extra-judicially, has reiterated the deterrent function of damages for defamation. Commenting in the Ebsworth Memorial Lecture (2010—see para.26.31, below) on the proposal of the English branch of PEN that damages should be capped at £10,000, he said:

> "If a newspaper is willing to bid a quarter of a million pounds for the story of a footballer's mistress, they are unlikely to be deterred by the prospect of having to pay £10,000 if a story that sells papers turns out to be a libel. The earliest laws of ancient Rome capped damages for defamation and all other forms of insult short of actual bodily harm at 25 bronze coins. Gaius says that 25 bronze coins may have been adequate for the poverty of early Rome, but the famous jurist Labeo, who wrote in the first century B.C., told the story of Lucius Veratius, who went round Rome slapping respectable people in the face, followed by a slave with a purse of bronze coins who counted out 25 for each of them. As a result, the law was amended and damages left at large to the judges. Labeo did not see the funny side of the story: he describes Veratius as *homo inprobus atque immani vecordia*, a wicked and brutal man, but he might nevertheless under the PEN scheme be an example for a modern tabloid editor."

On corporations and damage under Lord Lester's Defamation Bill see para.8.16, above.

*Note 29.* The proposition that the defendant must take his victim as he finds him is also to be found in *Cleese v Clark* [2003] EWHC 137 (QB); [2004] E.M.L.R. 37 at [40] and *Bowman v MGN Ltd* [2010] EWHC 895 (QB).

*Note 48.* It has been held in NSW that the statutory cap on damages for non-economic loss applies to a proceeding regardless of the number of causes of action that are pleaded or upheld in the proceeding: *Davis v Nationwide News Pty Ltd* [2008] NSWSC 693. And see *Buckley v Herald and Weekly Times Pty Ltd* [2009] VSCA 118 (consolidation). At the beginning of June 2010 the cap was A$ 294,500: 2009 NSW Gazette 3137.

**9.4**     **Role of the Court of Appeal.** On the current approach of the NSWCA see *Ali v Nationwide News Pty Ltd* [2008] NSWCA 183.

**9.5**     **Guidance for the jury: general.** For the approach in New Zealand see *Wells v Haden* [2008] DCR 859.

**Separate actions for defamation.** *Note 131.* See also *French v Triple M*   **9.12**
*Melbourne Pty Ltd* [2008] VSC 550.


Section 2. Aggravated Damages


**Aggravated damages.** *Note 142. Collins Stewart v Financial Times.* In *Clarke*   **9.14**
*(t/a Elumina Iberica UK) v Bain* [2008] EWHC 2636 (QB) Tugendhat J. was
clearly of opinion that damages might in principle be aggravated by subsequent
publications not sued on, though he said that it would "be an unusual case where
compensatory damages are increased by a very substantial amount to take
account of the aggravation caused by subsequent publications" (at [56]). There
are further complications in this area arising from the facts that injury to feelings
is not itself "damage" for the purposes of service out of the jurisdiction (see
Main Work, para.26.21) and that if the court has jurisdiction over a foreign
publisher it should only award damages for damage suffered here (see Main
Work, para.9.8): see *Clarke* at [62]–[67].


Section 3. Exemplary Damages


**Nature of exemplary damages.** *Note 171.* See also *Monks v Warwick DC*   **9.16**
[2009] EWHC 959 (QB) and *MoD v Fletcher* [2010] I.R.L.R. 25, EAT (a
discrimination case).

*Note 174.* New Zealand. See *Wells v Haden* [2008] DCR 859.


Section 4. Multiple Parties


**Co-defendants: exemplary and aggravated damages.** Eady J. in *Berezovsky*   **9.25**
*v Russian Television and Radio Broadcasting Co* [2010] EWHC 476 (QB) said
that the law on matters of aggravation in the case of joint tortfeasors could not
be definitively stated. He said:

> "I propose to ignore individual aggravating factors, as something of a distraction,
> because I think the lowest common denominator approach is likely to be preferred by
> a modern appellate court not least because it is more compatible with Article 10 of the
> European Convention on Human Rights. There would seem to be an inhibiting or
> 'chilling' effect on freedom of expression in so far as the law may render each
> individual contributor to an investigative story liable for the words or conduct of other
> people. In a genuine case of 'joint enterprise', that may be appropriate, but I am not
> persuaded that this is such a case. Yet I do not believe that for the purposes of this case
> I need to resolve this dilemma." (at [175]).

CHAPTER 10

## DEFENCES: GENERAL

**10.1**     **Defences.** *Ireland.* The Irish Defamation Act 2009 approaches close to being a code of defamation law. S.17 and 18 preserve defences of absolute and qualified privilege which existed before the passing of the Act (though they also contain detailed provisions on those matters). Otherwise, however, and subject to statute or European law, "any defence that, immediately before the commencement of [Part 3 of the Act], could have been pleaded as a defence in an action for libel or slander is abolished": s.15(1).

CHAPTER 11

## JUSTIFICATION (TRUTH)

**Terminology and policy.** *Lord Lester's Defamation Bill.* See para.1.12, above.   **11.1**
Cl.4 would rename the defence "truth", something which is likely to be entirely
uncontroversial (note that there is a clerical error in cl.5(3) and (4), where "a
defence of justification" should be read as "a defence of truth"). By cl.5(1) and
(2) it is clear that the burden of proof would remain on the defendant. As at
common law, substantial truth would be sufficient (cl.5(2)(a)) and cl.5(4) appears
substantially to reproduce s.5 of the Defamation Act 1952. The "single meaning"
rule is not affected and it may be that cl.5(2)(b) substantially reproduces the
present position (Main Work, paras 11.11–11.14), though the choice of the
phrase "less serious meaning" where the defendant seeks to depart from the
meaning alleged by the claimant is perhaps debatable (if the words will support
the meaning of a general charge of wrongdoing rather than simply of the specific
incident mentioned, is that a "less serious meaning"?). The explanatory notes
indicate (para.82) that cl.5(3) is meant to cover the "lesser meaning" situation of
cl.5(2)(b). The Bill does not, however, purport to do anything to ameliorate the
case management problems which arise on the pleading of meaning: explanatory
notes, para.79.

*Ireland.* The Irish Defamation Act 2009 provides:

"16.—(1) It shall be a defence (to be known and in this Act referred to as the 'defence
of truth') to a defamation action for the defendant to prove that the statement in respect
of which the action was brought is true in all material respects.
   (2) In a defamation action in respect of a statement containing 2 or more distinct
allegations against the plaintiff, the defence of truth shall not fail by reason only of the
truth of every allegation not being proved, if the words not proved to be true do not
materially injure the plaintiff's reputation having regard to the truth of the remaining
allegations."

**The burden of proof.** *Lord Lester's Defamation Bill.* See para.11.1, above.   **11.3**
In *Europa Press Holding DOO v Croatia* (2009) App. no.25333/06 the ECtHR
at [63], citing *McVicar* and *Steel and Morris*, reiterated that

"in principle it is not incompatible with art 10 to place on a respondent in defamation
proceedings the onus of proving to a reasonable civil standard of proof (that is, on the
balance of probabilities) that the defamatory statements were substantially true."

Although an application for summary judgment or striking out in advance of
particulars of justification on the basis that the defence of justification is bound
to succeed is a bold one, such an application succeeded in *Ali v Associated
Newspapers Ltd* [2010] EWHC 100 (QB) (allegation that claimant an Islamic
extremist supported by claimant's blog).

*Note 26.* Criminal convictions. Under s.43 of the Irish Defamation Act 2009 acquittals and convictions are treated in the same way, i.e. both are "admissible in evidence in a defamation action".

**11.4     Repetition and rumour: the repetition rule.** *Meaning conveyed by statement.* Although most commonly encountered in the context of justification, the repetition rule is closely connected with the question of the meaning of the statement. In *Brady v Norman* [2008] EWHC 2481 (QB) the defendant's statement was that the Certification Officer had ruled that the claimant had legitimately been excluded from membership of ASLEF for bringing the union into disrepute. The defendant's argument that this was not defamatory because it was not a statement about the claimant but merely of the ruling was rejected.

> "No reasonable reader would regard the Certification Officer's ruling as morally neutral: its effect was to confirm that the Claimant had been legitimately expelled from the union for a serious offence. On [the defendant's] argument, to say of someone that a court had ruled that he had been properly been found guilty of (for instance) multiple murder did not 'engage' that person, merely reported the ruling, and was not capable of reflecting adversely on him. That (likely defences apart) would plainly be wrong" (at [21]).

Cf. *Sands v Channel Seven Adelaide Pty Ltd* [2009] SASC 215 (statement by second defendant did not convey the imputation that there were or had been reasonable grounds to suspect plaintiff of murder since it was merely explaining that a judge who had granted an injunction against first defendant had taken that allegation into account; in the alternative the statement was privileged as a fair and accurate report of court proceedings; appeal dismissed [2010] SASC 202, where Gray J. at [118] said that

> "reasonable listeners and readers of the publications should be taken to understand that court proceedings involve the resolution of competing claims by opposing litigants, and that it is not until judgment that one or other of those versions is found to be true. A reasonable listener and reader would not assume that all allegations made in court proceedings have a reasonable basis, or that those allegations represent the truth. Rather, the reasonable listener and reader will approach allegations made in court on a somewhat sceptical basis, aware that the allegations represent only one side of the story".

**11.5     The repetition rule and privilege.** *Note 43.* So in *Coull v Nationwide News Pty Ltd* [2008] NTCA 10, where the reporting privilege failed because the report was not fair and accurate, the fact that a reader might have concluded that all that was being reported was what witnesses said did not affect the fact that the material was defamatory.

**11.6     Proof of justification: cases where the imputation is of suspicion.** Subject to one elaboration the Supreme Court of New Zealand adopted as New Zealand law the principles stated in *Musa King*: *APN New Zealand Ltd v Simunovich Fisheries Ltd* [2009] NZSC 93; [2010] 1 N.Z.L.R. 315. The elaboration (which is already implicit) relates to the proposition numbered (6) in the Main Work: "circumstantial evidence cannot contribute to reasonable grounds for suspicion unless it gives rise to an available inference concerning the conduct of the plaintiff" (at [35]). The principles were also applied in *Greig v WIN Television NSW Pty Ltd* [2009] NSWSC 632. See also para.12.12, below.

**Justification required of and limited to the imputation.** *Note 79.* The *Maisel*   **11.8**
principle. See *Habib v Nationwide News Pty Ltd* [2010] NSWCA 34 at
[313]–[335].

**Substantial justification sufficient.** *Lord Lester's Defamation Bill.* See   **11.9**
para.11.1, above.

**Justification and the case advanced by the claimant: scope and effect of**   **11.14**
**the plea.** *Note 132.* In *APN New Zealand Ltd v Simunovich Fisheries Ltd* [2009]
NZSC 93; [2010] 1 N.Z.L.R. 315 the Supreme Court of New Zealand held that
the effect of s.8(3)(b) of the Defamation Act 1992 (NZ)

> "prevents a plaintiff from selecting from a substantially true publication some relatively
> minor aspect which is untrue but which, in the context of the publication as a whole,
> does not affect the truth of the general picture painted by the defendant, and hence does
> no material damage to the plaintiff's reputation" (at [42]).

However, it is accepted in accordance with *Crush*'s case that in New Zealand "a
defendant cannot plead and attempt to prove defamatory meanings of less gravity
than those alleged by the plaintiff" (at [31]). This also seems to be the view of
the Australian "contextual truth" defence expressed in *Wookey v Quigley* [2009]
WASC 284 by Hasluck J. at [62]:

> "My understanding is that this provision covers the situation where the plaintiff draws
> a particular allegation out of the material complained of but ignores some other more
> serious allegation, possibly because the defendant might be able to justify it. In that
> situation it is open to the defendant to raise and justify the more serious imputation in
> order to establish that the plaintiff's reputation has not actually been damaged as alleged
> by the plaintiff in seeking to confine his complaint to the less serious imputation
> selected by him."

The relationship between what is pleaded by the plaintiff and the scope of
justification certainly continues to generate case law in Australia. The cases are
reviewed in *West Australian Newspapers Ltd v Elliott* [2008] WASCA 172,
where the view is taken that it is the other side of the coin of the ability of the
plaintiff to depart from the precise meaning he has pleaded. Steytler P. said at
[31] (citations omitted):

> "This review of the cases suggests that there is general, although not universal, support
> for the proposition that a plaintiff who has pleaded specific meanings by way of false
> innuendo may only succeed at trial on some other meaning if it is not substantially
> different from and not more injurious than the meanings pleaded. If that is correct
> then . . . the issue of whether the meaning was substantially different might be tested by
> asking whether the defendant would have been entitled to plead a different issue,
> adduce different evidence or conduct the case on a different basis or, possibly, whether
> the justification would be substantially different. If the *Polly Peck* imputation pleaded
> by the defendant is one that would have satisfied the test enunciated, had it been pleaded
> by the plaintiff, it will be allowed. If it would not have satisfied that test, it will not be
> allowed . . . "

In *Soultanov v The Age Co Ltd* [2009] VSC 145 (where the issue of competing meanings was considered from the point of view of fair comment) Kaye J. said at [42]:

> "[There are] two underlying purposes served by the tests developed by the courts . . . as to the requisite relationship between the imputations pleaded by the plaintiff and the issues to be agitated in the case, whether by the plaintiff (or the jury) travelling beyond the strict formulation of the imputations in the statement of claim, or by the defendant pleading and relying on a defence which does not address the imputations as they have been formulated by the plaintiff. The principal purpose served by tying the plaintiff to imputations, not substantially different from those pleaded, is to ensure fairness to the defendant. The same test has been held to apply to the defendant, principally in order to ensure that the defence does not create a 'false issue', by raising matters which do not meet the case to be put by the plaintiff to the jury, or to be considered by the jury. The various formulae developed by the courts—that the meaning relied on must be a nuance of, a variant of, or not substantially different from, the pleaded imputation— have been developed to serve those two fundamental purposes."

It has also been said in Western Australia that there are three variations on this theme: the situation where the defendant argues (1) that the publication does not convey the imputation pleaded by the plaintiff, but seeks to justify a different meaning that is capable of arising from the publication; (2) that the multiple imputations conveyed by a publication are not distinct, but have a common sting, and that proving the truth of one aspect of the common sting will justify the entire publication; (3) that the publication carries, in addition to the defamatory imputations of which the plaintiff complains, one or more other imputations that are substantially true and the defamatory imputations do not further harm the reputation of the plaintiff because of the substantial truth of the contextual imputations (which is said to be the case covered by the statutory contextual truth defence): *JWH Group Pty Ltd v Buckeridge (No 3)* [2009] WASC 271 (at [38]) (which contains a useful review).

Before 2005 only NSW had the contextual truth defence. It has been held that although the legislative history indicates that the purpose of the current provision (Defamation Act 2005, s.26) was simply to replicate the former one (Defamation Act 1974, s.16) allowing for the changes made in the basic defence of truth, it has not, as a matter of language, achieved this: *Kermode v Fairfax Media Publications Pty Ltd* [2010] NSWSC 852. The 1974 Act allowed the defendant to "plead back" imputations relied on by the plaintiff so as to balance such of them as were proved to be true against those which were not; but the words "in addition to the defamatory imputations of which the plaintiff complains" in s.26 of the 2005 Act preclude this.

**11.15**      **Section 5 of the Defamation Act 1952.** *Lord Lester's Defamation Bill.* See para.11.1, above.

**11.16**      **Justification and damages.** *Note 152.* In *Williams v MGN Ltd* [2009] EWHC 3150 (QB), where the allegation was that the claimant was a henchman of a notorious gun criminal the claim was struck out as an abuse of process "because having regard to the Claimant's background and serious criminal convictions . . . it would be inappropriate to regard the article . . . and its references to him as constituting a 'real and substantial tort' ".

CHAPTER 12

# FAIR COMMENT

SECTION 1. INTRODUCTION

**The basis of the defence.** In *British Chiropractic Association v Singh* [2010]   **12.1**
EWCA Civ 350; [2011] E.M.L.R. 1 the court referred at [35] to the criticism in
the Main Work of the terminology used by the law and said:

> "The law of defamation surely requires that language should not be used which
> obscures the true import of a defence to an action for damages. Recent legislation in a
> number of common law jurisdictions—New Zealand, Australia, and the Republic of
> Ireland—now describes the defence of fair comment as 'honest opinion'. It is not for
> us to alter or add to or indeed for that matter reduce the essential elements of this
> defence, but to describe the defence for what it is would lend greater emphasis to its
> importance as an essential ingredient of the right to free expression. Fair comment may
> have come to 'decay with . . . imprecision'. 'Honest opinion' better reflects the real-
> ities."

However, it seems unwise to retitle the chapter in a mere Supplement. References
to the Australian and New Zealand legislation will be found in fn.7. It has been
said that the common law has been essentially reproduced in s.31 of the NSW
Act: *Fraser v Holmes* [2009] NSWCA 36 at [75].

*Lord Lester's Defamation Bill.* See para.1.12, above. Cl.2 renames fair comment "honest opinion". Cl.3 would then make some substantial changes in the
newly-named defence. As at common law the statement must relate to a matter
of public interest: cl.3(2). The words must be such as an ordinary person would
consider to be opinion: cl.3(3). And there must have existed at the time of the
publication facts or material on the basis of which an honest person could form
the opinion: cl.3(4) and (5). All these matters ("conditions" in terms of the Bill)
must be established by the defendant. The defendant loses the defence if the
claimant shows that the defendant did not in fact hold the opinion: cl.3(7). So far
that may be regarded as more or less restating the present law in the post *Tse Wai
Chun v Cheng* era, though it would become clear from cl.3(6)(c) that it is not

necessary that the statement must refer to the facts or material which is the basis of the opinion (though that issue may be very relevant to the question whether an ordinary person would perceive the statement to be opinion). However, by cl.3(4)(b) it is expressly provided that the "facts or material" which may be the basis of the defence include not only facts and material which is privileged (whether by common law or statute) but material which falls within the Bill's revamped version of the *Reynolds* defence ("responsible publication on matters of public interest"). This is a point which does not seem to have been squarely addressed in the post-*Reynolds* cases (though it is assumed in Main Work, para.12.21 that fair comment might extend to comment on *Reynolds* statements), perhaps because (a) fair comment continued to be regarded as an "easier" defence requiring "honesty" not "responsibility" and (b) there has been equivocation over whether *Reynolds* was to be regarded as truly a species of privilege at all. Furthermore, fair comment was perhaps perceived not to fit very well with the requirement of responsible journalism under *Reynolds*: it seems odd to say that you must investigate the facts you report, adopt a "fair" tone and even give the other side an opportunity to put its case but are then able to comment on all this in ways which are irrational, stupid, offensive or prejudiced (see Main Work, para.12.23). Cl.3(7)(c) specifically excludes any requirement that facts or material forming the basis of the comment should be referred to in the statement. So the justification once advanced for the defence, that the reader could judge for himself how far the comment was fair, vestigial perhaps since *Kemsley v Foot* in relation to facts, disappears altogether. This would be particularly significant for opinion based on privileged material, for the present law goes further in such cases and requires the commentator to give a fair and accurate account of the privileged occasion on which the statement commented on was made (see Main Work, para.12.21). The point is significant in relation to opinion based on *Reynolds*-type material: once A makes a statement about C complying with cl.1, C then appears to be fair game for the expression of any honest opinion, no matter how exaggerated, by all and sundry without any necessity to set out the background circumstances.

One feature of cl.3 which is likely to be very controversial is (6)(b). The present law of fair comment requires that the commentator be aware at the time of publication, at least in a general way, of supporting facts upon which he relies. This is not so under the Bill. One wonders why it does not go the whole hog, take the American stance and simply provide that opinion cannot be defamatory at all.

*Ireland.* The Irish Bill (fn.7) was passed as the Defamation Act 2009. It provides:

"**20.**—(1) It shall be a defence (to be known, and in this section referred to, as the "defence of honest opinion") to a defamation action for the defendant to prove that, in the case of a statement consisting of an opinion, the opinion was honestly held.

(2) Subject to *subsection (3)*, an opinion is honestly held, for the purposes of this section, if—

(a) at the time of the publication of the statement, the defendant believed in the truth of the opinion or, where the defendant is not the author of the opinion, believed that the author believed it to be true,

(b) (i) the opinion was based on allegations of fact—

(I) specified in the statement containing the opinion, or

(II) referred to in that statement, that were known, or might reasonably be expected to have been known, by the persons to whom the statement was published, or

(ii) the opinion was based on allegations of fact to which—

(I) the defence of absolute privilege, or

(II) the defence of qualified privilege,

would apply if a defamation action were brought in respect of such allegations, and

(c) the opinion related to a matter of public interest.

(3) (a) The defence of honest opinion shall fail, if the opinion concerned is based on allegations of fact to which *subsection (2)(b)(i)* applies, unless—

(i) the defendant proves the truth of those allegations, or

(ii) where the defendant does not prove the truth of all of those allegations, the opinion is honestly held having regard to the allegations of fact the truth of which are proved.

(b) The defence of honest opinion shall fail, if the opinion concerned is based on allegations of fact to which *subsection (2)(b)(ii)* applies, unless—

(i) the defendant proves the truth of those allegations, or

(ii) where the defendant does not prove the truth of those allegations—

(I) the opinion could not reasonably be understood as implying that those allegations were true, and

(II) at the time of the publication of the opinion, the defendant did not know or could not reasonably have been expected to know that those allegations were untrue.

(4) Where a defamatory statement consisting of an opinion is published jointly by a person ("first-mentioned person") and another person ("joint publisher"), the first-mentioned person shall not fail in pleading the defence of honest opinion in a subsequent defamation action brought in respect of that statement by reason only of that opinion not being honestly held by the joint publisher, unless the first-mentioned person was at the time of publication vicariously liable for the acts or omissions, from which the cause of action in respect of that statement accrued, of the joint publisher."

Like s.10(1) of the New Zealand Act of 1992 this places the burden of proof squarely on the defendant to show that the opinion was honestly held. Under s.31 of the 2005 NSW Act the position is the reverse.

SECTION 2. COMMENT

(a) *Comment and fact*

**The distinction.** *British Chiropractic Association v Singh* [2010] EWCA Civ **12.6** 350; [2011] E.M.L.R. 1 attracted much attention. It does not make new law but it does emphasize the critical importance of the context of the material. The claimants sued in respect of the following words in an article written by the defendant in a newspaper (the newspaper was not sued, perhaps because the author was a softer target):

> "The British Chiropractic Association claims that their members can help treat children with colic, sleeping and feeding problems, frequent ear infections, asthma and prolonged crying, even though there is not a jot of evidence. This organization is the respectable face of the chiropractic profession and yet it happily promotes bogus treatments".

The judge below had held that these words meant that the BCA knew that there was no evidence to support the claims, that by making them it knowingly promoted bogus treatments and that these were assertions of fact. Reversing him, the CA held that the natural meaning of the words was "not that the BCA was promoting what it knew to be bogus treatments but that it was promoting what [the defendant] contended were bogus treatments without regard to the want of reliable evidence of their efficacy" (at [30]). "It is one thing to defame somebody in terms which can only be defended by proving their truth, even if this ineluctably casts the court in the role of historian or investigative journalist. It is another thing to evaluate published material as giving no evidential support to a claim and, on the basis of this evaluation, to denounce as irresponsible those who make the claim" (at [22]).

The court at [32] said that it might be that the pair of questions posed for the judge

> "was based on a premise, inherent in our libel law, that a comment is as capable as an assertion of fact of being defamatory, and that what differ are the available defences; so that the first question has to be whether the words are defamatory even if they amount to no more than comment. This case suggests that this may not always be the best approach, because the answer to the first question may stifle the answer to the second."

It is not clear exactly what is meant in practical terms by this.

In *Joseph v Spiller* [2009] EWCA Civ 1075; [2010] E.M.L.R. 7 D's website stated that "[D] is no longer able to accept bookings for [C's band] . . . as [C's band] . . . are not professional enough to feature in our portfolio and have not been able to abide by the terms of their contract". It went on to state that C had asserted that "contracts hold no water in legal terms", that "for this reason" any bookings might not be met and advised taking legal advice before booking the band. The CA, reversing the judge below ([2009] EWHC 1152 (QB)) held that this was capable of being comment. The first sentence quoted was essentially a value judgment; the words following "for this reason", stated the inferences which the reader was invited to draw from the facts stated and similarly, the "recommendation" to the reader was capable of being a comment upon the facts on the basis of which the recommendation was made. However, the judge's decision to strike out the defence of fair comment was upheld on the basis that the allegation about contracts holding no water was untrue and D could not rely on a breach of contract by C with a third party some 14 months before, which had had no repercussions on the relationship between C and D and which was not even remotely referred to in the publication. Permission to appeal: UKSC 2009/0210, hearing July 2010, judgment expected October.

The subtlety of the distinction between fact and comment is illustrated by *Grant v Torstar Corp, Toronto Star Newspapers Ltd* [2009] SCC 61 (for which see para.15.23, below). One of the imputations was that an application for development approval was a "done deal", the context being that the plaintiff had political influence. The SCC said that it was arguable that this was a comment as "an idiomatic expression of an opinion about the *likelihood* of something, namely government approval, that had not yet come to pass" (at [137]). Alternatively, "it can be taken as an assertion that government approval for the development was actually already sealed, either formally behind closed doors or by tacit understanding" (at [139]). But arguably it is not simply a matter of futurity. If one reads it as meaning "his political influence is so great that it is bound to happen" is not that a statement of fact?

The ECtHR has frequently reiterated the distinction between statements of fact and "value judgments" but the dichotomy is not, it seems, a simple one. There may be "value-laden" statements of fact: *Karsai v Hungary* (2009) App. no.5380/07 at [33].

See also *Horlick v Associated Newspapers Ltd* [2010] EWHC 1544 (QB) at [24]; *Dee v Telegraph Media Group Ltd* [2010] EWHC 924 (QB); [2010] E.M.L.R. 20 ( para.2.8, above) and *French v Herald and Weekly Times Pty Ltd* [2010] VSC 155 ("drug cheat" still an assertion of fact even though preceded by "disgraced"—the latter was a comment on the former (untrue) fact).

**Inferences of fact as comment.** It is necessary to distinguish between infer-    **12.7** ences of fact which a reasonable reader might draw from the direct terms of the statement and his inference that the statement represents the opinion of the publisher: *Buckley v Herald and Weekly Times Pty Ltd* [2008] VSC 459.

> "[The] recipient of the publication is not confined to an understanding of the words conveyed in their literal sense; rather, as the authorities to which I have referred make plain, the law takes into account that the recipient of the material may indulge in deduction, inference or implication. However, to postulate that an imputation may derive from a publication by a process of implication or inference by the reader or listener of the publication, is not to say that the imputations, thus derived, were understood by the ordinary reasonable reader or listener as the comment or opinion of the publisher. That is, there is an important distinction between inferences or implications by the hypothetical ordinary reasonable reader of the publication complained of, on the one hand, and, on the other hand, an understanding by the ordinary reasonable reader of the publication that imputations, pleaded by a plaintiff, were conveyed to that reader as the opinion or comment of the writer of the articles" (at [28]).

The use of the word "viewed" in "The father of two is viewed by those who have had professional dealings with him as having a violent temper, acting like a commercial thug, and 'a man with eight different personalities'" could not justify a reasonable jury in regarding this as an expression of the writer's opinion. See also *Cleary v Hore-Lacy (No 2)* [2009] VSCA 132.

**Fact and comment: the significance of "supporting facts".** *Lord Lester's*    **12.8** *Defamation Bill.* See para.12.1, above.

The approach of the CA in *Joseph v Spiller* [2009] EWCA Civ 1075; [2010] E.M.L.R. 7 is not perhaps entirely consistent with that in *Lowe v Associated Newspapers*, since the court (disagreeing with the trial judge) regarded the matter as comment but held that the defence could not succeed in the absence of a reference to a single, true supporting fact. The passage from Lord Nicholls in *Tse Wai Chun* (quoted, Main Work, para.12.80) is cited without comment at [32] but the view that the reader should on the basis of the facts referred to "be in a position to judge for himself how far the comment was well founded" is singularly difficult to reconcile with e.g. *Kemsley v Foot*. Compare the formulation of Sir Charles Gray in *Thornton v Telegraph Media Group Ltd* [2009] EWHC 2863 (QB) at [44]–[45]:

> "In appropriate circumstances the publisher of a review of a literary work or dramatic or artistic work will be held to have complied with the requirement that words should indicate, at least in general terms, the factual basis for the comment if the reviewer identifies for the benefit of his or her readers the book or play or film or picture as the case may be . . . In such a case the Defendant reviewer may freely comment on the dramatic quality of the play or film or the literary or artistic merits or demerits of the book or picture . . . The reader of the review can then, if so inclined, buy the book and read it or go to see the play or film or see the picture at an exhibition or gallery. The reader of the review is then in a position to make up his or her own mind whether the comment is a fair one."

On the facts, however, the defence failed because the review significantly misdescribed what the book had said about the claimant's methods.

*Note 63.*

"It is not to the point that no explicit example of bad service [in the restaurant] is set out in the matter complained of. A review constitutes an exception to the general rule that the facts on which the comment is based must be set out in the matter complained of, or be otherwise notorious. It would be, in practical terms, impossible to critique a film, a play, or a restaurant if the law were otherwise": *Gacic v John Fairfax Publications Pty Ltd* [2009] NSWSC 1403 at [163].

**12.12** **Facts relied on in support of the defence.** The Supreme Court of New Zealand has held that, subject to two qualifications, the principles stated by the English CA in *Musa King v Telegraph Group Ltd* (Main Work, para.11.6) are applicable to facts relied on in support of the defence of honest opinion (broadly equivalent to the English fair comment): *APN New Zealand Ltd v Simunovich Fisheries Ltd* [2009] NZSC 93; [2010] 1 N.Z.L.R. 315. The qualifications are (1) (as is recognised in *Musa King*) a defendant relying on honest opinion/ fair comment may rely only on facts of which he was aware at the time of the publication; (2) in the case of honest opinion, but not in the case of truth, a fact need not be independently proved if it is referred to as a fact in a fair and accurate report which attracts privilege and upon which the defendant is commenting.

(b) *Facts sufficiently true*

**12.14** **Facts upon which comment is based must be true.** In *Levi v Bates* [2009] EWHC 1495 (QB) (a trial by judge alone) the defence of fair comment failed because the publications were "riddled with material inaccuracies" (which had also defeated the justification defence); and see *Thornton v Telegraph Media Group Ltd* [2009] EWHC 2863 (QB). See also para.12.17, below.

**12.17** **Illustration: court proceedings.** The example in the text of a statement that B was convicted without explanation that his conviction was quashed is regarded by the BCCA in *Creative Salmon Co Ltd v Staniford* [2009] BCCA 61 at [61] as an illustration of a general principle that:

"[T]he requirement to state the facts truly means in the present context that the commentator may not omit to state important or material facts that would falsify or alter the complexion of the facts stated in the commentary. It is not necessary to state all facts of a nature that may influence the opinion of the person hearing or reading the commentary. In order to defeat the defence, the omitted facts must be sufficiently fundamental that they undermine the accuracy of the facts expressed in the commentary to the extent the stated facts cannot be properly regarded as a true statement of the facts."

**Comment on privileged statement.** *Lord Lester's Defamation Bill.* See **12.21** para.12.1, above.

In *French v Herald and Weekly Times Pty Ltd* [2010] VSC 155 at [43] Beach J. said that he took

"leave to doubt that the defence can be established on the basis of facts which must be proved to be true (as distinct from published on an occasion of qualified privilege) by merely establishing that a third party has found or stated the underlying facts which it would be necessary to establish if one was trying to establish a truth defence."

### (c) *Words capable of being comment*

**The domain of comment.** The Supreme Court of Canada in *WIC Radio Ltd* **12.23** *v Simpson* [2008] SCC 40; [2008] S.C.R. 420 held that the "objective" element of fair comment was whether an honest person could hold the opinion. Speaking for the court, Binnie J. said at [28]:

"In my respectful view, the addition of a qualitative standard such as 'fair minded' should be resisted. 'Fair-mindedness' often lies in the eye of the beholder. Political partisans are constantly astonished at the sheer 'unfairness' of criticisms made by their opponents. Trenchant criticism which otherwise meets the 'honest belief' criterion ought not to be actionable because, in the opinion of a court, it crosses some ill-defined line of 'fair-mindedness'. The trier of fact is not required to assess whether the comment is a reasonable and proportional response to the stated or understood facts."

### (d) *"Malice"*

**Words not the defendant's opinion.** *Lord Lester's Defamation Bill.* See **12.25** para.12.1, above.

*Note 174. Cheng* was applied in *French v Triple M Melbourne Pty Ltd* [2008] VSC 553.

The Supreme Court of Canada in *WIC Radio Ltd v Simpson* [2008] SCC 40; [2008] S.C.R. 420 at [28] stated the Canadian law of fair comment as follows, adopting what had been said by Dickson J., dissenting, in *Chernesky v Armadale Publishers* [1979] 1 S.C.R. 1067 at [1099]:

"(a) the comment must be on a matter of public interest;
(b) the comment must be based on fact;
(c) the comment, though it can include inferences of fact, must be recognisable as comment;

(d) the comment must satisfy the following objective test: could any [person] honestly express that opinion on the proved facts?

(e) even though the comment satisfies the objective test the defence can be defeated if the plaintiff proves that the defendant was [subjectively] actuated by express malice."

The last point appears inconsistent with the view now taken in England that "honesty of belief", rather than improper motive, is the touchstone. However, the point of *WIC Radio* was that "the defendant had intended to convey one meaning in his comments but was objectively held to have conveyed a different meaning. He honestly believed the opinion he intended to convey but did not honestly believe the meaning he was taken to have conveyed": *Creative Salmon Co Ltd v Staniford* [2009] BCCA 61 at [24]. In other words, the point is similar to that in *Loveless v Earl* (Main Work, para.3.14) where it is said that where the defendant speaks on an occasion of qualified privilege one may depart from the objective meaning of the words and consider malice against what the defendant intended. The issue is perhaps hinted at in *British Chiropractic Association v Singh* [2010] EWHC 1101 at [31].

SECTION 3. A MATTER OF PUBLIC INTEREST

**12.33** **The management of institutions and companies.** The management of an investment fund is plainly a matter of public interest: *Horlick v Associated Newspapers Ltd* [2010] EWHC 1544 (QB) at [25].

**12.35** **The administration of justice.** Eady J. In *Hughes v Risbridger* [2010] EWHC 491 (QB) had doubts whether an email to fellow employees about a theft could be regarded as a matter of public interest but the point did not arise.

**12.40** **Public performances and performers.** In *Joseph v Spiller* [2009] EWCA Civ 1075; [2010] E.M.L.R. 7 at [37] a comment relating to the reliability in contract performance of artists in the entertainment business was regarded as arguably in the public interest.

CHAPTER 13

# ABSOLUTE PRIVILEGE

SECTION 1. INTRODUCTION

**General principles.** *Ireland.* The Irish Defamation Act 2009 provides in  **13.1**
s.17(1) that it

> "shall be a defence to a defamation action for the defendant to prove that the statement
> in respect of which the action was brought would, if it had been made immediately
> before the commencement of this section, have been considered under the law in force
> immediately before such commencement as having been made on an occasion of
> absolute privilege."

However, without prejudice to the generality of that (and subject to section 11(2)
of the Committees of the Houses of the Oireachtas (Compellability, Privileges
and Immunities of Witnesses) Act 1997) s.17(2) specifically provides a defence
of absolute privilege where it is proved that the statement was

> "(a) made in either House of the Oireachtas by a member of either House of the
>     Oireachtas,
> (b) contained in a report of a statement, to which *paragraph (a)* applies, produced by
>     or on the authority of either such House,
> (c) made in the European Parliament by a member of that Parliament,
> (d) contained in a report of a statement, to which *paragraph (c)* applies, produced by
>     or on the authority of the European Parliament,
> (e) contained in a judgment of a court established by law in the State,
> (f) made by a judge, or other person, performing a judicial function,
> (g) made by a party, witness, legal representative or juror in the course of proceedings
>     presided over by a judge, or other person, performing a judicial function,

(*h*) made in the course of proceedings involving the exercise of limited functions and powers of a judicial nature in accordance with Article 37 of the Constitution, where the statement is connected with those proceedings,

(*i*) a fair and accurate report of proceedings publicly heard before, or decision made public by, any court—

    (i) established by law in the State, or
    (ii) established under the law of Northern Ireland,

(*j*) a fair and accurate report of proceedings to which a relevant enactment referred to in section 40 of the Civil Liability and Courts Act 2004 applies,

(*k*) a fair and accurate report of proceedings publicly heard before, or decision made public by, any court or arbitral tribunal established by an international agreement to which the State is a party including the Court of Justice of the European Communities, the Court of First Instance of the European Communities, the European Court of Human Rights and the International Court of Justice,

(*l*) made in proceedings before a committee appointed by either House of the Oireachtas or jointly by both Houses of the Oireachtas,

(*m*) made in proceedings before a committee of the European Parliament,

(*n*) made in the course of proceedings before a tribunal established under the Tribunals of Inquiry (Evidence) Acts 1921 to 2004, where the statement is connected with those proceedings,

(*o*) contained in a report of any such tribunal,

(*p*) made in the course of proceedings before a commission of investigation established under the Commissions of Investigation Act 2004, where the statement is connected with those proceedings,

(*q*) contained in a report of any such commission,

(*r*) made in the course of an inquest by a coroner or contained in a decision made or verdict given at or during such inquest,

(*s*) made in the course of an inquiry conducted on the authority of a Minister of the Government, the Government, the Oireachtas, either House of the Oireachtas or a court established by law in the State,

(*t*) made in the course of an inquiry conducted in Northern Ireland on the authority of a person or body corresponding to a person or body referred to in *paragraph (s)*,

(*u*) contained in a report of an inquiry referred to in *paragraph (s)* or *(t)*,

(*v*) made in the course of proceedings before an arbitral tribunal where the statement is connected with those proceedings,

(*w*) made pursuant to and in accordance with an order of a court established by law in the State."

The effect of s.17(1) is to preserve the Irish common law on absolute privilege as it stood on December 31, 2009. That may cause potential problems since the Irish common law, like the English version, presumably adheres to the declaratory theory of precedent. For example, in 2008 English law held that a victim's complaint to the police was subject to absolute privilege, though before then it was thought that only qualified privilege applied (see Main Work, para.13.12). That situation does not appear to fall within the list in s.17(2). As far as can be determined the issue was never considered in Ireland. Perhaps the likely answer is that the existence of the statutory list will incline the courts to be resistant to pleas for "creative" interpretations of the common law. A similar point could arise in relation to qualified privilege, where the pre-Act common law is similarly preserved: see para.14.1, below.

Section 2. Statements Made in or in Connection with Judicial
Proceedings

**General rule.** Immunities for other torts. In *Walsh v Sprecher Grier Halber-*     **13.5**
*stam Llp* [2008] EWCA Civ 1324 claims for deceit and conspiracy in connexion
with litigation were struck out.

(b) *Privilege of Witnesses*

**Extent of privilege.** Does *Westcott* (fn.106) apply to a person who makes a     **13.12**
complaint in the course of his employment, for example a shop assistant who
accuses a customer of theft? That was held arguable for the purpose of setting
aside a default judgment in *Hughes v Alan Dick & Co Ltd* [2008] EWHC 2695
(QB) (statement to immigration authorities that passenger carrying improperly
obtained money). Compare *P and W v Manny* [2010] ACTSC 50. In *Coles Myer
Ltd v Webster* [2009] NSWCA 299 the assistant was found to have concocted a
story to the police about fraud because she had taken offence at their behaviour.
This was held to be malice for the purposes of qualified privilege, which was
assumed to be the only defence applicable (there was a concurrent, successful
claim for false imprisonment). In *P and W v Manny*, above, it was said that *Taylor
v Director of the Serious Fraud Office* and *Westcott v Westcott* involved exten-
sions of absolute privilege in a way rejected by the HCA in *Mann v O'Neill*
(1997) 191 C.L.R. 204 (though on the facts the statement could not fairly be said
to be part of the process of investigating crime).

*Note 100.* See also *McDaniel v McDaniel* [2009] BCCA 53.

*Note 103.* Negligence of expert witnesses. A "leap frog appeal" certificate was
given on this issue in *Jones v Kaney* [2010] EWHC 61 (QB) and the Supreme
Court granted permission to appeal on April 6, 2010.

Section 3. Statements made before other Tribunals having Functions of
a Judicial Nature

**Examples: tribunals of a judicial nature.** *Notes 202 and 203.* See also     **13.23**
*Vaidya v GMC* [2010] EWHC 984 (QB).

Section 5. Proceedings in Parliament

**Extent of the privilege.** The NSWCA in *Stewart v Ronalds* [2009] NSWCA     **13.30**
277 expressed the tentative opinion that the Bill of Rights did not apply to an
inquiry commissioned by the Executive, with the result to be reported to the
Executive, and only subsequently tabled in Parliament; nor did such a situation
fall within s.16(2)(c) of the Parliamentary Privileges Act 1987 (Cth) (which is in
the same terms as s.13(5)(c) of the Defamation Act 1996).

**13.32**      **The Defamation Act 1996.** *Lord Lester's Defamation Bill.* See para.1.12, above. Cl.16 would repeal s.13 of the Defamation Act 1996 and recast the basis of the law. In effect it takes up in a modified form the suggestion of the Joint Committee on Privilege referred to in fn.283. The member suing for defamation would not have the right to waive privilege but the Speaker might do so. If he did not, the claim might have to be stayed under *Prebble*.

<br>

SECTION 6. REPORTS, ETC. PUBLISHED BY ORDER OF PARLIAMENT

**13.34**      **The Parliamentary Papers Act.** *Lord Lester's Defamation Bill.* See para.1.12, above. Cl.18 and Sch.2 would repeal the Parliamentary Papers Act 1840. Cl.7(1)(c) would confer absolute privilege on any copy of, extract from or summary of anything published by the authority of Parliament (or the Northern Ireland or Welsh Assemblies). There continues to be a (simplified) procedure for staying proceedings which relate to such documents. Cl.7(1)(c) relates to the document published by the authority of Parliament (what the 1840 Act called a "report, paper, votes or proceedings"). Media reports of such documents and of proceedings in Parliament would also be absolutely privileged: see para.15.32, below.

<br>

SECTION 7. REPORTS OF JUDICIAL PROCEEDINGS

**13.35**      **Defamation Act 1996.** *Lord Lester's Defamation Bill.* See para.1.12, above. Cl.6 would replace s.14 of the Defamation Act 1996. The essential nature of the protection would be the same but the scope of the proceedings covered would be much extended, not only to various "international" tribunals, but to those of "any court established under the law of a country or territory outside the United Kingdom". The overlap with the statutory qualified privilege (see Main Work, para.16.8) and the vestigial common law qualified privilege (see Main Work, para.15.31) would therefore be even greater, though the absolute privilege would continue to have a requirement of contemporaneity as well as fairness and accuracy.

     In *Karim v Newsquest Media Group Ltd* [2009] EWHC 3205 (QB) a report of Law Society disciplinary proceedings was held to fall within the Act. In effect the law on statements before such a tribunal (see Main Work, para.13.23) is transferred across to reports of such proceedings.

**13.36**      **Meaning of "contemporaneously".** In *Crossley v Newsquest (Midlands South) Ltd* [2008] EWHC 3054 (QB) Eady J. held (1) that a report of county court proceedings published three days afterwards was contemporaneous and absolutely privileged and (2) that in so far as it contained material from earlier hearings necessary to understand the proceedings directly reported that was also absolutely privileged. He was also of the view that even in the case of non-contemporaneous reports, the requirement of "public interest and public benefit" for qualified privilege under s.15 and Sch.1 of the Defamation Act 1996 did not create any additional hurdle beyond fairness and accuracy in the case of reports of English proceedings (see para.16.5, below).

**Fairness and accuracy.** The claimant cannot complain if an accurate report **13.37** presents a one-sided story because he did not participate in the proceedings: *Karim v Newsquest Media Group Ltd* [2009] EWHC 3205 (QB).

*Note 323.* See also *Sands v Channel Seven Adelaide Pty Ltd* [2009] SASC 215 (common law report privilege) where the point is made at [326] that the fairness and accuracy required is that of the report, not some popular notion of fairness to the plaintiff (appeal dismissed [2010] SASC 202).

CHAPTER 14

# QUALIFIED PRIVILEGE AT COMMON LAW PART I

SECTION 1. INTRODUCTION

**14.1** **Introduction: the "classical" forms of qualified privilege.** *Ireland.* The Irish Defamation Act 2009, s.18(1) provides that

> "it shall be a defence to a defamation action for the defendant to prove that the statement in respect of which the action was brought would, if it had been made immediately before the commencement of this section, have been considered under the law (other than the [Defamation] Act of 1961) in force immediately before such commencement as having been made on an occasion of qualified privilege"

but without prejudice to the generality of that, there is a defence of qualified privilege under s.18(2) if the defendant proves that

> "(a) the statement was published to a person or persons who—
>
>> (i) had a duty to receive, or interest in receiving, the information contained in the statement, or
>> (ii) the defendant believed upon reasonable grounds that the said person or persons had such a duty or interest, and
>
> (b) the defendant had a corresponding duty to communicate, or interest in communicating, the information to such person or persons."

By s.18(7) duty and interest mean a legal, moral or social duty or interest. In other words, there is a statutory restatement of the classical duty/interest model. Compare the similar technique with regard to absolute privilege, para.13.1, above. S.18(3) and (4) make provision for the equivalents of the statutory forms of qualified privilege under Sch.1 of the English Defamation Act 1996.

**14.3** **Arrangement of the material.** On the point that the communication must be warranted by the exigency of the occasion see *Papaconstantinos v Holmes à Court* [2009] NSWSC 903 (letter to club about employment of plaintiff's son, a matter which had been addressed by the club some time earlier).

The common law and the Human Rights Act. The suggestion in *W v JH* (fn.42) that the common law on qualified privilege might have to be adapted to take account of the Convention has been further explored. In *Clift v Slough BC* [2009] EWHC 1550 (QB); [2009] 4 All E.R. 756 the claimant had criticised the response of the defendants to a complaint she had made and, after an investigation by the defendants of a telephone conversation between her and a representative of the defendants, she had been placed on their "Violent Persons Register". That decision was published by email within the defendants' organisation and to some "partner organisations" outside it. In considering whether qualified privilege applied to those publications, Tugendhat J. held that in order to support the defendants' case on interest or duty it had to show that it had complied with its statutory duties under the Human Rights Act 1998. On this basis qualified privilege applied to the publication to the defendants' staff who dealt directly with the public because that was rational and proportionate but it did not apply to the publication to other staff even if that had been administratively convenient. Tugendhat J. was of the view that if the case had not been affected by the legislation, privilege would have covered publication to all the defendants' staff.

"The ruling I made would have been different if I had followed *Kearns* [*v General Council of the Bar*, fn.26]. So far as publication to fellow Council employees is concerned, there was an existing relationship, and so no occasion to enquire into the circumstances. Publication to all employees of the Council would have been on an occasion of qualified privilege, including to those employees who did not need to know, such as those in the Licensing Department. In the case of publication to partner organisations, or nonemployees, these were not with in an existing relationship, and the ruling would have been the same. These were not on an occasion of qualified privilege" (at [99]).

The claimant's submissions on privilege were made only on the basis of the Human Rights Act but Tugendhat J. was of the view that the Data Protection Act 1998 might also have to be taken into account in such cases.

"The conclusions I have reached in this case may have some impact upon defences of qualified privileged raised by defendants who are not public authorities, but who have published information in breach of DPA. I have not so decided. Whether they do or not must remain open for another case. Even if the position of some personal or private sector defendants is to be assimilated to that of the Council in this case by reason of the DPA, there will remain communications to which the neither the HRA nor the DPA apply" (at [104]).

It can therefore no longer necessarily be said that no question of having to act responsibly (as opposed to honestly) arises in cases where qualified privilege is afforded by the common law (at [123]). This certainly adds a layer of uncertainty to situations where there is an established "off the peg" category of privilege. Furthermore, *Clift* raises the possibility (at [123]) that the reverse position may have to be considered: whether a defendant will fail if he has complied with the legislative requirements but cannot establish a relevant duty/interest at common law.

A related point is the treatment in *Flood v Times Newspapers Ltd* [2010] EWCA Civ 804; [2010] E.M.L.R. 26 of *De Buse v McCarthy* (fn.32). It is suggested that since that case involved a statement by a public authority it would now have to be considered "under the Human Rights Act 1998 s.6(1) and Article 8 directly, or, if applicable, under the Data Protection Act 1998": at [42], approving what Tugendhat J. said below.

For another view on the impact of data protection legislation on traditional tort rules see para.22.18, below.

*Note 28.* Permission to appeal was refused in *Seray-Wurie v Charity Commission* [2009] EWCA Civ 153.

SECTION 3. DUTY AND INTEREST: PARTICULAR SITUATIONS

(a) *Communications made in discharge of a duty*

**14.6**        **Duty and interest.** Ipp J.A. in *Bennette v Cohen* [2009] NSWCA 60 at [25] distilled the "classical" form of qualified privilege in Australia as follows:

"The following propositions may be extracted from the authorities . . .

(a)  The test for common law qualified privilege is usually expressed at a very high level of generality and abstraction;

(b)  In practice, however, the close scrutiny required of all the circumstances of each case results in common law qualified privilege having a relatively limited or narrow practical application;

(c)  The scrutiny required depends on the facts of each case and there is no closed set of criteria that must be applied or considered, and;

(d)  Guidelines have been established that assist in the scrutiny that is required. These include:

(i)  As a matter of public policy, it must be in the general interest of the whole community that the type of material in question be published, notwithstanding that it is defamatory of a third party;

(ii)  The occasion must not be used for some purpose or motive foreign to the interest that protects the making of the statement. Further, there must be a significant connection between the defamatory material and the privileged occasion;

(iii)  The interest that gives rise to qualified privilege must be real and direct;

(iv)  Ordinarily, a volunteered statement is privileged only where there is a pressing need to protect the interests of the defendant or a third party, or where the defendant has a duty to make the statement;

(v)  If a publication is made to a large audience, a claim of qualified privilege at common law will fail unless the members of the audience all have an interest in knowing the truth, and;

(vi)  The interest should not give officious and interfering persons a wide licence to defame."

**14.25**        **Inquiries as to credit.** In *Dale v Veda Advantage Information Services and Solutions Ltd* [2009] FCA 305 Lindgren J. held that qualified privilege applied to statements made via the defendants' credit database to providers of credit, nothwithstanding *Macintosh v Dun*. The defendants had begun as mutual association of credit providers but had become a profit-making company, though the credit providers were still the sole sources of information to the defendants and the sole recipient of information from them. That in itself was sufficient to distinguish the case from *Macintosh*, where the information appears to have been gathered from a range of undisclosed sources. No claim was made for breach of statutory duty under the Privacy Act 1988 (Cth).

**Volunteered statements in aid of justice.** See para.13.12, above.          **14.34**

(b) *Communications in pursuance of an interest*

**Common and reciprocal interests.** *Hyer v Cabbie Pty Ltd* (fn.270) was          **14.42**
upheld by the NSWCA, sub nom *Lindholdt v Hyer* [2008] NSWCA 264 but only on the basis that there was malice. Only one judge addressed the issue of whether there was a privileged publication. See para.14.67, below.

**Business and commercial interests.** The NSWCA upheld the decision in the          **14.43**
*Aktas* case (fn.278) that qualified privilege applied to the endorsement "Refer to Drawer" by a paying banker on dishonoured cheques: *Aktas v Westpac Banking Corp Ltd* [2009] NSWCA 9. The paying bank had a duty to communicate its decision to the payees and they had an interest in receiving it. However, this was reversed by a bare majority of the HCA: *Aktas v Westpac Banking Corp Ltd* [2010] HCA 25. The majority said at [41]:

> "The bank has an interest in communicating because it refuses to pay. But the payee has no interest in receiving a communication of refusal to pay a cheque which is regular on its face in a case where the drawer of the cheque has funds sufficient to meet its payment. And where a notice of dishonour is defamatory, the defamation will lie in the assertion either that the cheque is not regular, or that the drawer does not have funds sufficient to meet the payment ordered on the cheque. When a notice of dishonour is defamatory, the communication goes beyond informing the recipient that the bank refuses to pay the cheque; the communication gives the bank's reason for refusal. The defamatory imputation will be found in that reason, not in the bare fact of refusal. That being so, it is wrong to identify some community of interest in the communication actually made as arising out of a need or desire on the part of the bank to say that payment is refused or as founded in some more general notion of the payee needing or wanting to know 'the fate' of the cheque. As explained earlier, the bank acts as it does in what it perceives to be *its* interests. And for the payee of the cheque, there will be no need for any communication from the bank about the fate of the cheque, if it is met on presentation."

The decision is based on the view that to "hold banks responsible to their customers not only in contract, but also for damage to reputation, is conducive to maintaining a high degree of accuracy in the decisions that banks must make about paying cheques" (at [42]). No doubt there is something to be said for that from a policy point of view but against the background of the general law of qualified privilege the decision is surprising. To say that "the payee has no interest in receiving a communication of refusal to pay a cheque which is regular on its face in a case where the drawer of the cheque has funds sufficient to meet its payment" is in effect to follow the view of Hilbery J. in *Davidson v Barclays Bank* (fn.278) that the bank could not create a privileged occasion by its own mistake, but as Heydon J. points out, dissenting, the occasion "commenced when cheques were drawn on the first respondent by the second respondent and continued at least until the time when the first respondent informed payees and collecting banks of its decision not to honour those cheques. The first respondent was not mistaken about those facts. A mistake underlay what it communicated to its customers and the collecting banks. But that mistake was not a mistake about the occasion" (at [62]).

The approach of Hilbery J. in *Davidson* "creates an exception, in the case of banker and customer, to the application of settled principle" (Keifel J., dissenting, at [113]).

**14.45      Other common interests.** *Note 287.* On *De Buse v McCarthy* see the remarks in relation to the Human Rights Act in *Flood v Times Newspapers Ltd* [2010] EWCA Civ 804; [2010] E.M.L.R. 26 at [42].

The NSWCA reversed the decision in *Bennette v Cohen* [2009] NSWCA 60. The purpose of the meeting at which the statement was made was to raise funds for a party to a legal dispute; there was no reciprocal interest in making and receiving statements about the other party and even if there had been what was said was foreign to the occasion. In *Ryan v Premachandran* [2009] NSWSC 1186 privilege was denied for publication of complaints about the competence of a teacher to other parents of children in a class (though on the facts it had not been proved that all publishees were such). Nicholas J. said:

"The recipients were not persons with authority over, or responsible for, the plaintiff's performance as the principal. Thus they were not persons to whom a complaint about her conduct might properly be directed as having the relevant interest in knowing of its existence, or were persons capable of acting so as to further or protect the defendant's interest. In other words, in my opinion, it cannot be said that the defendant was under a social or moral duty to make the publication to the recipients or had an interest to protect in doing so, or that they had a relevant interest in knowing of defamatory statements relating to his personal concerns in support of his call for the plaintiff's resignation . . . Furthermore, in my opinion, the defendant did not show the existence of any occasion or exigency which warranted publication of his grievances against the plaintiff" (at [84]–[85]).

**14.49      Reply to retort.** See also *French v Herald and Weekly Times Pty Ltd* [2010] VSC 155.

**14.51      Responses to attacks on others.** *French v Herald and Weekly Times Pty Ltd* [2010] VSC 155 at [62] (though on the facts the statement was a reply to questions rather than a response to an attack).

**14.54      Defence of principal's interests.** See also *Khader v Aziz* [2010] EWCA Civ 716; [2011] E.M.L.R. 2 at [27].

(d) *Relevance*

**14.61      A limited role for relevance.** *Note 404.* See also *Sands v Channel Seven Adelaide Pty Ltd* [2009] SASC 215 at [246] (appeal dismissed [2010] SASC 202); and *Aktas v Westpac Banking Corp Ltd* [2009] NSWCA 9, where McClellan C.J. at C.L. said at [75]:

"If a bank returned a cheque to the payee having correctly determined that there were insufficient funds with two endorsements, one being 'Refer to Drawer' and the other, the 'drawer is a thief', the imputations arising from the publication of the first statement, made necessary by the bank's decision to refuse payment, will be an occasion of qualified privilege. The publication of the second will not, there being no interest or duty on the part of the bank to publish that the drawer is a thief, with whatever defamatory imputation may be found to arise from the publication of that statement. An occasion on which matter which gives rise to defamatory imputations is published may not be used for some purpose or motive foreign to the duty or interest that protects the making of the statement."

On appeal the majority of the HCA held that the first statement in the example would not be privileged if the determination had been incorrectly made: para.14.43, above.

### (e) *Excessive publication*

**Unnecessary publication.** In *Brady v Norman* [2008] EWHC 2481 (QB), a    **14.67** case rather similar to *Trumm v Norman* (para.14.73, fn.469) it was held that publication in ASLEF's *Loco Journal* to 131 persons (of a total circulation of approximately 18,000) who were not members or ex-members of the union was not privileged. Note that the defendant accepted that he could, if he wished, communicate with ASLEF members alone (at [15]). In *Levi v Bates* [2009] EWHC 1495 publication in football programmes sold to club members was privileged but not that in programmes sold to others (e.g. away supporters).

In *Lindholdt v Hyer* [2008] NSWCA 264 the publication was a magazine for cab drivers but was easily accessible to the public, indeed drivers were encouraged to show it to them. At trial the judge had found that there was qualified privilege but that it was defeated by malice. Upholding the latter finding, the majority of the NSWCA declined to deal with the argument in the defendant's Notice of Contention that the finding of privilege was wrong. However, McColl J.A. thought the defendant's argument was correct:

"Many . . . mono-topic magazines exist. A glance along a newsagent's shelf reveals magazines dedicated to sports, computers etc. Publishers of such magazines do not have a 'community of interest' with their subscribers in the sense required for an occasion of qualified privilege. The interests of society in general do not require that a communication made to any person with an interest in such topics should be protected . . . Once it is concluded that *Cabbie* is published to the general public, then . . . it cannot be said that the interests of society in general required the publication to it of matters concerning the economic welfare of taxi drivers/operators. Such publications were not made for the welfare of society. The fact that some readers may have been interested in the subject matter does not elevate it to that level . . . This was not a case where publication to the public beyond the taxi industry was reasonable, and no wider than was necessary for the effective communication of the imputations" (at [160]–[161]).

# CHAPTER 15

QUALIFIED PRIVILEGE AT COMMON LAW PART II

SECTION 2. THE CASE LAW FROM *REYNOLDS V TIMES NEWSPAPERS*

**15.2**    *Reynolds v Times Newspapers Ltd. Lord Lester's Defamation Bill.* See para.1.12, above. "*Reynolds* privilege" would be recast in statutory form by cl.1, with the sidenote name of "responsible publication on matters of public interest". As to cl.1 and reportage see para.15.16, below. One clear difference is that the defence would apply to opinions as well as statements of fact, thereby producing some common ground with fair comment, or honest opinion as it would be called under the Bill: cl.1(2). This would not duplicate honest opinion or render it redundant since presumably the opinion has to be arrived at "responsibly" under cl.1. However, as has already been noted (para.12.1, above) factual material "responsibly" published under cl.1 may also be supporting material for the purposes of the opinion defence so the defendant would get a second bite at the cherry, so to speak, but on a different basis. Otherwise it is very difficult to predict what difference the provision would make. The explanatory notes say that cl.1 "builds on" *Reynolds* (para.47) but are coy about stating how much new build there is in the resulting structure. However, the following (somewhat speculative) points may be made.

■ Even where the draftsman's instructions are to reproduce the common law as nearly as may be (e.g. the Sale of Goods Act 1893) the tendency is to discourage reference back to the law before the statute, the words of which are now the source of the law. The Bill does not purport to "codify" *Reynolds* in this sense but to build on it. Opinions differ on whether Lord Nicholls' hoped-for valuable body of case law has been built up (if it has *Jameel* culled it) but in any event we are back to square one.

■ The foundation in cl.1(1) is that (a) the words were published for the purpose of, or otherwise in connexion with, a matter of public interest and (b) the defendant acted responsibly in publishing. It would be hopeless to seek a watertight "definition" in the existing case law but the general sense seems to be that the public interest justifies the publication (after such verification as may be appropriate) of the story as a whole, including the parts of which complaint is made. It is not enough that the general subject matter is something of public interest (see *Flood v Times Newspapers Ltd*, paras 15.12–15.13, below). Read literally cl.1(2)(a) is arguably much wider—it is enough that the words were "published ... in connexion with ... the discussion of a matter of public interest". Of course the question of the justifiability of the inclusion of the allegations complained of may be swept up in the "responsible journalism" element (as the Supreme Court of Canada does in *Grant v Torstar*, see para.15.23, below, factor (f) in the list) but there is nothing in cl.1(4) which very clearly fulfils this role. Compare s.26(2)(b) of the Irish Act, para.15.24, below.

■ If we turn to the question of whether the defendant acted responsibly, cl.1(3) and the opening words of cl.1(4) may fairly be regarded as making Lord Nicholls' point in *Reynolds* that no list can be exhaustive. Some of the *Reynolds* factors are missing from cl.1(4) or at least are not expressly mentioned—anything can fall into "all the circumstances of the case". There is nothing about *Reynolds* factor (9), the "tone of the article". Now this may be a deliberate omission based on the no doubt correct view that it is not the law's job to teach taste to tabloid editors, but what Lord Nicholls made clear he had in mind was more the "rush to judgment" problem, the media not simply raising issues for investigation but acting as judge, jury and executioner—see *Grobelaar* and *Galloway*, Main Work, para.15.15. The point may also be of significance for the purposes of the inclusion of statements of opinion within this defence. Cl.1(4)(c) is drafted in a remarkably neutral fashion. It is capable of including *Reynolds* factors (3) (reliability of source) and (5) (status of information) but it would be more reassuring if it was more specific.

**The impact of the European Convention on Human Rights.** The point is  **15.4**
made in the Main Work that the Strasbourg case law has (understandably) not figured large in the cases interpreting and applying *Reynolds*. See, however, *Flood v Times Newspapers Ltd* [2010] EWCA Civ 804; [2010] E.M.L.R. 26, paras 15.12–15.13, below. *Flood* was a case of the reporting of allegations of criminal conduct before the completion of an investigation which eventually led to the conclusion that they were unfounded and in which the application of *Reynolds* privilege was rejected. After the hearing the CA's attention was drawn to *A v Norway* (2009) App. no.28070/06. The facts were much more extreme, involving the attribution by the media of serious suspicion of two sex murders to A, who had been convicted of a murder 13 years before and who had served his sentence, although at the time he was still subject to "security measures". A was not named but was identifiable from the material; he had been given the opportunity to declare his innocence on the front page of the newspaper. The ECtHR found that there had been a violation of art.8 and that the Norwegian courts in dismissing (by majority) his claim for defamation had not struck a fair balance between his rights and those of the media under art.10. The reasoning and conclusion is very brief but the case is perhaps a corrective to the not uncommonly held view that under art.8 the media are always protected provided they are dealing with matters of public concern and make no egregious errors of fact. Lord Neuberger M.R. said in *Flood* at [85] that it might well provide some support for the result in that case but that it was unnecessary to say anything more about it.

**15.5**     **Jameel (Mohammed) v Wall Street Journal Europe SPRL.** In view of the defendants' success in the HL a Strasbourg application in relation to the application of the presumption of falsity was declared inadmissible on February 10, 2009: App. no.28577/05.

**15.10**    **Subject matter of sufficient public interest.** *Note 86.* Now that it is recognised that reputation is an interest falling within art.8 of the Convention, there must in any case be a balancing exercise between the protection of that interest and of freedom of expression and Lord Nicholls' statement that "any lingering doubts should be resolved in favour of publication" can no longer stand: *Flood v Times Newspapers Ltd* [2010] EWCA Civ 804; [2010] E.M.L.R. 26 at [21], referring to *S (A Child) (Identification: Restriction on Publication), Re* [2004] UKHL 47; [2005] 1 AC 593 and *BBC, Re* [2009] UKHL 34; [2010] 1 A.C. 226.

**15.12 to**    *Second sentence.* In *Flood v Times Newspapers Ltd* [2010] EWCA Civ 804;
**15.13**    [2010] E.M.L.R. 26 Lord Neuberger M.R. said at [22]:

> "*Jameel* was fairly heavily referred to in argument before us, as both parties were keen to identify differences or similarities between that case and the instant case. Given that the law relating to *Reynolds* privilege is at a relatively early stage of development, and in the light of Lord Nicholls's reference to 'a valuable corpus of case law [being] built up', this is understandable. However, there is a risk of unnecessarily protracting hearings and losing sight of the wood for the trees if there is too minute a comparison of the various factors in previous decided cases and those in the case at issue. Each case turns on its own facts, and the court has to apply the normal sharp focus on the competing factors, which is required where there are tensions between Convention rights. Too much concentration on the facts of other cases can distract from the exercise."

The recognition that reputation is protected by art.8 (para.15.10, above) means that particular factors in *Reynolds* may have to be considered from the point of view of both the claimant and the defendant.

> "So, for example, Lord Nicholls states that 'the more serious the charge, the more the public is misinformed and the individual harmed'. That is focussing on the right to reputation. But as he also said, investigative journalism is part of the vital role of the press. Investigative journalism tends to result in serious allegations. The seriousness of the allegation may also support the journalist's contention that there is a public interest in the making of the allegation. A recent example may be certain allegations that MPs have been claiming as expenses money spent for private purposes" *Flood v Times Newspapers Ltd* [2009] EWHC 2375; [2010] E.M.L.R. 8 at [149] per Tugendhat J.

The decision was reversed on appeal and this point does not seem to be mentioned. However, there is nothing which could be taken as disapproval of it.

The CA's decision on *Flood* is the most important on *Reynolds* privilege since *Jameel.* The defendants in June 2006 published a story to the effect that there were reasonable grounds to suspect that the claimant, a serving police officer, had corruptly received payments from a security company with Russian clients in return for providing confidential information about the possible extradition of Russians here. The allegations were said to have originated with an insider at the security firm who had passed a dossier to the police anti-corruption squad. The story went on to say that the police were investigating the claimant. The article was also published on the defendants' website. The claimant began proceedings for libel in respect of both publications in May 2007. The police investigation concluded in December 2006 and was unable to find any evidence of wrongdoing on the part of the claimant, though this was not communicated to the parties until September 2007. On an appeal and cross-appeal from Tugendhat J.'s decision on a preliminary issue the CA had to consider whether the publications were covered by *Reynolds* privilege, the main publication in June 2006, the website publication on a continuing basis thereafter.

There was no doubt that allegations of police corruption were a matter of serious public interest and concern; so was the publication of the fact that there was a police investigation into those allegations, if only because that gave the public confidence that the police would pursue "one of their own" (see Moses L.J. at [116]). Indeed the reporting of the investigation would have fallen squarely within para.9 of Sch.1 of the Defamation Act 1996 since it was based on a police press statement and, while strictly speaking that would not cover the identification of the claimant (since that information was not in the press notice), the claimant was prepared to concede that this would have been privileged (a sort of "combination" of *Reynolds* and Sch.1—see para.16.15, below). On that basis the facts would quite closely resemble those of *Jameel*, where the story (a) identified the claimant and (b) reported the fact of the monitoring of the accounts. However, the story in *Flood* went considerably further than this in including details of the allegations which underlay the investigation. The main content of the article was the allegations plus some material about Russian emigres:

> "[In *Jameel* the] basis on which SAMA had chosen to co-operate with the United States was never disclosed. Nothing that was published suggested justification for the inclusion of the claimant's bank accounts amongst those to be monitored. Monitoring embraced those whose accounts might be used unwittingly.
>
> Of course, the details in the *Times*' article [in *Flood*] added spice to the story; of course those details might make it more likely that a reader would notice the article. Editors know how to attract the attention and interest of their readers and the courts must defer to their judgement of how best to achieve that result . . . But non sequitur that it can be left to them to judge whether publication of the impugned details is of public interest" (Moses L.J. at [117]–[118]).

In order to cast the protection of privilege around the publication of the details it would be necessary to show that sufficient steps to verify them had been taken and the defendants' case fell well short of that. No attempt had been made to rely on the reportage principle (Main Work, paras 15.16–15.18). Whether or not that extends beyond the even-handed reporting of disputes:

> "[t]he fact that an unidentified insider has given specific information which, if true, may incriminate a claimant, will very rarely be justifiable reportage. Of course, it will add something to the substance and newsworthiness of the story that the police are investigating the claimant, but it seems to me that it would be tipping the scales too far in favour of the media to hold that not only the name of the claimant, but the details of the allegations against him, can normally be published as part of a story free of any right in the claimant to sue for defamation just because the general subject matter of the story is in the public interest. The fair balancing of Article 8 and Article 10 would normally

require that such allegations should only be freely publishable if to do so is in the public interest and the journalist has taken reasonable steps to check their accuracy. If they are true, a claim for defamation will fail; if they are untrue, but their publication was in the public interest, and a reasonable check was carried out, there is good reason why a claim for defamation should fail, even though it is hard on the claimant; if they are untrue and their publication cannot be said to be in the public interest or no reasonable check was carried out, it seems quite unjust that the claimant should have no remedy in law" (at [62]).

This was not a piece of investigative journalism but a simple repetition of the substance of what the insider had told the police embroidered to some extent with speculation and when the allegations were published in the article,

"they were, as the passages . . . quoted from the judgment [of Tugendhat J.] show, and as the journalists must have appreciated, no more than unsubstantiated unchecked accusations, from an unknown source, coupled with speculation. The only written evidence available to the journalists did not identify any police officer, let alone DS Flood, as the recipient of money from ISC at all, let alone for providing confidential information" (at [73]).

The dangers in allowing the details of charges to be ventilated in the press before they have been investigated are emphasised by Moore-Bick L.J. at [104]:

"In my view responsible journalism requires a recognition of the importance of ensuring that persons against whom serious allegations of crime or professional misconduct are made are not forced to respond to them before an investigation has been properly carried out and charges have been made. It is very easy for allegations of impropriety or criminal conduct to be made, to the police, professional bodies and others who may have a duty to investigate their truth, out of malice, an excess of zeal or simple misunderstanding. If the details of such allegations are made public, they are capable of causing a great deal of harm to the individual concerned, since many people are inclined to assume that there is 'no smoke without fire'. Moreover, there is a serious risk that once the allegations have been published the person against whom they are made will feel obliged to respond to them publicly, thereby depriving himself of the safeguard of the ordinary process and risking a measure of trial by press. I am not dealing here with the publication of the simple fact that a complaint has been made against a person, without any details being given, or with the publication of the fact that a person has been charged with a criminal offence. Such information is likely to be a matter of public interest. It is routinely made public in statements issued by the police and when that occurs a report of the statement is protected under section 15 of the Defamation Act. However, it is unnecessary and inappropriate for such reports to set out the details of the allegations made against the person charged; the description of the charge itself is sufficient to inform the public of what it has an interest in knowing. The alternative is trial by press without proper safeguards, which is clearly not in the public interest."

As Moses L.J. put it at [119]:

"That a person is accused is generally of far greater interest than his or her subsequent triumphant acquittal. Once an accusation is dismissed, the blaring headline of accusation on page 1 becomes a tepid reference in the graveyard of page 2."

Tugendhat J. below had said that he did not find *Miller v Associated Newspapers* and *Henry v BBC* (fnn.127 and 128) of assistance because they now had to be read subject to *Jameel*. Since in both cases the privilege claim failed in part because of the fact that investigations had not been completed, the CA decision would seem to support them.

The journalist in *Flood* had in fact been in contact with the insider via two unidentified sources "A" and "B" which had led the insider to go to the police so that in a sense it was the journalist himself who had prompted the investigation. However, the argument that this of itself prevented reliance on *Reynolds* was rejected (see at [52]). As Tugendhat J. had said below:

> "Even if it had been precipitated by the journalists, that would not have been a reason why they should not report it (assuming other conditions necessary for reliance on a *Reynolds* public interest defence were fulfilled). This is not a case which is circular in the sense that TNL were simply reporting that they had made allegations to the police. They were not reporting that at all. What they were reporting was that there was an investigation by the police. The police do not automatically investigate every allegation that is made to them. They decide what to investigate and what not to investigate. So there is a very important difference between what the journalists may have alleged to the police, and the fact that the police were carrying out an investigation (even if that investigation may have resulted from what the journalists alleged)" [2009] EWHC 2375; [2010] E.M.L.R. 8 at [191].

Another important point which emerges from the case is the correct analysis of the appellate court's role in these cases. It had been said in *Galloway v Telegraph Group Ltd* [2006] EWCA Civ 17; [2006] E.M.L.R. 11 at [68] that

> "[t]he right to publish must . . . be balanced against the rights of the individual. That balance is a matter for the judge. It is not a matter for an appellate court. This court will not interfere with the judge's conclusion after weighing all the circumstances in the balance unless he has erred in principle or reached a conclusion which is plainly wrong."

This is now held to be an incorrect approach. The applicability of *Reynolds* is not a matter of "discretion" but a decision on a matter of law so that in principle there can only be one correct answer, even if one has to recognise that in practice sensible people may come to different conclusions. Lord Neuberger M.R. at [49] said:

> "In my view, a decision in a case such as this does not involve the exercise of a discretion and cannot therefore be approached as the court suggested in *Galloway* . . . Where a first instance court carries out a balancing exercise, the appeal process requires the appellate court to decide whether the judge was right or wrong, but it should bear in mind the advantage that the trial judge had in the ways described [by Lord Bingham] in *Jameel* [2007] 1 AC 359, paragraph 36. Where the determination is a matter of balance and proportionality, it is, generally speaking, difficult for an appellant to establish that the judge has gone wrong."

And Moore-Bick L.J. said at [107]:

> "There is an intrinsic difference between exercising a discretion and deciding a question of law. In cases where the court is called upon to exercise its discretion views may legitimately differ about the order that should be made. For that reason the judge's decision cannot be overturned otherwise than on well-recognised grounds which, if established, undermine the basis on which the discretion was exercised. When a

question of law is to be decided there is only one correct answer, however difficult it may be to find. Thus, if the true meaning of a document is in issue, the fact that the construction preferred by the judge is plausible does not prevent an appellate court from deciding the matter for itself. Nonetheless, where newspapers and broadcasters are involved striking a balance between freedom of speech and the protection of reputation will often depend to a large extent on an assessment of the behaviour of the journalists involved in the publication. Factors of the kind identified by Lord Nicholls require a careful assessment of the evidence and an appellate court should be cautious before overturning the decision of the judge below, particularly since it has not itself had the advantage of seeing the witnesses."

There may be a number of people involved in different ways in the "production" of a news item for which *Reynolds* privilege is claimed. Does the defence apply to a claim against one of them if he has not followed the requirements of the case even though others have? Tugendhat J. considered this issue in *Hays Plc v Hartley* [2010] EWHC 1068 (QB) though it was unnecessary to decide it since the claim was struck out as an abuse of process (see para.9.1, above). Put shortly, the defendant, via a journalist, supplied a story to a newspaper which published it but which was not sued. The defendant was sued in respect of the publication to the journalist and the republication in the newspaper was relied on in support of damages. The newspaper had an arguable *Reynolds* defence (either in the standard form or as reportage). However, since the defendant was in effect acting as an independent news agency rather than publishing to the world, he had followed his usual practice and relied on the journalist and newspaper to carry out the investigations required for responsible journalism. In the normal news media situation of a commercial publisher and employed journalists Tugendhat J.'s provisional view was that if the commercial publisher had complied via the collective action of its employees the same defence must be available to the individuals, even though, for example, each of them had carried out only one aspect of the task. Had the issue arisen the question would have been how far this could be applied to a freelance supplier of news stories.

*Reynolds and internet publication.* The availability of previously published material in archives, primarily on the internet but also to some extent in physical form, raises a number of difficulties in relation to privilege where circumstances have changed since the initial publication (see, e.g. Main Work, paras 13.36 and 16.4). Where there is litigation it is common to attach a qualification to internet material which may have the effect of removing the sting from the material (see para.6.3, above) but it will not necessarily do so. The issue arose in the *Reynolds* context in *Flood v Times Newspapers Ltd* [2010] EWCA Civ 804; [2010] E.M.L.R. 26. For the facts see above. A *Reynolds* defence failed in respect of the initial, paper publication of the story in 2006 and therefore no further issue could arise in respect of the internet publication, which was continuing at the time of the hearing. However, Tugendhat J. below ([2009] EWHC 2375; [2010] E.M.L.R. 8) had applied *Reynolds* to the paper publication and on that basis it was significant that, although the claimant had been cleared by the police investigation in 2006/2007 the website version in 2009 still simply had a note "this article is subject to legal complaint". Technically, no complaint was made of continuing publication after the commencement of proceedings but no point was taken on that. Tugendhat J. held that the qualified website article was not protected by privilege from the time of the release of the report of the investigation. The qualification failed to make clear who had made the complaint (it could just as well have been other persons named in the article), the status of the information relied on in relation to the paper publication had changed for the worse and the article could no longer be regarded as a fair representation of the claimant's position. It was true that the defendants had offered to publish a "news in brief" item referring to the report and that this had been rejected by the claimant on the wording. That might be relevant on any eventual award of damages but it could not support privilege.

> "[T]he risk in relation to the *Reynolds* public interest defence lay on TNL, and not on the Claimant. It is for a defendant to make good his defence. It may well be good practice to seek to agree a form of follow-up publication in a case such as this. But if there is no agreement, then the publisher must take his own course, and then defend it if he can at trial. He cannot offer the claimant a form of words which the claimant refuses to accept, and then rely on that refusal to relieve him of the obligation of acting responsibly and fairly, at least when the claimant's refusal is reasonable, as it was here" (at [244]).

In the CA Lord Neuberger M.R. (with whom Moore-Bick L.J. agreed) said that he would adopt what Tugendhat J. had said, subject to qualifying the last sentence:

> "The fact that the claimant's refusal is unreasonable will, save perhaps in the most unusual circumstances, not be enough to justify the defendant doing nothing if responsible journalism would otherwise require him to retract or modify a website publication if further relevant information comes to light. The essential point is that it is for a defendant to decide on the appropriate course to take. As well as being contrary to principle, it seems to me to be literally adding insult to injury to enable a defendant to require a claimant, after new evidence has come to light, to agree a form of words to amend a publication, which is defamatory of him but against which he cannot protect himself in law, so as to ensure he still cannot protect himself against it in law" (at [81]).

**Reportage.** See *Flood v Times Newspapers Ltd* [2010] EWCA Civ 804;          **15.16**
[2010] E.M.L.R. 26, paras 15.12–15.13, above.

*Lord Lester's Defamation Bill.* See para.1.12, above. See clause 1(5). Para.20 of the explanatory notes says that this would clarify the position on reportage. With respect, it is difficult to see how it will clarify things at all, since it simply provides as an example the situation of a dispute, where the defence is established, and says that it *may* be other situations. It refers to reports on a pre-existing matter but almost all defamatory statements are likely to be about a "pre-existing matter", e.g. what the claimant is alleged to have done. On the other hand, the form of the provision might suggest that it would not allow us to jettison the repetition rule altogether. Cl.1(6) provides that in determining the public interest for the purposes of cl.1(5) the court may disregard any question as to the truth of what is reported. But a central plank of *Jameel* is that the truth of the allegation is irrelevant right across the board of *Reynolds* privilege. The point is surely not that the court in a reportage case may disregard the truth of what is stated but that the *defendant* is not (at least in the case of reporting a dispute) required to investigate the truth of it.

**15.23**    *Canada.* The Supreme Court of Canada restated the law in *Grant v Torstar Corp, Toronto Star Newspapers Ltd* [2009] SCC 61 so as to incorporate a new defence, separate from qualified privilege, of "responsible communication on matters of public interest". Speaking for eight members of the court, McLachlin C.J. said that she would

> "formulate the test as follows. First, the publication must be on a matter of public interest. Second, the defendant must show that publication was responsible, in that he or she was diligent in trying to verify the allegation(s), having regard to all the relevant circumstances" (at [98]).

> The "public interest is not synonymous with what interests the public. The public's appetite for information on a given subject—say, the private lives of well-known people—is not on its own sufficient to render an essentially private matter public for the purposes of defamation law. An individual's reasonable expectation of privacy must be respected in this determination. Conversely, the fact that much of the public would be less than riveted by a given subject matter does not remove the subject from the public interest. It is enough that some segment of the community would have a genuine interest in receiving information on the subject" (at [102]).

On the other hand, the defence is not confined to government or political matters or the actions of public figures (at [106]) and guidance may be found in the cases on fair comment and on s.2(b) of the Canadian Charter of Rights (which deals with freedom of expression).

> "Public interest may be a function of the prominence of the person referred to in the communication, but mere curiosity or prurient interest is not enough. Some segment of the public must have a genuine stake in knowing about the matter published" (at [105]).

The question of public interest was for the judge: although the focus was on the publication rather than the occasion, as in traditional privilege, the judge had an analogous "gatekeeper" function. But the question of whether the defendant acted responsibly is for the jury and the judge should assess the publication in a broad way and not editorially excise particular passages on the basis that they were not necessary to the communication.

> "Deciding whether the inclusion of the impugned statement was justifiable involves a highly fact-based assessment of the context and details of the publication itself. Whereas a given subject matter either is or is not in law a matter of public interest, the justifiability of including a defamatory statement may admit of many shades of gray. It is intimately bound up in the overall determination of responsibility and should be left to the jury. It is for the jury to consider the need to include particular defamatory statements in determining whether the defendant acted responsibly in publishing what it did" (at [109]).

At the second stage the jury is to be guided by a list of factors resembling those in *Reynolds* and these are summarized at [126], the issue being whether "the publisher was diligent in trying to verify the allegation", having regard to

> "(a) the seriousness of the allegation;
> (b) the public importance of the matter;
> (c) the urgency of the matter;

(d) the status and reliability of the source;

(e) whether the plaintiff's side of the story was sought and accurately reported;

(f) whether the inclusion of the defamatory statement was justifiable;

(g) whether the defamatory statement's public interest lay in the fact that it was made rather than its truth ('reportage'); and

(h) any other relevant circumstances."

As under *Reynolds*, malice disappears from the picture: a "defendant who has acted with malice in publishing defamatory allegations has by definition not acted responsibly" (at [125]). It may be noted in the context of factor (g) that the expanded version at [120]–[121] is focused, like a number of the English cases cited therein, firmly on the reporting of *disputes*, so there is the same uncertainty as there is here on how far reportage can be applied more extensively. Although the application of all these factors would be for the jury, it would remain the case, as in the analogous context of malice and qualified privilege, that the judge could withdraw the defence on the basis that the facts are incapable of supporting it in law: at [129]. Under the new defence it is not necessary for the jury to find a single meaning: it is to assess whether responsibility has been shown in the light of the range of meanings the words are reasonably capable of bearing (at [124]—see Main Work, para.15.19).

Abella J. expressed himself in complete agreement with the Chief Justice's judgment except on the role of the jury and he would have made the whole issue of the applicability of the defence one for the judge alone, leaving to the jury only the determination of disputed matters of fact. Although "the jury's participation in defamation cases is firmly entrenched in the psyche of defamation law" (at [144]) yet,

"By adopting the responsible communication defence, we are recognizing the sophistication and constitutional complexity of defamation cases involving communications on matters of public interest. What is most important is protecting the integrity of the interests and values at stake in such cases. This defence is a highly complex legal determination with constitutional dimensions. That takes it beyond the jury's jurisdiction and squarely into judicial territory" (at [145]).

Compare the majority at [127]–[135].

The article in *Grant* concerned an application for permission for a golf course development by the plaintiff, a person of political influence, which was being opposed by local residents. On the facts the SCC seems to have regarded it as more or less self-evident that the material complained of was capable of falling within the new defence. Indeed, there is little reference to the facts beyond the statement that:

"Overly narrow characterization [of the subject matter] may inappropriately defeat the defence at the outset. For example, characterizing the subject matter in this case simply as 'Peter Grant's business dealings' would obscure the significant public interest engaged by the article and thus restrict the legitimate scope of public interest. Similarly, characterizing the subject matter too broadly as 'Ontario politics' might render the test a mere rubber stamp and bring unworthy material within the protection of the defence" (at [107]).

On the same day the SCC decided *Quan v Cusson* [2009] SCC 62 (for the decision below see Main Work, para.15.23 fn.225) and applied the *Grant* law to that. The allegation was that in the aftermath of "9/11" the plaintiff, an Ontario police officer, had without permission, gone to New York, had purported to assist at "Ground Zero" and had possibly hampered the rescue efforts. The SCC regarded it as plain that the public interest test was met ("the Canadian public has a vital interest in knowing about the professional misdeeds of those who are entrusted by the state with protecting public safety"—at [31]) and ordered a new trial on the issue of "diligence". The lower appellate court had in fact accepted "*Reynolds* law" into Ontario—see fn.225) but had refused to allow the defendants to rely on it because it had not been raised at trial: see [2009] SCC 62 at [45].

**15.24**     **Ireland.** See now s.26 of the Defamation Act 2009.

"26.—(1) It shall be a defence (to be known, and in this section referred to, as the 'defence of fair and reasonable publication') to a defamation action for the defendant to prove that—

  (*a*)  the statement in respect of which the action was brought was published—

    (i)  in good faith, and
    (ii)  in the course of, or for the purpose of, the discussion of a subject of public interest, the discussion of which was for the public benefit,

  (*b*)  in all of the circumstances of the case, the manner and extent of publication of the statement did not exceed that which was reasonably sufficient, and

  (*c*)  in all of the circumstances of the case, it was fair and reasonable to publish the statement.

(2) For the purposes of this section, the court shall, in determining whether it was fair and reasonable to publish the statement concerned, take into account such matters as the court considers relevant including any or all of the following:

  (*a*)  the extent to which the statement concerned refers to the performance by the person of his or her public functions;

  (*b*)  the seriousness of any allegations made in the statement;

  (*c*)  the context and content (including the language used) of the statement;

  (*d*)  the extent to which the statement drew a distinction between suspicions, allegations and facts;

  (*e*)  the extent to which there were exceptional circumstances that necessitated the publication of the statement on the date of publication;

  (*f*)  in the case of a statement published in a periodical by a person who, at the time of publication, was a member of the Press Council, the extent to which the person adhered to the code of standards of the Press Council and abided by determinations of the Press Ombudsman and determinations of the Press Council;

  (*g*)  in the case of a statement published in a periodical by a person who, at the time of publication, was not a member of the Press Council, the extent to which the publisher of the periodical adhered to standards equivalent to the standards specified in *paragraph (f)*;

  (*h*)  the extent to which the plaintiff's version of events was represented in the publication concerned and given the same or similar prominence as was given to the statement concerned;

  (*i*)  if the plaintiff's version of events was not so represented, the extent to which a reasonable attempt was made by the publisher to obtain and publish a response from that person; and

  (*j*)  the attempts made, and the means used, by the defendant to verify the assertions and allegations concerning the plaintiff in the statement.

(3) The failure or refusal of a plaintiff to respond to attempts by or on behalf of the defendant, to elicit the plaintiff's version of events, shall not—

(*a*) constitute or imply consent to the publication of the statement, or

(*b*) entitle the court to draw any inference therefrom.

(4) In this section—
'court' means, in relation to a defamation action brought in the High Court, the jury, if the High Court is sitting with a jury;
'defamation action' does not include an application for a declaratory order."

In comparison with the Bill version (cl.24) set out in the Main Work, the following points may be noted. (1) The reasonableness of the manner and form of the publication in relation to the public discussion is made part of the substance of the defence rather than being relegated to an apparent "second stage" under cl.24(4)(d). (3) "Malice" (or "bad faith . . . spite, ill will or other improper motive" as cl.24(4)(b) formerly had it) disappears. It seems legitimate to apply the phrase "responsible journalism" to the factors set out in s.24(2) so the defence is more like *Reynolds*. (4) The requirement in cl.24(4)(a) of the Bill that the defendant believed the statement to be true has disappeared, opening the way to reportage. "The person" in s.26(2)(a) is slightly linguistically odd but presumably refers to the plaintiff. It is thought that this paragraph should not confine the defence to statements about a person having a public office or function, though that will no doubt be satisfied in many cases

### SECTION 3. CANDIDATES FOR ELECTION

**Candidates for election.** In *Shavluk v Green Party of Canada* [2010] BCSC    **15.28**
804 an election press release regarding termination of the claimant's party candidacy was held to fall both under qualified privilege and the defence of responsible communication established in *Grant v Torstar* (para.15.23, above).

*Note 276.* It has been held that this form of privilege in Australia is not confined to to a statement by one candidate with respect to another candidate: *Fraser v Holmes* [2009] NSWCA 36 at [30] (statement about union leader opposed to candidate). See also *Megna v Marshall* [2010] NSWSC 686.

### SECTION 4. PRIVILEGED REPORTS AT COMMON LAW

**Reports of judicial proceedings.** *Last sentence.* Criminal libel was abolished    **15.31**
by s.73(b) of the Coroners and Justice Act 2009.

**Reports of parliamentary proceedings.** *Lord Lester's Defamation Bill.* Cl.7    **15.32**
would confer absolute privilege on fair and accurate reports of proceedings in Parliament, reports of anything published by the authority of Parliament and copies of or extracts from things so published. The same would apply to reports of proceedings etc of the Northern Ireland or Welsh Assemblies.

CHAPTER 16

QUALIFIED PRIVILEGE: STATUTE

SECTION 2. PRIVILEGE CONFERRED BY SCHEDULE 1 TO
THE DEFAMATION ACT 1996

**16.2**     **Background.** *Overlap between the common law and Sch.1.* There was a partial
overlap in *Flood v Times Newspapers Ltd* [2010] EWCA Civ 804; [2010]
E.M.L.R. 26. In that case the publication of a police notice announcing an
investigation would have fallen within para.9 of Part II (subject to the publication
of a statement by way of explanation or contradiction on request) but not the
publication of the ex parte allegations which had led to the investigations. The
argument that this meant that common law *Reynolds* privilege could not apply
because it was inconsistent with s.15 and Sch.1 was rejected. Lord Neuberger
M.R. said:

> "Subject to complying with section 15(2) and being unmalicious, publication by a
> defendant of a statement made by the police will be privileged irrespective of whether
> publication of the statement is in the public interest, and without the defendant being
> under any duty to check the accuracy of the statement. On the other hand, if it is
> potentially covered by *Reynolds* privilege, publication of an allegation made to the
> police will only attract privilege if it is in an article which, taken as a whole, is on a
> matter of public interest, if its inclusion in the article is justifiable, and if the steps taken
> to gather and publish the information were responsible and fair.
>
> While these seem to be two conceptually rather different sets of criteria, I accept Mr
> Price's point that, if one considers the matter more closely, there is, in practice, more
> overlap between the section 15(1) criteria and the *Reynolds* privilege criteria than may
> at first appear. Thus, reporting a police statement unmaliciously might well normally be
> expected to satisfy all the *Reynolds* privilege criteria. However, that rather misses the
> point; in some cases, absent section 15, it is quite conceivable that the court might take
> the view that publicising such a statement would not be in the public interest, or even
> that a competent journalist would have checked the original source of the contents of
> the statement before publishing it. One can analyse the legislative balancing exercise as
> involving section 15(2) being a quid pro quo for removing the risk of such a possibility
> in a case where the publication is of a police statement, and there is nothing inconsistent
> with that analysis in the notion that *Reynolds* privilege can apply to publication of the
> information which led to the statement" (at [31]–[32]).

"Public interest" must of course here be read in the *Reynolds* sense, though Sch.1 is inapplicable to matter which is not of public concern and the publication of which is not for the public benefit (see Main Work, para.16.5). The meaning of this is not entirely clear (see para.16.5, below) but it is thought that it is inconceivable that publication of a copy of a notice issued by the English police for the information of the public could fall within this restriction.

*Law of Libel Amendment Act 1888, s.4.* Since criminal libel has been abolished (see para.1.13, above) this provision is entirely repealed: Coroners and Justice Act 2009, Sch.23, Part 2.

*Lord Lester's Defamation Bill.* See para.1.12, above. Cl.8 and Sch.1 of the Bill would replace s.15 and Sch.1 of the Defamation Act 1996 with a similar structure but with changes of detail. Perhaps the most significant of these is that the Schedule list would become fully "internationalised". At the moment, for example, a fair and accurate report of court proceedings anywhere in the world is privileged under Part I of the Schedule but the privilege for fair and accurate reports of public meetings under Part II is confined to meetings in a member State. New entrants to the Part II list would be:

(1) fair and accurate copies, extracts from and summaries of online archives which have been publicly available for twelve months and in respect of which no defamation challenge has been made "whether in the courts or otherwise". An archive need have no particular status—by cl.17(1) it includes "any collection of sound recordings, images or other information" (for the purposes of cl.10—see para.6.3, above—it is not confined to online material).

(2) Reports of press conferences given by or on behalf of persons and bodies falling within the Schedule are identified as an express category. At the moment, by a somewhat artificial construction, at least some press conferences are treated as public meetings: see Main Work, para.16.18.

No change would be made to the principle that the privilege does not apply to the publication of matter which is not of public concern and the publication of which is not for the public benefit. This element causes some difficulty (see the remarks of Eady J. in *Crossley v Newsquest (Midlands South) Ltd*, para.16.5, below) and goes some way to deprive the Schedule of certainty. However, given the wholesale internationalisation which is proposed some such restriction probably remains necessary.

*Ireland.* The Irish equivalent of Sch.1 is now to be found in the Irish Defamation Act 2009, Sch.1. The structure is similar, i.e. Part 1 cases are privileged without explanation or contradiction; under Part 2 the privilege is lost if the defendant has failed to comply with a request to publish a reasonable statement by way of explanation or contradiction (see s.18(4)). Similarly, the privilege is lost by proof of malice (s.19(1)). There are many differences of detail. Part 1 is considerably longer than the English version, having 19 paragraphs, but five of them relate to the Press Council and the Press Ombudsman (as to which see

Sch.2 of the Act). Part 2 is rather shorter than the English version, mainly because all "associations" are put in one category under para.1, rather than being enumerated at length as in para.14 of the English version. Reports of notices issued for the information of the public fall under Part 1, not Part 2 as in the English Act.

**16.4**    **Fairness and accuracy.** *Court reports.* In this context fairness and accuracy is closely related to malice. In *Crossley v Newsquest (Midlands South) Ltd* [2008] EWHC 3054 (QB) (where in fact the report was held to be subject to absolute privilege) Eady J. remarked at [45] that it

> "is, of course, elementary that newspaper reports have almost always to be selective: what is more, there is generally scope for argument over the judgment as to what should be included or left out. This is therefore not fertile ground in which to find evidence of malice."

**16.5**    **Public concern and public benefit.** Reports of court proceedings are absolutely privileged when contemporaneous. Other reports fall within s.15 and Sch.1 and on the face of it there is the further requirement that the publication be of public concern and for the public benefit (s.15(3)). However, in *Crossley v Newsquest (Midlands South) Ltd* [2008] EWHC 3054 (QB) Eady J. was of the view that this did not create any additional hurdle for reports of English proceedings. He said:

> "[25] It may be that the significance of s 15(3) is to be found in the different wording of s 14. Absolute privilege is confined to reports of domestic and European courts. It does not extend to courts elsewhere. The categories covered by s 15, by contrast, are very wide indeed: see the contents of Sch 1 to the 1996 Act. Thus, it may be that the additional hurdles set up in s 15(3) would have to be overcome in relation to matters taking place elsewhere in the world. For example, the privilege would attach to reports of 'proceedings in public before a court anywhere in the world'. If a British citizen were to be defamed in the course of such proceedings, it may be that the Defendant would have to show 'public concern' and 'public benefit' before being entitled to rely on the statutory privilege . . .
> [26] That is a possible clue to Parliament's intention in the enactment of s 15(3). Be that as it may, I am quite satisfied that the present Defendant does not require to overcome any additional hurdles in relation to a report of proceedings in the Worcester County Court. Citizens in this jurisdiction are entitled to know what goes on in public hearings before any of Her Majesty's courts."

(b) *Statements privileged under Schedule 1 subject to explanation or contradiction*

**16.15**    **Notices from governments, etc.** In *Flood v Times Newspapers Ltd* [2010] EWCA Civ 804; [2010] E.M.L.R. 26 the claimant conceded that privilege for the publication of a copy of a notice issued by the police of an investigation into an unnamed officer would extend to the newspaper naming the officer. Lord Neuberger M.R., remarked at [29] that "technically, it is probably wrong to refer to the privilege going any further than the statute provides, but it is, I think, a fair description of the effect of [the] concession." Clearly, however, the statutory privilege cannot extend to the reporting of the ex parte allegations which led to the investigation (at [30]). As to common law, *Reynolds* privilege in this context see paras 15.12–15.13, above.

CHAPTER 17

# MALICE AND QUALIFIED PRIVILEGE

SECTION 1. GENERAL

**17.2** **"Presumed" and "express" malice.** *Ireland.* The provision of the Irish Defamation Bill referred to in fn.2 was changed. S.19 of the 2009 Act now reads:

> "**19.**—(1) In a defamation action, the defence of qualified privilege shall fail if, in relation to the publication of the statement in respect of which the action was brought, the plaintiff proves that the defendant acted with malice.
>
> (2) The defence of qualified privilege shall not fail by reason only of the publication of the statement concerned to a person other than an interested person if it is proved that the statement was published to the person because the publisher mistook him or her for an interested person.
>
> (3) Where a defamation action is brought against more than one defendant, the failure of the defence of qualified privilege in relation to one of the defendants by virtue of the application of *subsection (1)* shall not cause the failure of the defence in relation to another of the defendants unless that other defendant was vicariously liable for such acts or omissions of the first-mentioned defendant as gave rise to the cause of action concerned.
>
> (4) [Repeal of s.11(4) of the Civil Liability Act 1961].
>
> (5) In this section 'interested person' means, in relation to a statement, a person who, under *section 18(2)(a)*, had a duty or interest in receiving the information contained in the statement."

*Note 9.* See also *Henderson v London Borough of Hackney* [2010] EWHC 1651 (QB) at [35].

**17.4** **Malice as "improper" or "indirect" motive.** *Note 26.* See also *Dillon v Cush* [2010] NSWCA 165.

**17.5** **Matter believed to be true but purpose to injure.** *Note 45.* See also *Hughes v Risbridger* [2010] EWHC 491 (QB) at [25].

**17.8** **Ill will or desire to injure not necessary.** In *Bray v Deutsche Bank AG* [2009] EWHC 1356 (QB) the form of malice alleged (but not established) was not that D "was aware that he was saying anything false about the Claimant, but . . . that he abused the occasion by saying something which he knew was false in circumstances where (unknown to him) his words referred to, and defamed, [C]."

**Untruth, belief and wilful blindness.** *Note 122.* See also *Fraser v Holmes*  **17.17**
[2009] NSWCA 36.

**Unreasonable belief or carelessness in arriving at belief not malice.** See  **17.18**
also *Fraser v Holmes*, above.

CHAPTER 18

# REHABILITATION OF OFFENDERS ACT 1974

SECTION 3. EFFECTS OF REHABILITATION

**18.13**    **Extrajudicial consequences.** In *CC Humberside v Information Commissioner* [2009] EWCA Civ 1079; [2010] 1 W.L.R. 1136 the court reversed the decisions of the Information Tribunal (Main Work, fn.58) in relation to the removal of records of old convictions. The case turned on the interpretation of the Data Protection Act 1998 and this aspect of the case is considered at para.22.20, below. However, the gravamen of the complaints of the data subjects was not simply about the *retention* of the data but the effects of its *disclosure* so the case is of interest for the purposes of this Chapter. In four cases the issue had arisen because the convictions had been disclosed to employers who were exempt under the 1975 Exceptions Order and had been entitled to obtain disclosure (see fn.58). Hughes L.J. made the following remarks about the present position at [112]–[113]:

"I fully understand the concern of the [Information] Commissioner at the combination of the extent of a comprehensive database of conviction information and the range of those who have access, directly or indirectly, to it. The greater concern is perhaps related to indirect access. The Tribunal was told in 2005, in a similar appeal (*Chief Constable of West Yorkshire and others v Information Commissioner*) that at that time approximately 2.6 million CRB certificates were issued in a year and of those 90% or thereabouts enhanced. Some 13,000 organisations are, it would seem, entitled to seek such certificates. But this concern is with policy, and with what ought or ought not to be in the legislation, rather than with the application of the law as it stands. It is for Parliament, and not for the Commissioner alone, to consider any limitation on the indirect access of others to the contents of the PNC. I would respectfully agree that the time may well have come to review the accretions which there have been to the Rehabilitation of Offenders Act 1974 (Exceptions) Order. It currently includes amongst the exceedingly long list of those who must answer questions relating to spent convictions persons as diverse as those who wish to hold a National Lottery licence, or to be a doctor's receptionist, dental nurse, steward at a football ground, or traffic officer designated under the Traffic Management Act 2000 as having the power to direct traffic. Given that it does not follow that old convictions will in fact be treated as a bar to such employment, it might nevertheless be thought that consideration of the ambit of the Order might be useful. There might also be a case for reviewing the rehabilitation periods applicable to offences, and extending some. There might well be a case for implementing section 56 Data Protection Act in order to prevent employers and others who are *outside* the Exceptions Order from in effect circumventing the Rehabilitation of Offenders Act. But none of this is for me; it is for Parliament. And it is not for the Commissioner to try to modify the effect of statute by construction of the data protection principles. For the same reason I can understand why over the years the police and the Commissioner have actively discussed a so-called 'step down' regime, under which some information on the PNC would become available only to the police. This may have potential as a policy, although to my mind the criminal and family courts and child protection professionals engaged in working together with police officers would all need continued access to unexpurgated information. It would, however, require modification of the Rehabilitation of Offenders Act and of the Police Act 1997, which at present requires the police to provide the Secretary of State with everything in the record. Moreover, it would require immensely detailed programmes for organisation of the database: the March 2006 edition of the Retention Guidelines, which attempts the exercise, has 25 different categories of offender/outcome combination and no less than 200 pages of a closely-typed list of offences; yet it would still remove from the record convictions which would, for example, disqualify from jury service for life, and some which might plainly be relevant even many years later (for example wounding with intent, bigamy or importing Class A drugs). It would require, thirdly, as it seems to me at least, a method of accommodating fixed penalty notices as they are currently issued for offences which include not only public disorder but dishonesty. But again, if a workable and fair restricted access scheme can nevertheless be devised, this is not to be achieved through the Data Protection Act."

CHAPTER 19

## OTHER DEFENCES

SECTION 1. THE OFFER OF AMENDS PROCEDURE

**19.1**  **Background.** *Ireland.* The Irish Defamation Act 2009 provides:

"22.—(1) A person who has published a statement that is alleged to be defamatory of another person may make an offer to make amends.

(2) An offer to make amends shall—

(*a*) be in writing,

(*b*) state that it is an offer to make amends for the purposes of this section, and

(*c*) state whether the offer is in respect of the entire of the statement or an offer (in this Act referred to as a 'qualified offer') in respect of—

(i) part only of the statement, or

(ii) a particular defamatory meaning only.

(3) An offer to make amends shall not be made after the delivery of the defence in the defamation action concerned.

(4) An offer to make amends may be withdrawn before it is accepted and where such an offer is withdrawn a new offer to make amends may be made.

(5) In this section 'an offer to make amends' means an offer—

(*a*) to make a suitable correction of the statement concerned and a sufficient apology to the person to whom the statement refers or is alleged to refer,

(*b*) to publish that correction and apology in such manner as is reasonable and practicable in the circumstances, and

(*c*) to pay to the person such sum in compensation or damages (if any), and such costs, as may be agreed by them or as may be determined to be payable, whether or not it is accompanied by any other offer to perform an act other than an act referred to in *paragraph (a), (b)* or *(c)*.

23.—(1) If an offer to make amends under *section 22* is accepted the following provisions shall apply:

(*a*) if the parties agree as to the measures that should be taken by the person who made the offer to ensure compliance by him or her with the terms of the offer, the High Court or, where a defamation action has already been brought, the court in which it was brought may, upon the application of the person to whom the offer was made, direct the party who made the offer to take those measures;

(*b*) if the parties do not so agree, the person who made the offer may, with the leave

[104]

of the High Court or, where a defamation action has already been brought, the court in which it was brought, make a correction and apology by means of a statement before the court in such terms as may be approved by the court and give an undertaking as to the manner of their publication;

(c) if the parties do not agree as to the damages or costs that should be paid by the person who made the offer, those matters shall be determined by the High Court or, where a defamation action has already been brought, the court in which it was brought, and the court shall for those purposes have all such powers as it would have if it were determining damages or costs in a defamation action, and in making a determination under this paragraph it shall take into account the adequacy of any measures already taken to ensure compliance with the terms of the offer by the person who made the offer;

(d) no defamation action shall be brought or, if already brought, proceeded with against another person in respect of the statement to which the offer to make amends applies unless the court considers that in all the circumstances of the case it is just and proper to so do.

(2) Subject to *subsection (3)*, it shall be a defence to a defamation action for a person to prove that he or she made an offer to make amends under *section 22* and that it was not accepted, unless the plaintiff proves that the defendant knew or ought reasonably to have known at the time of the publication of the statement to which the offer relates that—

(a) it referred to the plaintiff or was likely to be understood as referring to the plaintiff, and

(b) it was false and defamatory of the plaintiff.

(3) Where the defendant in a defamation action made a qualified offer only, *subsection (2)* shall apply in relation to that part only of the action that relates to the part of the statement or the meaning, as the case may be, to which the qualified offer relates.

(4) A person who makes an offer to make amends is not required to plead it as a defence in a defamation action.

(5) If a defendant in a defamation action pleads the defence under this section, he or she shall not be entitled to plead any other defence in the action, and if the defence is pleaded in respect of a qualified offer only he or she shall not be entitled to plead any other defence in respect of that part of the action that relates to the part of the statement or the meaning, as the case may be, to which the qualified offer relates."

There appears to be a difference of substance from English law in s.23(2) in that the defence of unaccepted offer is defeated by proof that the defendant knew *or ought reasonably to have known* that the statement referred to him and was false and defamatory of him. Compare the Main Work, para.19.6.

**Requirements of statutory offer of amends.** An offer which concedes that **19.3** the words are defamatory but denies that they refer to the claimant is not an offer within the meaning of the Act. Although meaning and reference are commonly treated separately a statement cannot, in a litigation context, be defamatory in the abstract and it makes no sense to require the defendant to make a suitable correction of a statement which does not refer to the complainant: *Club La Costa (UK) Plc v Gebhard* [2008] EWHC 2552 (QB).

**If offer accepted.** The court has power under the offer of amends regime to **19.4** allow the person aggrieved to make a statement in court: *Winslet v Associated*

*Newspapers Ltd* [2009] EWHC 2735 (QB); [2010] E.M.L.R. 11. See para.31.10, below.

*Note 33. Warren v Random House* is reported at [2009] Q.B. 600.

**19.5**    **The amount of compensation.** For another illustration, where the procedure was promptly invoked and a 50 per cent discount given, see *Bowman v MGN Ltd* [2010] EWHC 895 (QB).

SECTION 3. CONSENT

**19.10**    **Consent.** *Carrie v Tolkien* [2009] EWHC 29 (QB); [2009] E.M.L.R. 9 is a neat illustration of this defence. The defendant published a potentially defamatory comment on the claimant's blog. The claimant discovered this a maximum of four hours 19 minutes later but allowed it to remain there for 22 months. He had therefore acquiesced in the publication of the libel from the time of discovery and there was no evidence in the short, initial period of any substantial publication to others.

In *Flood v Times Newspapers Ltd* [2010] EWCA Civ 804; [2010] E.M.L.R. 26, dealing with a situation of non-correction of internet material after a change of circumstances, Lord Neuberger M.R. said at [82]:

"If a claimant says in clear terms that he does not want the publication to be amended or withdrawn, or even that he does not care whether it is amended or withdrawn, then, at least as at present advised, I consider that he could be held to have lost any right to contend that the defendant's failure to amend or withdraw the article was actionable: it could be a simple case of waiver or estoppel, or even, if there was consideration, of contract."

That would seem to be consent under another name.

*Ireland.* The Irish Defamation Act, s.25 makes the plaintiff's consent to publication a defence.

SECTION 4. LIMITATION

**19.13**    **Basic principle and history.** *Ireland.* Under the Irish Defamation Act 2009, amending the Statute of Limitations 1957, a defamation action shall be brought within one year of the accrual of the cause of action or such longer period, not exceeding two years, as the court may direct where the interests of justice so require and the prejudice that the plaintiff would suffer if the direction were not given would significantly outweigh the prejudice that the defendant would suffer if the direction were given (see s.38(1)). Furthermore, the date of accrual of the cause of action "shall be the date upon which the defamatory statement is first published and, where the statement is published through the medium of the internet, the date on which it is first capable of being viewed or listened to through that medium."

**Exercise of the discretion.** See also *Vaidya v GMC* [2010] EWHC 984 (QB).   **19.21**
In personal injury cases in the context of the similar s.33 of the Limitation Act
1980 it is now held that mere loss of the limitation defence is not "prejudice" to
the defendant: what counts is the impact of the delay upon his ability to defend
himself: *Cain v Francis* [2008] EWCA Civ 1451; [2009] Q.B. 754. But *Cain* did
not consider the unusual context of defamation cases and there the loss of the
defence may still have some relevance, if only because being sued is an interference with freedom of expression, a factor absent from personal injury cases:
*Brady v Norman* [2010] EWHC 1215 (QB).

*Note 124.* Permission to appeal on various points in the *Gentoo* case was
refused but the limitation point was not pursued in these proceedings: [2008]
EWCA Civ 968.


SECTION 6. RELEASE, ACCORD AND SATISFACTION


**Generally.** *Note 163.* In *McLaughlin v Newall* [2009] EWHC 1925 (QB) the   **19.27**
correspondence made it clear that that the discharge of the defamation claim was
dependent on performance of the offer to apologise. In any event, no terms of
apology had ever been agreed and in most defamation cases agreement on that
will be central to a binding compromise rather than merely peripheral: *Western
Broadcasting Services v Seaga* [2007] UKPC 19; [2007] E.M.L.R. 18.

CHAPTER 21

# MALICIOUS FALSEHOOD

SECTION 1. INTRODUCTION

**21.1**  **Generally.** The alternative name, "injurious falsehood", is used by Eady J. in *Quinton v Peirce* [2009] EWHC 912 (QB).

There must be a reference to the claimant, his property, his business or his economic interests, otherwise there would be a danger of parasitic claims for secondary economic loss from statements aimed at other persons: *Marathon Mutual Ltd v Waters* [2009] EWHC 1931 (QB); [2010] E.M.L.R. 3. However, for striking out purposes it was arguable on the pleadings that a statement directly referring to Company M also referred for this purpose to Company R, which managed Company M's fund, as the defendant knew.

*Ireland.* The Irish Defamation Act 2009 provides:

"42.—(1) In an action for slander of title, slander of goods or other malicious falsehood, the plaintiff shall be required to prove that the statement upon which the action is founded—

(*a*)  was untrue,

(*b*)  was published maliciously, and

(*c*)  referred to the plaintiff, his or her property or his or her office, profession, calling, trade or business.

(2) In an action for slander of title, slander of goods or other malicious falsehood, the plaintiff shall be required to prove—

(*a*)  special damage, or

(*b*)  that the publication of the statement was calculated to cause and was likely to cause financial loss to the plaintiff in respect of his or her property or his or her office, profession, calling, trade or business."

**21.3**  **Malicious falsehood and other torts.** Although there was no abuse of process in *Joyce v Sengupta*, there was an abuse in *Tesco Stores Ltd v Guardian News & Media Ltd* [2009] E.M.L.R. 5 (no neutral citation) because to allow the malicious falsehood claim to proceed would conflict with the policy on offers of amends under the Defamation Act 1996. See also para.21.5, below.

On the overlap with the Data Protection Act 1998 see para.22.18, below.

SECTION 2. MALICIOUS FALSEHOOD

**Falsity.** *The single meaning rule.* The CA in *Ajinomoto Sweeteners Europe*   **21.5**
*SAS v Asda Stores Ltd* [2010] EWCA Civ 609 (reversing Tugendhat J., [2009]
EWHC 1717 (QB); [2010] Q.B. 204) held that the single meaning rule of
defamation does not apply to malicious falsehood. Although the rule seemed to
have caused little practical difficulty in defamation (see para.3.15, above) it
would have the effect, in the context of malicious falsehood, of

> "denying any remedy to a claimant whose business has been injured in the eyes of some
> consumers on the illogical ground that it has not been injured in the eyes of others, or
> alternatively . . . giving such a claimant a clear run to judgment when in the eyes of
> many customers the words have done it no harm";

whereas "trial of plural meanings permits the damaging effect of the words to be
put in perspective and both malice and (if it comes to it) damage to be more
realistically gauged" (Sedley L.J. at [34]). The legend on the defendants' product
was "No hidden nasties" and "No artificial colours or flavours and no aspartame". The claimants contended that this was capable of meaning at least that
there was a risk that aspartame is harmful or unhealthy and the judge had found
that a substantial body of consumers would so understand it; but a substantial
body would have read it as meaning simply that it was a product for customers
who found aspartame objectionable; and, on the basis of the single meaning rule,
he had found that the latter was the meaning to be ascribed. Rimer L.J. said at
[41]:

> "If the case were allowed to go to trial and the claimant were able to prove that [the
> former] . . . meaning was false, uttered with malice and calculated to damage it, why
> should it not be entitled to damages for the injury which the falsehood will have caused
> it? More importantly—and this is the primary remedy the claimant wants—why, if it
> can prove its case, should it not be entitled to have the defendant restrained by
> injunction from doing that which it wants to do, namely (presumably for its own
> commercial benefit) to continue to publish a falsehood that will continue to damage the
> claimant in the eyes of a substantial body of consumers? The result, however, of the
> application by the judge of the single meaning rule is that that body of consumers is
> removed from the court's radar. The court instead satisfies itself with the fiction,
> contrary to its own finding, that the entire consuming public will interpret the defen-
> dant's packaging as bearing a single innocuous meaning."

Where a malicious false statement reflects on the claimant's reputation malicious
falsehood overlaps with defamation, even though it is only defamation which
provides damages for injury to reputation as such. It is not very likely that a
claimant will embark instead on the generally more onerous task of establishing
a claim for malicious falsehood, though he may occasionally have tactical
reasons for doing so (see, e.g. *Joyce v Sengupta* [1993] 1 W.L.R. 337, Main
Work, para.21.3, though the particular reason in that case is no longer relevant).
In theory at least this case adds another possible tactical reason. Indeed, it is
possible to have concurrent claims for defamation and malicious falsehood (see,
e.g. *Tesco Stores Ltd v Guardian News & Media Ltd* (though the malicious
falsehood claim was stayed there) and *Thornton v Telegraph Media Group Ltd*
[2010] EWHC 1414 (QB); [2010] E.M.L.R. 25). If that happened and the trial

were by jury there would be obvious problems in having different rules on meaning. In *Ajinomoto* at [18] Sedley L.J. says that such a case would not be tried by jury "since malicious falsehood carries no such right". However, s.69(1) of the Senior Courts Act 1981 (formerly the Supreme Court Act 1981) simply provides that "where there is in issue . . . a claim for libel or slander, the action shall be tried with a jury . . . ". Claims for false imprisonment and malicious prosecution carry a right to trial by jury, claims for assault (or battery) do not. Yet if there is a claim for the third along with either or both of the first two the whole action would be tried by jury: see *Thompson v MPC* [1998] Q.B. 498.

# MISUSE OF PRIVATE INFORMATION

Section 1. Introduction

**Other systems of law.** *Note 17.* On appeal in *Giller v Procopets* equitable    **22.2**
damages for breach of confidence were awarded and it was not thought necessary
to consider whether a general tort of invasion of privacy should be recognized:
*Giller v Procopets* [2008] VSCA 236.

Section 2. Liability under the Human Rights Act 1998

**The European Convention on Human Rights.** *R (Wood) v M.P.C.* [2009]    **22.3**
EWCA Civ 414; [2010] 1 W.L.R. 123 is a claim which involved action by a
public authority and is based squarely on interference with Convention rights.
However, since it involves photographing a person, which has arisen several
times in a common law context, it is considered at para.22.9, below.

*Retention of DNA etc.* In *S and Marper v UK*, App. nos 30562/04 and
30566/04 the ECtHR held that:

> "the blanket and indiscriminate nature of the powers of retention of the fingerprints,
> cellular samples and DNA profiles of persons suspected but not convicted of
> offences . . . fails to strike a fair balance between the competing public and private
> interests and that the [United Kingdom] has overstepped any acceptable margin of
> appreciation in this regard. Accordingly, the retention at issue constitutes a dispropor-
> tionate interference with the applicants' right to respect for private life and cannot be
> regarded as necessary in a democratic society" (at [125]).

The court was impressed by the fact that no other member of the Council of
Europe allowed indefinite retention of such records from unconvicted persons
(see at [47]). Following consultation the Home Office on November 11, 2009
announced that it was proposed to remove all profiles of persons not convicted
after six years but that profiles of persons convicted of a recordable offence
would continue to be kept indefinitely. However, until the matter is finalised the
courts are bound by the contrary decision in *R(S) v CC South Yorkshire* [2004]
UKHL 39; [2004] 1 W.L.R. 2196; *R(GC) v M.P.C.,* July 16, 2010.

*Level of seriousness of interference.* In *R (Gillan) v M.P.C.* [2006] UKHL 12; [2006] 2 A.C. 307, dealing with "stop and search" legislation, Lord Bingham said at [28]:

> "It is true that 'private life' has been generously construed to embrace wide rights to personal autonomy. But it is clear Convention jurisprudence that intrusions must reach a certain level of seriousness to engage the operation of the Convention, which is, after all, concerned with human rights and fundamental freedoms, and I incline to the view that an ordinary superficial search of the person and an opening of bags, of the kind to which passengers uncomplainingly submit at airports, for example, can scarcely be said to reach that level."

While not denying the basic premise that there is a certain threshold of seriousness the ECtHR disagreed on the facts (*Gillan v UK* (2010) App. no.4158/05). It distinguished the situation of airport searches because the subject would know in advance what would happen.

> "The Court is unable to accept [the view that a superficial search which does not involve the discovery of items like address books or diaries does not engage Art. 8]. Irrespective of whether in any particular case correspondence or diaries or other private documents are discovered and read or other intimate items are revealed in the search, the Court considers that the use of the coercive powers conferred by the legislation to require an individual to submit to a detailed search of his person, his clothing and his personal belongings amounts to a clear interference with the right to respect for private life. Although the search is undertaken in a public place, this does not mean that Article 8 is inapplicable. Indeed, in the Court's view, the public nature of the search may, in certain cases, compound the seriousness of the interference because of an element of humiliation and embarrassment" (at [63]).

The court provided the following general description of the nature of art.8 (citations omitted):

> "[T]he concept of 'private life' is a broad term not susceptible to exhaustive definition. It covers the physical and psychological integrity of a person. The notion of personal autonomy is an important principle underlying the interpretation of its guarantees . . . The Article also protects a right to identity and personal development, and the right to establish relationships with other human beings and the outside world. It may include activities of a professional or business nature. There is, therefore, a zone of interaction of a person with others, even in a public context, which may fall within the scope of 'private life'. There are a number of elements relevant to a consideration of whether a person's private life is concerned in measures effected outside a person's home or private premises. In this connection, a person's reasonable expectations as to privacy may be a significant, though not necessarily conclusive, factor . . . " (at [61]).

*Note 25. W v Westminster CC* seems to have been the inspiration for the attempted amendment in *H v Tomlinson* [2008] EWCA Civ 1258; [2009] E.L.R. 14. A claim in respect of statements made in connexion with the claimant's exclusion from school was bound to fail because there was justification for the sting of the libel. There was no basis for allowing an amendment alleging breach of the art.8 right to privacy because the information was in the public domain. Nor was there a basis for an amendment alleging injury to the claimant's reputation under art.8 because the claimant's reputation was already such that the allegations made no difference. For art.8 and the law of privilege see para.14.3, above.

**Public authorities.** In *BKM Ltd v BBC* [2009] EWHC 3151 (Ch) an unsuc-  **22.4**
cessful attempt was made to obtain an injunction against the use of material
clandestinely filmed in a care home. Though it is not entirely clear from the
judgment (and probably makes no difference in practice) the case seems to have
been framed as one under the Human Rights Act rather than for common law
misuse of private information. The claim was based on the privacy rights of
residents of the home and the defendants did not contest that the proprietors of
the home had locus standi to take action to protect those rights.

SECTION 3. MISUSE OF PRIVATE INFORMATION

**The "classical" law of confidence.** Individuals may in some cases have a  **22.6**
right of privacy under the next section in relation to their business affairs but
"companies' rights of confidentiality will usually be governed in this jurisdiction
by the equitable principles of 'old-fashioned' breach of confidence or by specific
contractual provisions": *Ambrosiadou v Coward* [2010] EWHC 1794 (QB) at
[33]. On confidence between spouses see *Tchenguiz v Imerman* [2010] EWCA
Civ 908.

*Note 70.* But in *Napier v Pressdram Ltd* [2009] EWCA Civ 443 Toulson L.J.
said at [53]:

> "I would not attach significance to the fact that correspondence was headed 'Private and
> Confidential'. Many letters are marked in that way when they are intended by the sender
> to be for the eyes of the person to whom they are addressed, without prior reading by
> others, but without necessarily intending to limit the use which the receiver may decide
> to make of them."

*HEFCE v Information Commissioner*, January 13, 2010, EA/2009/0036 before
the Information Tribunal is a case of the "classical" type, turning on the
exception for information disclosed in confidence under the Freedom of Information Act 2000 and the potential public interest defence.

**What information is private.** Copying and retention of private material for  **22.8**
use in divorce proceedings was not *misuse* of the information in *White v Withers
Llp* [2008] EWHC 2821 (QB). This aspect was not pursued on the appeal, which
was concerned with trespass to goods and conversion: *White v Withers Llp* [2009]
EWCA Civ 1122. But cf. *Tchenguiz v Imerman* [2010] EWCA Civ 908.
A blogger on police matters who was a serving constable did not have a
reasonable expectation of privacy so as to be able to prevent a newspaper
revealing his identity where that had been obtained by "detective work": blog-
ging is a public activity. In any event, even if there were such an expectation it
would be likely to be outweighed at trial by the legitimate public interest in the
identity of the police officer engaged in the activity. *Author of a Blog v Times
Newspapers Ltd* [2009] EWHC 1358 (QB); [2009] E.M.L.R. 22. By the time of
the hearing the police force had got to know of his identity but even if this had

not been the case, it was not "part of the court's function to protect police officers who are, or think they may be, acting in breach of police discipline regulations from coming to the attention of their superiors (whose task it is to make judgments about such matters, at least in the first instance)" (at [28]).

*Privacy and court proceedings.* In *Crossley v Newsquest (Midlands South) Ltd* [2008] EWHC 3054 (QB) Eady J. said:

"[58] . . . While I would accept that ordinarily people may expect their financial affairs to be accorded privacy, once information of that kind has entered the public domain it may very well be, depending on the particular circumstances, that such protection has been lost. Unfortunately, once something is mentioned in open court, it is difficult to see how there can any longer be such an expectation. The basic rule is that anything said in open court may be reported: see eg *R v Arundel Justices, ex parte Westminster Press Ltd* [1985] 1 WLR 708.
[59] It is true that in CPR 39.2(3)(c) it is provided that a court hearing, or any part of it, *may* be held in private if it involves confidential information (including information relating to personal financial matters) and publicity would damage that confidentiality. There is no provision that such a hearing *must* take place in private; nor was there any application in the present case for the details of Mr and Mrs Crossley's financial affairs to be addressed in private session. The court would have had a discretion to make such an order, if it thought it appropriate, after balancing privacy considerations against the general principle of open justice and the right of the public to be informed as to what takes place in court proceedings. As I have already said, however, the hearing was in fact in open court and a representative of the press was present. In those circumstances, any suggestion that publication in the newspaper of the information discussed in open court constituted a breach of confidence, or an actionable infringement of the Claimants' privacy, is misconceived."

"The fact that [a person is acquitted] . . . is not of itself private information the publication of which would be incompatible with his right to privacy. This has nothing to do with his private life. The trial was held in public, and the media were at liberty to publish [the defendant's] name along with other details of the case other than the identity of the complainant": *BBC, Re* [2009] UKHL 34; [2010] 1 A.C. 145 at [20] per Lord Hope.

However, this case involved the further issue that the broadcaster proposed to air a programme advocating consideration of the retrial of D (under the Criminal Justice Act 2003) on a charge of rape of which he had been acquitted. Following the acquittal there had been an Attorney General's Reference on a question of law and in this an "anonymity order" had been made in respect of D. The HL in *BBC, Re* discharged this order. Art.8 was engaged because the programme would not merely reveal D's acquittal but the possibility that his DNA profile retained after his acquittal—and retained in breach of art.8, see *S and Marper v UK*, para.22.3, above—might provide compelling evidence of his guilt. However, the balance came down in favour of the broadcaster's art.10 rights. The purpose of the programme was legitimate and to allow the use of D's name was a proportionate interference with his rights.

"The programme that the BBC wish to broadcast has been inspired by the removal of the double-jeopardy rule. What this means in practice for our system of criminal justice is a matter of legitimate public interest. Among the issues which can be so described are the kinds of offences to which Pt 10 of the 2003 Act applies, and the circumstances in which an application for a person who has been acquitted to be retried would be appropriate. These issues could, of course, be discussed in the abstract by reference to hypothetical facts and circumstances. But the arguments that the programme wishes to present will lose much of their force unless they can be directed to the facts and circumstances of actual cases. The point about D's name is that the producers of the programme believe that its disclosure will give added credibility to the account which they wish to present. This is a view which they are entitled to adopt and, given the content of the programme as a whole, it is an aim which can properly be regarded as legitimate" (at [26]).

*Note 118.* The CA allowed appeals against the decision of the Information Tribunal in the *CC Humberside* case, see para.22.20, below.

**Photographs in public places.** *R (Wood) v M.P.C.* [2009] EWCA Civ 414;     **22.9**
[2010] 1 W.L.R. 123 (reversing [2008] EWHC 1105 (Admin), fn.142) is an important decision in this area. This was an application for judicial review of police action in taking and retaining photographs of the claimant in the street as he was leaving a meeting of a company the subsidiary of which organized an arms trade fair. The claimant was a prominent campaigner against the arms trade but had never been arrested and had no convictions. Dyson L.J. and Lord Collins agreed with Laws L.J.'s analysis of the applicability of art.8 in such circumstances. The basic principle was that the mere act of taking a photograph of a person in a public place did not engage art.8. "The snapping of the shutter of itself breaches no rights, unless something more is added": at [35] (compare, however, *Reklos v Greece*, below). That something else might be the fact or threat of publication in the media (as in *Murray*); but it might also be the circumstances in which the photograph was taken, as where the person was pursued and harassed by a mob of photographers (note, though, that in practice this will almost always be accompanied by threat of publication). On the facts the conduct of the police fell into neither category, but art.8 was still engaged. As Laws L.J. put it:

"[I]n my judgment it is important to recognise that state action may confront and challenge the individual as it were out of the blue. It may have no patent or obvious contextual explanation, and in that case it is not more apparently rational than arbitrary, nor more apparently justified than unjustified. In this case it consists in the taking and retaining of photographs, though it might consist in other acts. The Metropolitan Police, visibly and with no obvious cause, chose to take and keep photographs of an individual going about his lawful business in the streets of London. This action is a good deal more than the snapping of the shutter. The police are a state authority. And as I have said, the claimant could not and did not know why they were doing it and what use they might make of the pictures.

In these circumstances I would hold that article 8 is engaged. On the particular facts the police action, unexplained at the time it happened and carrying as it did the implication that the images would be kept and used, is a sufficient intrusion by the state into the individual's own space, his integrity, as to amount to a prima facie violation of article 8(1). It attains a sufficient level of seriousness and in the circumstances the claimant enjoyed a reasonable expectation that his privacy would not be thus invaded" (at [45]–[46]).

The taking and retention of the photographs was in pursuit of a legitimate aim, namely for the prevention of disorder and crime and the protection of the rights of others. However, Dyson L.J. and Lord Collins (Laws L.J. dissenting on this point) held that there had been an infringement of art.8 because the police conduct could not satisfy the requirement of proportionality. The purpose of the operation had been to gather evidence about any offences committed at the company meeting. It was quickly apparent that there had been none (though two persons had been ejected for chanting slogans) and the claimant was certainly not involved in any misconduct and the suggestion that the photographs could be retained on the basis that the claimant might commit an offence at the arms fair several months later was "plainly an afterthought" (at [97]). The claimant's

> "behaviour [at the company meeting] was beyond reproach, even though he was subjected to what he considered to be an intimidating experience. There was no more likelihood that the claimant would commit an offence if he went to the fair than that any other citizen of good character who happened to go to the fair would commit an offence there" (at [89]).

Note the remark of Lord Collins at [100]:

> "[I]t is plain that the last word has yet to be said on the implications for civil liberties of the taking and retention of images in the modern surveillance society. This is not the case for the exploration of the wider, and very serious, human rights issues which arise when the state obtains and retains the images of persons who have committed no offence and are not suspected of having committed any offence."

*Murray v Big Pictures* (fn.136) has an echo in the ECtHR's decision in *Reklos v Greece* (2009) App. no.1234/05. The new born child of the applicants was photographed in an area of the clinic where he was born (to which only medical staff were supposed to have access) by a "resident photographer" without the applicants' consent and their demand for the negatives was refused. The failure of the Greek courts to provide a remedy was held to be a violation of art.8. The court referred to the general nature of the right to control one's image at [40]:

> "L'image d'un individu est l'un des attributs principaux de sa personnalité du fait qu'elle dégage son originalité et lui permet de se différencier de ses congénères. Le droit de la personne à la protection de son image constitue ainsi l'un des composants essentiels de son épanouissement personnel et présuppose principalement la maîtrise de celle-ci par l'individu. Si la maîtrise de son image implique dans la plupart des cas la possibilité, pour l'individu, de refuser la diffusion de son image, elle comprend en même temps le droit de chacun de s'opposer à la captation, la conservation et la reproduction de celle-ci par autrui. En effet, l'image étant l'une des caractéristiques attachées à la personnalité de chacun, sa protection effective présuppose, en principe et dans des circonstances similaires au cas d'espèce . . . , le consentement de l'individu dès sa captation et non pas seulement au moment de la diffusion éventuelle de l'image au public. Dans le cas contraire, un attribut essentiel de la personnalité pourrait être retenu captif par autrui sans que l'intéressé ait la maîtrise sur son éventuel usage ultérieur."

Although there was nothing demeaning about the photographs, nevertheless:

> "l'élément prépondérant dans le cas d'espèce n'est pas la représentation anodine ou non du fils des requérants sur les photographies incriminées, mais le fait que le photographe les a conservées sans avoir obtenu le consentement des requérants. L'image du nouveau-né a été ainsi retenue captive par le photographe sous une forme identifiante et pouvait faire l'objet d'une exploitation ultérieure, contraire à la volonté de l'intéressé et/ou de ses parents" (at [42]).

It will be observed that although in this case there was no intention to publish the photographs on a general basis the court was of the view that the mere taking of a photograph without consent could infringe art.8. In effect the "right to control one's image", highly developed in some legal systems but hardly at all in others, is becoming part and parcel of art.8.

In *Egeland v Norway* (2009) App. no.34438/04 two editors were convicted of an offence under Norwegian law of publishing photographs of B which had been taken while she was leaving court in a distressed situation after receiving a 21 year sentence for murder. The ECtHR held that the convictions were not a disproportionate restriction on the editors' freedom of expression in view of the intrusion into B's art.8 rights. For English law on the restriction of photography of persons leaving court, see Criminal Justice Act 1925, s.41(2)(c).

**Untrue information.** The difficult relationship between misuse of private   **22.10**
information and defamation has twice been considered by Tugendhat J. In *RST v UVW* [2009] EWHC 2448 (QB); [2010] E.M.L.R. 13 an interim injunction was granted restraining disclosure of past sexual encounters but the learned judge said that it was a case in which the question whether it was in reality a "reputation" case or a "privacy" case was one which could realistically be debated at some future substantive hearing: at [27]. In *Terry (formerly LNS) v Persons Unknown* [2010] EWHC 119 (QB); [2010] E.M.L.R. 16 an injunction was discharged on the basis, among other things, that the nub of the complaint concerned reputation rather than privacy but Tugendhat J. made the following remarks about the general position:

"In broad terms the cases may be considered in at least four different groups. The first group of cases, where there is no overlap, is where the information cannot be said to be defamatory ... It is the law of confidence, privacy and harassment that are likely to govern in such cases. There is a second group of cases where there is an overlap, but where it is unlikely that it could be said that protection of reputation is the nub of the claim. These are cases where the information would in the past have been said to be defamatory even though it related to matters which were involuntary, e.g. disease. There was always a difficulty in fitting such cases into defamation, but it was done because of the absence of any alternative cause of action. There is a third group of cases where there is an overlap, but no inconsistency. These are cases where the information relates to conduct which is voluntary, and alleged to be seriously unlawful, even if it is personal (e.g. sexual or financial). The claimant is unlikely to succeed whether at an interim application or (if the allegation is proved) at trial, whether under the law of defamation or the law of privacy. The fourth group of cases, where it may make a difference which law governs, is where the information relates to conduct which is voluntary, discreditable, and personal (e.g. sexual or financial) but not unlawful (or not seriously so). In defamation, if the defendant can prove one of the liable defences, he will not have to establish any public interest (except in the case of *Reynolds* privilege, where the law does require consideration of the seriousness of the allegation, including from the point of view of the claimant). But if it is the claimant's choice alone that determines that the only cause of action which the court may take into account is misuse of private information, then the defendant cannot succeed unless he establishes that it comes within the public interest exception (or, perhaps, that he believes that it comes within that exception)" (at [96]).

See further, in particular on the point that reputation as well as privacy is now regarded as an art.8 right, para.27.21A, below. The implications of what is said in *McKennit v Ash* troubled Sir Charles Gray in *WER v REW* [2009] EWHC 1029; [2009] E.M.L.R. 17, where the claimant declined to confirm or deny the story he was seeking to stop and proposed to serve the injunction on every national newspaper:

"I have to confess that at first blush I found it troubling that a judge should be asked to grant an injunction restraining not just the defendant publication but a whole number of other media organisations from publishing certain information, in complete ignorance whether the information is true or false and in complete ignorance of the extent to which the information, true or false, had entered the public domain" (at [8]).

See further, para.27.34, below.

**22.11**    **Justified disclosure.** In *BKM Ltd v BBC* [2009] EWHC 3151 (Ch) a claim for an injunction to restrain the use of footage clandestinely obtained at a care home failed. Mann J. said at [38]:

"[M]y decision is based on the deployment of material for Article 10 purposes which it is strongly arguable has been obtained within guidelines, and which it is clearly if not strongly arguable can be properly deployed in the public interest with all proper steps being taken to ensure either that there is no (further) infringement of the residents' Article 8 rights, or no infringement beyond that which can be justified by that public interest. It is, of course, the case that the BBC will have to consider very carefully whether the clandestinely obtained material can be properly deployed in the programme, particularly in the light of the points made during the hearing before me. I am deciding that I will not restrain the broadcast of any material. I am not deciding that that broadcast will be justified or justifiable. That will depend on the ultimate content."

He considered that:

"it may be that contraventions of the Article 8 rights are not completely removed by taking cinematic steps to obscure the identities of those depicted . . . However, that does not mean that those means are irrelevant. The level of an invasion of privacy is relevant to the balancing act that I have to perform. An invasion of privacy should not be allowed beyond that which is necessary in the public interest. It is hard to imagine that the public interest would ever justify the un-pixilated broadcasting of an image of a resident using a commode. It might well justify broadcasting a heavily obscured image. Other examples can be given. So one cannot say that any portrayal of the residents will give rise to a sufficiently serious infringement of privacy rights to outweigh any public interest justification coupled with Article 10 rights" (at [33]).

**22.13**    As is indicated in the Main Work, the law may anyway have moved on since *A v B Plc* and *Theakston v MGN* but in *RST v UVW* [2009] EWHC 2448 (QB); [2010] E.M.L.R. 13 it was held that those cases were distinguishable because (a) the sexual encounters involved had taken place at the claimant's home and (b) the other party had signed an agreement not to disclose them.

SECTION 4. DATA PROTECTION

**22.18**    **The Data Protection Act 1998.** At various points in the Main Work and this Supplement reference is made to the uncertainty which arises about the relationship between the data protection and human rights legislation and the common law of torts (see, e.g. Main Work and Supplement para.9.1 on declarations of falsity and Supplement para.14.3 on qualified privilege). Something less than enthusiasm is expressed by Eady J. in *Quinton v Peirce* [2009] EWHC 912 (QB) for the potential effect of the Data Protection Act 1998. The case was a claim for malicious falsehood made by a defeated council candidate in respect of statements in the election leaflet of his successful opponent. The claim failed because none of the statements could be said to be inaccurate in the sense required by this tort and anyway the bad blood which existed between the parties did not show malice in the required sense. Eady J. also held that the statements were not inaccurate for the purposes of the parallel claim under the Data Protection Act. But had that not been the case there would have been no simple answer to the claim since malice is not required under the Act and the question is whether they are accurate under the fourth Data Protection Principle, though for the purpose of a claim for damages the data controller may have a defence if he can show that he used reasonable care. Indeed, under s.14 the court may order the data controller to rectify, block, erase or destroy inaccurate data or opinions based on inaccurate data. As Eady J. pointed out such a scheme can only work where the data is absolutely verifiable and he would "have been at a loss to know how [he] could possibly order Mr Peirce to publish Mr Quinton's version of events baldly and without explanation or comment" (at [94]). Furthermore, since similar issues could arise in a claim parallel to one for libel, he was not:

"persuaded that it is necessary or proportionate so to interpret [the Act] as to give a power to the court to order someone to publish a correction or apology when the person concerned does not believe he has published anything untrue . . . Parliament rejected such a draconian step when addressing the remedies to be made available under the summary judgment regime contained in ss.8–10 of the Defamation Act 1996. The Act stops short of that. Where the parties are unable to agree the steps to be taken, a judge can order the defendant, at most, to publish a summary of the court's ruling: s.9(2). He or she cannot be compelled to adopt or endorse it . . . The legislature declined to provide for a power to require editors to publish corrections or factual accounts which they do not accept as accurate. This was for the same reasons as are contained in the reports of the Committee on Privacy and Related Matters (the Calcutt Committee, 1990 Cm. 1102) at para.11.4 and the Supreme Court Procedure Committee on Practice and Procedure in Defamation (the Neill Committee, 1991) at XVII 3–4. It would be surprising if only about two years later the legislators were prepared to provide for compulsion in such circumstances without that being unequivocally made clear" (at [88]–[90]).

Under the First Data Protection Principle data processing must also be "fair". Perhaps the ultimate absurdity lay in the suggestion that to comply with this the defendant should have notified the claimant before processing the information on his computer:

"Plainly, it cannot have been the intention of the legislature to require electoral candidates to give their opponents advance warning each time reference is to be made to them in a document that happens to be computer generated" (at [93]).

The plain truth is that the legislation (or rather the underlying Directive) is simply not thought through: something which is aimed at the dangers presented by the mass collection of data in automated systems is drafted in such a way that, read

**22.18**    CHAPTER 22—MISUSE OF PRIVATE INFORMATION

literally, it is capable of applying in a random way to communications which employ computer technology at some stage—probably the great majority of non-conversational communications nowadays. As Eady J. remarked at [73] (though counsel for the claimant denied the relevance of the proposition) the impact on the claimant would have been the same if the leaflet had been drafted by quill pen and ink.

**22.19    Data and systems to which the Act applies.** The European Court of Justice in *Tietosuojavaltuutettu v Satakunnan Markkinapörssi Oy* (2008), Case C–73/07 held that Directive 95/46 applied to the collection and processing of data already in the public domain about the tax affairs of individuals.

*Note 272.* The effect of the "confidence" exception in the Freedom of Information Act 2000 was considered by the Information Tribunal in *HEFCE v Information Commissioner*, January 13, 2010, EA/2009/0036. The decision was that the exception applied only if a claim for breach of confidence against the discloser would probably succeed. It was not enough that there was an arguable claim.

**22.20    The Data Protection Principles.** *First, third and fifth principles.* The CA allowed appeals against the decision of the Information Tribunal in the *CC Humberside* case (fn.300): *CC Humberside v Information Commissioner* [2009] EWCA Civ 1079; [2010] 1 W.L.R. 1136. The Chief Constables had registered purposes under the Act which went much wider than "core" operational police functions—for example the supply of records to the CPS, the courts and the Criminal Records Bureau. As long as the purpose was registered and lawful there were no further restrictions on the processing of data and the retention of old convictions was not therefore excessive. Furthermore the underlying Directive specifically contemplated that there might be a "complete register of criminal convictions", it was necessary to have such a register for the purposes of the courts and others and it was therefore impossible to say that the data was kept for longer than necessary. The real problems which needed to be addressed lay not in the retention of the data but in the circumstances in which it might be released to others, as to which see para.18.13, above. In one of the cases, that of SP, there was a further issue relating to whether data had been processed fairly under the First principle. SP had been given a reprimand for common assault at the age of 13 in 2001 and had been led to believe that this record would be removed when she reached the age of 18. This would in fact have happened had the policy not changed. The majority of the court (Carnwath L.J. dissenting) held that the First principle had not been infringed. Only Waller L.J. dealt with a further argument under art.8, which he did not consider was engaged because the complaint was about retention, not disclosure. That appears to be inconsistent with the reasoning of the CA in *R (Wood) v M.P.C.*, para.22.9, above, though his alternative conclusion that the processing was in accordance with law and necessary in a democratic society may very well be correct.

**22.23    Compensation for non-pecuniary loss.** See also *Hughes v Risbridger* [2010] EWHC 491 (QB) at [34].

CHAPTER 23

# OTHER CAUSES OF ACTION ARISING FROM STATEMENTS

SECTION 1. NEGLIGENCE

**Negligence and defamation.** The High Court of Australia in *Sullivan v Moody* **23.4** (fn.42) had declined to find a duty of care in relation to the investigation and reporting of suspicions of child abuse against the plaintiff. In *Stewart v Ronalds* [2009] NSWCA 277 the NSWCA similarly declined to find a duty of care in senior counsel retained to investigate allegations against a member of the NSW Parliament. However, at [104] Hodgson J.A. said:

"I do not read [*Sullivan*] as altogether ruling out a duty of care in all cases where the law of defamation might apply. In a footnote to that paragraph, the joint judgment referred, without expressing either approval or disapproval, to *Spring v Guardian Assurance Plc* . . . in which the House of Lords, by a four/one majority, held that an employer giving a reference in respect of a former employee owed that employee a duty to take reasonable care in its preparation. The majority considered that the fact that, in an action for defamation based on an inaccurate reference, the employer would have a defence of qualified privilege, did not bar an action in negligence where no such defence was available. In my opinion, while it is by no means clear that this case would be followed in Australia, it is at least arguable that, because defamation applies irrespective of any particular relationship between a defendant and a plaintiff and irrespective of any particular vulnerability of a plaintiff to injury by defamatory assertions by a defendant, defamation does not necessarily cover the field and exclude a duty of care in cases where there is some particular relationship created by assumption of responsibility by a defendant and where the plaintiff has particular vulnerability to injury from defamatory assertions by the defendant."

In *Reeves v New South Wales* [2010] NSWSC 611 the plaintiff police officer alleged negligence in failing to give information to protect him from adverse comment in relation to evidence given to a Royal Commission. The defendants' argument that there was no duty of care because the exclusive remedy lay in the law of defamation was rejected. This was not a case, like *Sullivan v Moody*, where there was an "intersection" between defamation and negligence.

"Given the nature of the harm which flowed from the duties Mr Reeves was given; his statutory obligation to pursue them; his resulting vulnerability to allegations of corruption; the adverse attention to which he came before the Royal Commission as the result of the Police Service investigation . . . ; the resulting position into which he was placed at work and before the Police Board from . . . [the] false evidence about this investigation; that Mr Reeves undoubtedly had to rely on the Police Service to provide accurate information about the position into which he had been placed cannot be doubted. He was not in a position where he could protect himself without its support. That a duty of care existed in this situation must be accepted" (at [380]).

See, however, *Dale v Veda Advantage Information Services and Solutions Ltd* [2009] FCA 305, where a duty of care was denied in respect of privileged credit reports (para.14.25, above).

**23.5**    **Limits on liability for negligence.** In *Birkenfeld v Yachting New Zealand Ltd* [2008] NZCA 531; [2009] N.Z.L.R. 499 the plaintiff was injured in a marine accident caused by the defendants to which the New Zealand Accident Compensation scheme had no application. The defendant tendered NZ$560,000 plus interest and costs, which was the limit of its liability under the legislation implementing the convention on limitation of liability in maritime claims. The NZCA rejected the plaintiff's claims for a declaration that the accident was the defendants' fault because it would serve no useful purpose. However, the court was clearly influenced by the context of the maritime limitation legislation and its code for notifying and investigating accidents. In so far as the plaintiff was concerned about her reputation, the court remarked:

"The law protects reputation interests in various ways, including the tort of defamation and the evolving cause of action for breach of privacy. But this Court has been reluctant to develop a cause of action in negligence for that purpose, as to do so would cut across the proper scope of other causes of action" (at [53]).

Section 2. Harassment

**23.9**    **The Protection from Harassment Act 1997.** *What may amount to harassment.* Harassment involves tormenting a person by subjecting him to constant interference or intimidation: *R v Curtis* [2010] EWCA Crim 123; [2010] 1 Cr. App. R. 31 (sporadic outbursts of violent temper over nine months). See also *Ferguson v British Gas Trading Ltd* [2009] EWCA Civ 46; [2010] 1 W.L.R. 785 (persistent, unjustified demands for payment even if unknown to management); *DPP v Hardy* [2008] EWHC 2874 (QB) (legitimate inquiry may become harassment by reason of persistence and manner); *James v CPS* [2009] EWHC 2925 (continual abuse of person coming into contact with D even if contact voluntary).

*Note 98.* On the overlap of defamation and harassment see also *Bloom v Robinson-Millar*, October 7, 2009 (QB).

*Note 101.* The "prevention or detection of crime" defence is confined to acts specifically directed to those purposes: *Dowson v CC Northumbria* [2009] EWHC 907 (QB).

CHAPTER 24

## CRIMINAL LIBEL

SECTION 5. PENDING REFORM OF CRIMINAL DEFAMATION

**The Law Commission studies.** The long saga of the reform of criminal libel **24.20** has now come to an abrupt end. Without fanfare and with little discussion, the crime of defamatory libel in the common law of England and Wales as well as Northern Ireland was abolished by the Coroners and Justice Act 2009, s.73. The abolition was based on an initiative sponsored by Dr Evan Harris and Lord Lester (See *Hansard* HL vol 712 col 843, July 9, 2009). Though the crime survives, mainly in statutory format, in other jurisdictions (though it was abolished in Ireland by the Defamation Act 2009), it is not intended to maintain commentary on criminal libel in future editions of this book.

# CHAPTER 25

# THE EUROPEAN CONVENTION ON HUMAN RIGHTS AND REPUTATION

## SECTION 1. BACKGROUND

**25.5**  **Convention applicants.** In *Kubaszewski v Poland* (2010), App. no.571/04, local newspaper allegations that a municipal council had wasted money on a sewerage system were underscored with an even more serious accusation of "money-laundering" in collusion with local contractors. Civil liability for libel was found, with pending criminal proceedings. The allegations benefited from the special protection accorded to important party political matters of public interest (see Main Work, para.25.18 (1)). But what really saved the newspaper in the eyes of the European Court was that the allegations were not made personally against specific individuals but against the whole Municipal Board, and thereby against a collective of politicians in their public capacity who must endure public opprobrium from time to time. The Court's view that the domestic finding of liability breached article 10 again does not reach the point of automatic immunity for public bodies, as in *Derbyshire CC v Times Newspapers* [1993] A.C. 534, but it will be more difficult in the light of this decision to sustain liability when there is expression which does not directly identify individuals and instead asserts a corporate blame.

## SECTION 2. THE RIGHT TO REPUTATION AS A CONVENTION RIGHT

**25.10**  **The basis for the right to reputation in the Convention.** (1) The resort to privacy rights as a mode of restraining expression remains a manifest trend and one which cuts across the priority given to political speech under article 10. A number of instances have recently occurred.

In *Petrina v Romania* (2008), App. no.78060/01, a politician was accused in a television programme of prior collaboration with the state security services (*Securitate*) during the Communist era. It was later alleged in a number of newspaper articles that the applicant had been a captain in the *Securitate* and had acted as an informant on others in his political party. The applicant brought criminal proceedings for insult and defamation (with linked civil actions), but the journalists were acquitted because their allegations had been accepted in the domestic courts as general and imprecise—value judgments rather than facts—and were set in the context of humorous satire. The European Court considered the case under art.8 as an unrequited attack on reputation which was an aspect of private life which can apply even within the context of public allegations against a public figure. On that basis, there had been a violation of art.8. It counted against the journalists that there was no clearly established historical or official evidence and no admissions from the applicant. There was justification for giving priority to art.8 since the allegation that the applicant had effectively posed as a defender of democracy was a criticism of his personal character and not just his public persona.

In *Petrenco v Moldova* (2010), App. no.20928/05, the official government newspaper made negative comments about the applicant's professional competence as an historian and claimed that his career had owed much to his past cooperation with the KGB. After he failed to obtain satisfaction in the domestic courts, the European Court found a breach of art.8. The applicant was a public figure—the Chairman of the Association of Historians of the Republic of Moldova, a university professor, and the author of the 1996 school curriculum on "Universal History". But in contrast to the treatment of those attributes under art.10 (which had originally been invoked in the application), they did not appear so weighty under art.8. Instead, the Court talked about "balance" between values and found a breach of art.8 in respect of the allegation that the applicant had collaborated with the KGB in the absence of any factual justification.

Art.8 was next the weapon of choice in *A v Norway* (2009), App. no.28070/06. The applicant complained about the rejection of his defamation action against the *Fædrelandsvennen* newspaper which published two articles concerning the preliminary investigation into the murder of two young girls in which he was said to be implicated. The domestic court had found the reports to be defamatory as implying he was a prime suspect in the murder case but accepted a defence for the newspaper based on the public interest in the murders. The applicant had been convicted of another murder for which he had been released from prison a year before the murder of the two girls. He was questioned about the murders as a possible witness but not charged, and two other men were subsequently convicted of those crimes. The newspaper reports covered his involvement in the police investigations and also disclosed his past criminal convictions, his place of work, residence and neighbourhood, and a large though somewhat indistinct photograph of him. As a result, though he was not named, he was identifiable. He also brought a successful defamation action against a television station, TV2, which reported press interest in him and showed an interview with him on his way to the area of the murders. Because of the media reports, he was unable to continue his work, had to move house, and had become socially isolated. The European Court concluded that the damage to his reputation and to his private life more generally had not adequately been remedied, and so there was a breach of art.8. It is striking in this case how little margin of appreciation seems to be afforded under art.8 compared to art.10, for the European Court reached its verdict despite "the careful and thorough review carried out by the national courts of the various factors that are relevant under the Convention" (at [74]).

Privacy also remains a value protected within art.10(2) and thereby a restraint on free expression. In *Standard Verlags GmbH v Austria (No.2)* (2009), App. no.21277/05, the Austrian newspaper, *Der Standard*, reported "A society rumour" under the general heading of "Gossip mongering" to the effect that the soon to retire President of Austria and his wife were to separate because of the wife's liaisons with a prominent politician and the husband of a diplomat. Both the President and his wife brought legal actions for breach of privacy and were awarded compensation. The prominent politician also sought and won damages for breach of privacy and defamation based on the original hard copy publication in the paper and repetition on the newspaper's website and obtained an injunction to stop the newspaper from publishing further allegations. The European Court held that these sanctions on speech did not violate article 10. Though the allegations had concerned one of the most prominent public figures in Austria, they impinged on the private aspects of the lives of that person and of persons connected. The aspects under scrutiny did not impinge directly on the exercise of their public functions (in a way which might be true, say, of the health of a politician) but merely served to satisfy the curiosity of the public.

Similarly, the operation of art.10 was subordinated to privacy interests in *Egeland and Hanseid v Norway* (2009) App. no.34438/04. The editors in chief of two major national newspapers in Norway, the *Dagbladet* and *Aftenposten*, were convicted for the publication of photographs of a woman leaving a court building where, following a notorious trial, she had just been convicted and sentenced to 21 years' imprisonment for a triple murder of her parents-in-law and sister-in-law. The woman had been arrested inside the courthouse and was in a distraught state as she was being taken to an unmarked police car. The offence of the newspapers was under section 131A of the Administration of Courts Act 1915, which prohibits photographing an accused or convicted person on their way to or from a court hearing without their consent. The section was viewed as aiming to protect both privacy and the administration of justice. The Supreme Court refused to admit any special considerations, such the immediacy of the conviction or the enhanced public interest in such a shocking case. Similarly, the European Court considered this form of reporting to be particularly intrusive of a person who was in great distress and at her most vulnerable psychologically. So there had been no violation of art.10, and one must conclude that photography is more likely to be impugned on this reasoning than the printed word.

Lest it be thought that art.8 has completely nullified free speech interests, three corrective cases are now provided. In *Kuliś v Poland* (2008), App. no.15601/02, the applicant was the publisher of a weekly magazine which contained an interview with the lawyer who had acted for persons accused of kidnapping the daughter of Andrzej Kern, the then Deputy Speaker of the *Sejm* (Poland's lower House of Parliament). The criminal proceedings against the accused had just been discontinued, and the lawyer accused Kern of deceit and abuse of power in the investigation of his daughter's alleged kidnapping and that he had tried to place her in a psychiatric clinic and had been deficient as a parent. Kern, his wife and daughter brought civil proceedings against the magazine for protection of their personal rights and were awarded an apology and compensation. The European Court inevitably viewed Kern as a public figure and noted that he had made the alleged kidnapping a matter of public interest by involving the prosecution authorities, the media, politicians and important State institutions in the case. Thus, his family life became closely linked to his standing as a politician and contributed to a public debate. The publications hardly embodied sensitivity to the situation but did not exceed what was tolerable in a public debate and had sufficient factual basis. It had to be accepted that political invective could spill over into the personal sphere. Thus, there was a breach of art.10. It should, however, be noted that Kern had courted publicity, especially by an appeal on television for assistance. In this way, in the inelegant language of the Court, "mediatisation of this case was triggered by Mr Kern himself" (at [44]). A more passive politician might therefore be treated differently.

Another corrective to the predominance of art.8 is *Karakó v Hungary* (2009), App. no.39311/05, though this was given in the context of political elections, where free speech is of particular importance. The applicant was a member of parliament who was standing as a candidate in the 2002 parliamentary elections. During the hustings, a flyer was distributed in his electoral district, signed by a rival politician. The flyer stated that the applicant regularly voted against the interests of his district. The applicant's action for criminal libel was dismissed by the court. He complained to the European Court under art.8 that his reputation had not been adequately protected, but account was taken of the fact that the flyer had expressed a value judgment regarding the public record of an active politician during an election campaign in which he had been a candidate. There could be no doubt that the flyer was protected by art.10 and in the circumstances art.8 should not be given in priority.

Third, in *Gillan and Quinton v UK* (2010), App. no.4158/05, the complaint was sustained under the rubric of art.8 that a relatively superficial search can constitute an interference, contrary to the view of the House of Lords that art.8 had not been engaged (*R (on the application of Gillan) v M.P.C.* [2006] UKHL 12; [2006] 2 A.C. 307). The search had occurred in the exercise of stop and search powers under the Terrorism Act 2000, s.44. Both applicants were stopped in 2003 near to an arms trade fair being held at the ExCel Centre, Docklands. The searches were of outer clothing and bags; nothing incriminating was found; the length of the transaction was up to thirty minutes. One applicant was a protester against the arms industry; the other was a journalist seeking to cover the events. Their potential claims under arts 5, 10, 11, and 14 were left aside rather than dismissed, but the case does give an indication of art.8 being used as a sword rather than a shield in the furtherance of rights of expression and free association when the authorities seek to suppress them.

Art.8 does, of course, remain as a form of unique restraint on expression where the charge is one of excessive media intrusion per se rather than damage to reputation. A recent example is *Reklos and Davourlis v Greece* (2009), App no.1234/05, where the applicant complained about photographs having been taken of their new-born baby without their consent contrary to art.8. The photographs had been taken by a professional photographer who was allowed into the clinic where the baby had been born without their prior consent, and the photographer refused to hand over the negatives but had not in any way published the photographs. In this way, art.8 can impact on the preparations for publication as well as the publication itself. It is as if the existence of a negative has a "chilling effect" on privacy, just as has been held to be the case in regard to the storage of data for criminal justice purposes (*S and Marper v United Kingdom* (2008), App. nos 30562/04, 30566/04.

**Problems of excessive enforcement of the right to reputation.** (1) The     **25.13**
quantum of damages has been considered in *Armoniene v Lithuania* (2008), App.

no.36919/02. The problem was the opposite to that encountered in cases such as *Tolstoy Miloslavsky v UK* (App. no.18139/91, Ser.A, Vol.316, 323 (1995) 20 E.H.R.R. 442). In other words, the libel laws were attacked as unduly restricting damages and so failing to allow the courts to vindicate a person's reputation under art.8. In the case, a leading daily newspaper in a front-page story article alleged that her husband was HIV-positive and had had a relationship with a woman who had AIDS. The statutory maximum award (which had been granted) was €2,896. Even recognising that heavy sanctions on press transgressions could have a chilling effect, this sum was deemed by the European Court to be insufficient to redress the damage suffered by the applicant and deter the recurrence of such abuses. The Court's own award was €6,500 for non-pecuniary damage (the applicant had claimed €26,065).

**25.14**    **Problems of inadequate substantive support for the right to reputation.** (2) An illustration of the recognition of a situation akin to qualified privilege, where disclosure is damaging but is necessary for a potential investigation in the public interest is *Juppala v Finland* (2008), App. no.18630/03. A doctor reported to the child welfare authorities, against the wishes of the applicant (the mother), evidence of an injury to the child of the applicant which was alleged to be the result of violence by the applicant's partner. The partner was acquitted in subsequent proceedings, whereupon the doctor was convicted of criminal libel. Given that there is an important societal need to protect children (and given the child had accused the partner), the conviction breached art.10 since it failed to answer any "pressing social need". A similar point arose in *Frankowicz v Poland* (2008), App. no.53023/99, where the applicant, a medical specialist, had been disciplined for writing a report about a client's medical condition for the purposes of claiming an invalidity allowance. In the course of the report, he commented that part of the treatment by a local clinic failed to show adequate diligence. This restriction on expression was excessive. Next, in *Kurłowicz v Poland* (2010), App. no.41029/06, the president of a city council was convicted of defamation regarding the financial and organisational actions of a school manager. The remarks had been uttered during sessions of the council convened to consider the finances of the school. In those circumstances, the European Court felt that there should be protection for such an important aspect of public debate: "It is precisely the task of an elected representative to ask awkward questions when it comes to public spending" (at [47]).

**25.14**    (3) The remedy of a right to reply was not disapproved, as represented by *Csánics v Hungary* (2009), App. no.12188/06. The applicant, the chairman of a trade union, attacked the domestic court decisions which had ordered him to rectify assertions he had made in an interview concerning a demonstration organised by his trade union. The remedy was held to be in breach of art.10, but because of the disproportionate finding that he had overstepped the bounds of tolerable criticism rather than because of the "relatively mild sanction" (at [46]).

By contrast, in *Karsai v Hungary* (2009), App. no.5380/07, the obligation placed on an historian to publish a rectification breached art.10. The applicant was a university professor of history who published an article critical of those, including a named author, who had praised the former Prime Minister, Pál Teleki (who, during his tenure of office from 1939 until he committed suicide in 1941, collaborated with Nazi Germany and allowed the passage of anti-Semitic legislation). The stance of his sympathisers was described as revisionism and "Jew-bashing". The author brought a civil action, and the Court of Appeal ordered the publication of a rectification. The applicant feared that this remedy impugned his own credibility as a historian. The European Court depicted the dispute as a discussion about the standing of the former Prime Minister, a debate of utmost public interest which had a bearing on responses to Hungary's totalitarian era. The author had himself widely published on the subject and so had voluntarily exposed himself to public comment. Thus, harsh criticism was to be permitted between such protagonists. The obligation to publish a rectification was judged to affect unduly the applicant's professional credibility as a historian and was therefore capable of producing an intimidating effect which would dampen public debate to the detriment of art.10.

**Problems of inadequate procedural support for the right to reputation.** A    **25.15**
number of issues were tested by the European Court arising from the domestic litigation between Grigori Loutchansky and *The Times* in *Times Newspapers (nos 1 and 2) v UK* (2009), App. nos 3002/03 and 23676/03 (the admissibility decision (on 11 October 2005) is discussed in relation to qualified privilege at Main Work 25.18(1)(g)). Prominent amongst them was the special limitation period applicable to libel actions under the Limitation Act 1980, s.4A, which the Court simply stated was a matter for individual states (at [46]). The more protracted inquiry was about the repetition of a libel on the archive website of a newspaper, a form of publication which has the potential to create endless further liability as the webpage is accessed repeatedly over time and thereby falls under the rule in the *Duke of Brunswick v Harmer* [1849] 14 QB 154. The Court viewed it as fair treatment under art.10 to put the publisher at risk of such liability and to reject a "single publication rule" (liability only for the first instance of publication). In this way, the newspaper is placed under an implied responsibility to publish a qualification or correction on its website (as later occurred) or even remove the offending material from its own server. Such a duty was proportionate under art.10. However, internet news archives were recognised by the Court as "an important source for education and historical research" by the public (at [45]), so endless separate causes of action arising after "a significant lapse of time" (at [48]) would constitute a disproportionate threat to freedom of expression. One qualification is that this social utility was accorded to news archives which are "readily accessible to the public and are generally free", attributes which *The Times* has recently shied away from. In addition, the Court warned that it expected higher standards of responsible journalism to be applied to ensuring the accuracy of historical stories, compared to the standards applicable to "perishable" information which was produced in circumstances of the urgency of a current publishing deadline. The Court did not consider the liability to alter the website which may arise from a change of circumstances (as in *Flood v Times Newspapers Ltd* [2010] EWCA Civ 804; [2010] E.M.L.R. 26).

**Equal treatment in the protection of reputations.** Parliamentary immunity    **25.16**
as a limitation on the vindication of reputation arose in *Kart v Turkey* (2009), App. no.8917/05, in the somewhat unusual circumstances not of preventing

someone bringing action against a parliamentarian but of stopping a member of the National Assembly from defending criminal defamation actions which had commenced before that person's election. The actions against him could not proceed so he was no longer at risk of conviction, but that outcome was not satisfactory as he felt that he was then unable to clear his name in respect of suspended criminal process which could be resurrected when his term of office ended. The criminal defamation prosecutions arose from activities undertaken during his prior work as a lawyer rather than as a member of the National Assembly. The European Court viewed the result as being part and parcel of his voluntary choice of standing for election and becoming a member of the National Assembly, while the precise formulation of parliamentary immunity belonged to the realm of parliamentary law, in which a wide margin of appreciation was left to member States. As a result, there was no breach of art.6.

A rather more familiar problem of parliamentary immunity arose in yet another Italian case—*C.G.I.L. and Cofferati v Italy* (2009), App. no.46967/07. The trade union organisation, C.G.I.L., and its General Secretary complained about the publication in *Il Messaggero* of an interview by a government minister (and member of parliament), Umberto Bossi, who drew a connection between the social climate allegedly created by the leftist movements such as the C.G.I.L. and the murder of a Government consultant by the Red Brigades. An action for defamation was brought against Bossi, as well as the newspaper's journalist involved in the interview, the editorial director, and the publishing company. The action against Bossi was halted by the Rome District Court on grounds of parliamentary immunity, and therefore the actions against the others, based solely on the reproduction of Bossi's statements, also fell. It will be noted that the indulgence granted in Italian law was remarkable as it extended to remarks made outside the context of the parliamentary debate and having no clear connection with a parliamentary activity. On that basis, this undue interference with normal legal process was a breach of art.6(1).

SECTION 3. CONFLICTS BETWEEN THE PROTECTION OF A REPUTATION AND OTHER CONVENTION RIGHTS

**25.18**    **Restrictions on the right to free expression.** (2) Matters of comment on public affairs of wide interest were the subject of *Andreescu v Romania* (2010), App. no.19452/02. The applicant, a well-known human rights activist, had applied for access to personal files held by the *Securitate* (the Romanian intelligence service under the former regime). The application was made through a statutory body, the National Council for the Study of the Archives of the Securitate (*Consiliul Naţional pentru Studierea Arhivelor Securităţii*, CNSAS), but it made no response to his two requests—one concerning an intelligence file on him, and the other seeking information on whether the members of the Synod of the Romanian Orthodox Church had collaborated with the *Securitate*. After a year had passed, the applicant organised a press conference about the non-response and raised suspicions regarding the links to the former regime of a named member of the CNSAS. His remarks received widespread media attention. The officer made a criminal complaint of insult and defamation. The appellate court (the Bucharest County Court) found the applicant guilty without hearing evidence from him, after he had been acquitted by the first-instance court, and he was fined. The European Court found a breach of art.6(1) because of the unfair process. As for art.10, there was also a breach, having regard to the fact that the applicant had emphasised that he was voicing suspicions rather than certainties , that there was some supporting evidence (the official's conduct, his past links, and the modus operandi of *Securitate* agents), and also because of the particularly high level of the fine.

The protection under art.10 for allegations levelled against the police was emphasised once again in two Russian cases. In *Dyundin v Russia* (2008), App. no.37406/03, a journalist was responsible for a newspaper interview with two former suspects who alleged that the police had beaten them in order to obtain confessions. The journalist then criticised the authorities' failure to investigate the allegations of abuse. The senior operational police officer at the police station where the ill-treatment had allegedly occurred successfully sued the applicant and the newspaper's founder for defamation. The European Court held that the domestic court had attached undue weight to the fact that the prosecution authorities had refused to bring criminal proceedings against the policemen because of the lack of reliability of the allegations by the former suspects. However, the standard of proof for criminal charges should be distinguished from the worth of journalism on a matter of public concern. The publication had amounted to fair comment on a matter of public concern with a sufficient factual basis and not exceeding the acceptable limits of criticism.

Also on the subject of criminal investigation, in *Godlevskiy v Russia* (2008), App. no.14888/03, the journalist-applicant alleged that investigative officers had corruptly discontinued the prosecution of drug-dealers in order to share the profits from drug sales. Subsequently those officers sued in civil defamation and obtained judgment against him. The European Court noted that the newspaper article had not mentioned the plaintiffs by name but had referred collectively to "the police" or "the anti-narcotics unit". The article was viewed as reasonably constructed, being particularly reliant upon an interview with a former drug-addict and police informant, and amounted to a discussion on a matter of public interest rather than a gratuitous attack on the reputation of named police officers. The domestic court's decision to protect unnamed officers, based on their subjective perception of the impact of the publication was interpreted by the European Court to be "of primordial importance" (at [44]) as it meant that there had been no pressing social need for putting the protection of the investigators' personality rights above the applicant's right to freedom of expression. Consequently, the European Court concluded that the publication had not exceeded the acceptable limits of criticism within art.10 and should not have been penalised.

Another topic of public interest is education, and in *Sorguç v Turkey* (2009), App. no.17089/03, the European Court not only recognised the public importance of discussion about the operation of that sector but began to elevate academic freedom as especially prioritised speech within it. The applicant, a professor of construction management at Istanbul Technical University, distributed a paper at an academic conference in which he criticised the selection procedure for assistant professors, without mentioning specific names. Later that year, an assistant professor sought to bring civil defamation proceedings, and the domestic court accepted that the allegations had been an attack on the individual's reputation rather than a general criticism of the academic system and related institutions. The European Court readily described the comments as being on an issue of public importance. The speech was essentially a presentation of the type of value judgments which, being based on experience, were at least in part susceptible of proof. Since the Turkish courts treated them as primarily a personalised attack, he had not received the opportunity to substantiate his statements and had been denied the freedom of expression which should be accorded to an academic in public debate. The Court underlined the importance of academic freedom, especially in the context of opinions about the education institution or system in which the academic worked. Accordingly, there had been a violation of art.10.

(4) The fact/value judgment distinction remains prominent, somewhat haphazard, and often crucial. Examples include *Azevado v Portugal* (2008), App. no.20620/04, where literary criticism of the efforts of a rival author were value judgments and, accordingly, were not susceptible of proof. In *Chalabi v France* (2008), App. no.35916/04, denigration of management capabilities and the religious knowledge of the director of the Grand Mosque of Lyon in a local magazine were trenchant but not excessive, given that the director was a prominent figure and under official investigation for misappropriation and fraud.

(7) Comments arising from legal proceedings were further considered in *July and Sarl Liberation v France* (2008), App. no.20893/03. The French daily newspaper, *Libération*, reported statements made at a press conference concerning the death in Djibouti of Judge Bernard Borrel. His widow had been critical of the subsequent investigation, alleging bias, delay, and "a catalogue of errors", of which the charge of bias alone was sanctioned as a criminal libel. The European Court found a breach of art.10. The journalists had been careful to use quotation marks and speakers' names to make clear what was reportage and what amounted to the newspaper's own analysis, and the terms used were not personally insulting against any official.

(8) A failure to undertake sufficient journalistic research undermined the protection of the newspaper in *Flux v Moldova (No.6)* (2008), App. no.22824/04, where allegations of financial irregularities by a high school principal were contained in an anonymous letter published by a newspaper. The journalist concerned had met the author but had not sought to verify the facts or to contact the school, and a right to reply had been denied.

The same point arose in *Europa Press Holding DOO v Croatia* (2009), App. no.25333/06; [2010] E.M.L.R. 10. A popular news magazine, *Globus*, published an article about an incident which took place in a government building a week earlier. The Croatian Minister of Finance and Deputy Prime Minister had allegedly expressed displeasure about an article by a journalist of another publisher who was present with him and had told her that she should be killed. The article described how he had taken a handgun from a security officer and pointed it at the journalist, saying that he would kill her, after which he had laughed at his own joke. In a civil action for defamation, the domestic court, after hearing several eyewitnesses, decided that the published information had been untrue and that the reports about the incident had not been properly verified. The European Court accepted that the very specific factual assertions of seriously reprehensible conduct were not value judgments and therefore should be verified. The magazine had not produced evidence to counter that of the politician beyond the journalist immediately involved, and the European Court considered that more should have been done to verify the story, especially by hearing the other side's version of events. Thus, the domestic courts' decisions were proportionate to the injury to reputation suffered.

But it is recognised that mistakes can be made even within a protected publication. In *Niskasaari v Finland* (2010), App. no.37520/07, a Finnish publishing company, a freelance journalist and an editor complained about their criminal convictions for defamation, arising from a publication of a magazine article which contained some inaccuracies about the removal from frontline work and assignment to inappropriate research work of the Child Ombudsman in the Mannerheim League for Child Welfare. The implication was that the officer was being transferred due to poor performance. A later edition of the magazine included a correction by the press officer of the Mannerheim League for Child Welfare, asserting that the information concerning the reassignment was misleading because the officer had been awarded a grant for three months and also had three months' research leave, none of which had affected her status. The European Court was struck by the fact that no consideration was given by the Finnish courts to the correction, whereas the European Court considered that the timely correction of incorrect information was an appropriate form of redress for damage to reputation. In contrast, the Finnish court had imposed substantial criminal fines and compensation, going beyond the bounds allowed by art.10, which at most required some kind of civil law response.

(9) Support for free speech in the context of court affairs, as in *Nikula v Finland* (2002), App. no.31611/96 (see further *Schöpfer v Switzerland* (1998–III), App. no.25405/94) emerged again in *Mariapori v Finland* (2010), App. no.37751/07, where accusations of perjury made in court by a tax expert, who was acting as the defendant's witness against a tax inspector in the context of tax fraud proceedings, were protected by art.10. The proceedings had been reported without identification of the tax inspector, but the verbatim proceedings were open to public access. It was noted that the trial judge did not intervene or ask the applicant to retract her statement, nor was she held to be in contempt of court. The conviction for aggravated defamation breached art.10, and the same applied to conviction for repetition of the accusation made against an anonymous tax inspector in a "book" written by the applicant. Though this amounted to no more than a polemical document or pamphlet, it did contribute to a public debate about the actions of the tax authorities and so was deserving of protection.

The treatment of lawyers who, in the setting of a courtroom, make comments which exceed the strict presentation of evidence was analysed with sympathy in *Nikula v Finland*. However, there comes a point where lawyers become equivalent to politicians or journalists—advocates for the cause of their clients but not accorded the special protection applicable to their role in a forensic setting. This point was perhaps reached in *Coutant v France* (2008), App. no.17155/03, where a member of the Paris Bar was fined for public defamation of a public authority because of her criticisms in a press release of the authorities during the "Chalabi" trial of around 600 Algerians who were implicated in terrorism in 1998. She denounced the use of "terrorist methods", "police raids using methods worthy of the Gestapo and the Militia", and "brutality and torture during four days of police custody, under the supervision of judges from the special section". As a lawyer in the trial, she argued that her professional duties required her to censure official practices incompatible with human rights. However, her complaints were brought under art.10 and not art.6. This distinction was also followed by the European Court, which found that the applicant had not argued in court for a nullity of the proceedings but instead had issued the impugned press release which raised general criticisms beyond the bounds of her client's criminal defence. As for art.10, the applicant lacked justification since she had failed to substantiate her case, had not acted in good faith, and had expressed herself in partial and vindictive terms, taking her beyond the limits required for the protected discussion of ideas.

**25.21**     **Procedural safeguards for persons exercising freedom of expression.** Procedural guarantees were found to be insufficient in *Mihaiu v Romania* (2008), App. no.42512/02. The domestic Court of First Instance acquitted the applicant because one of the constituent elements of criminal defamation, namely, intent, had not been made out. In June 2002 the Bucharest County Court set aside the judgment on appeal, following a hearing at which the applicant was absent but was represented by his lawyer. The European Court felt this unexpected reversal in the absence of the accused amounted to a breach of article 6(1).

CHAPTER 26

# THE INITIAL STAGES

SECTION 1. INTRODUCTION

**Risks.** *Add new note 3A after "ample means" in second line.* It is well known    **26.2**
that legal aid is not available in defamation except in cases which are so
exceptional that, as far as the authors are aware, none has yet qualified: see
Access to Justice Act 1999, Sch.2, para.1(f), and s.6(8): see also *Steel & Morris
v UK* [2005] E.M.L.R. 15 at [41]–[42]. The equivalent Scottish provisions, which
closely resemble the guidance given to the Legal Services Commission by the
Lord Chancellor as to the kind of case which he is likely to consider favourably
for funding under s.6(8)—which include a significant wider public interest in the
resolution of the case to which funded representation would contribute, the fact
that the case is of overwhelming importance to the person who seeks funding,
and the existence of exceptional circumstances such that without public funding
it would be practically impossible for the person to bring or defend the proceedings, or that the lack of public funding would lead to obvious unfairness in the
proceedings—were challenged unsuccessfully in *DW(AP), Petitioner* [2009]
CSOH 151.

**Defences.** *Note 16.* The Court of Appeal recently found an allegation that a    **26.4**
claimant "happily promotes bogus treatments" to be a statement of opinion,
defensible as comment: see *British Chiropractic Association v Singh* [2010]
EWCA Civ 350; [2011] E.M.L.R. 1. That decision may in large part be explained
by the scientific context of the allegations. It should be noted that the Court of
Appeal thought "honest opinion" a name that better reflected the importance of
the defence as an essential ingredient of the right to free expression.

*Note 22. Charman v Orion Publishing Group Ltd* is now also reported at
[2008] E.M.L.R. 16.

*Note 26.* More assistance has now been provided by the Court of Appeal's
decision in *Flood v Times Newspapers Ltd* [2010] EWCA Civ 804; [2010]
E.M.L.R. 26. *Charman v Orion Publishing Group Ltd* is now also reported at
[2008] E.M.L.R. 16.

SECTION 2. CHOICE OF DEFENDANTS

**26.17**    **Liability for aggravated and exemplary damages.** *Note 47.* For a recent examination of the principles which govern the award of aggravated damages, particularly in the contexts of subsequent publications and publication abroad, see *Clarke (t/a Elumina Iberica UK) v Bain* [2008] EWHC 2636 (QB).

In *Berezovsky v Russian Television and Radio Broadcasting Co* [2010] EWHC 476 (QB) at [174]–[175], Eady J. considered *Broome v Cassell* and *Hayward v Thompson* and concluded that question of whether any joint tortfeasor should be liable for aggravation of damages only to the extent of his joint liability—that is, at the lowest common denominator—could not be definitively answered. He decided, nonetheless, that the lowest common denominator approach was likely to be preferred by a modern appellate court, not least because it was likely to be more compatible with art.10, and therefore left individual aggravating factors out of account. In the event, he awarded damages only in respect of one meaning for which both defendants could be shown to be responsible, to avoid penalising the personal defendant for allegations which he could not be shown to have published.

SECTION 3. JURISDICTION

**26.25**    *Jurisdictional regime. Note 73. High Tech International AG v Deripaska* is reported at [2007] E.M.L.R. 15.

*Note 77. Atlantis World Group of Companies NV v Gruppo Editoriale L'Espresso SpA* is reported at [2009] E.M.L.R. 15.

**26.30**    **Application of the *forum conveniens* principle.** In *Mardas v New York Times Co* [2008] EWHC 3135 (QB); [2009] E.M.L.R. 8 the defendants asked the court to stay two actions or strike them out as an abuse. The claimant complained of publication within the jurisdiction of hard copy and internet articles published by the *New York Times* and the *International Herald Tribune*. Eady J. allowed an appeal from the master's order striking the actions out. He held that what mattered was whether there had arguably been a real and substantial tort within the jurisdiction, and that could not depend on a "numbers game, with the court fixing an arbitrary minimum according to the facts of the case". The scale of publication was uncertain and would have to be determined at trial. The allegations (of lying and charlatanry) were not trivial, and the claimant was well known within the jurisdiction, where his children lived: there was no artificiality about protecting his reputation in England and Wales. It was obvious that given the increasing recognition in the Strasbourg jurisprudence that the right to protect honour and reputation was protected by art.8, care must be taken on such applications not to deprive a litigant too readily of his art.6 right of unimpeded access to the courts in pursuit of his remedies. The Court of Appeal refused permission to appeal: [2009] EWCA Civ 633.

In *Baturina v Times Newspapers Ltd* [2010] EWHC 696 (QB); [2010] E.M.L.R. 18, the Russian claimant (the wife of the mayor of Moscow) sued over hard copy and online articles published both within the jurisdiction and in Russia by the *Sunday Times* concerning her alleged ownership of a mansion in Highgate. The claim was complicated by the fact that it was unsustainable without an innuendo meaning, namely the illegality of the claimant's supposed conduct under Russian law, which required officials and civil servants of the Russian Federation and their families to disclose all their property, something which the claimant had not done in respect of the Highgate mansion. Eady J. struck out the claims for hard copy publication within the jurisdiction (given the obscurity of the special facts relied on for the innuendo) and for internet publication both within the jurisdiction and in Russia (given both the obscurity of the special facts and the brevity of the period during which the article was available on the internet): reliance on any such publication would have required specific pleading of the readers with knowledge of the special facts. However, he saw no reason why the court should decline jurisdiction in respect of publication of hard copies of the *Sunday Times* in Russia. The defendant was based within the jurisdiction, primary publication of the newspaper took place there, and the defendant knew and intended that some publication would take place in Russia. The claimant also sued on repetitions of the *Sunday Times* allegations in the Russian media, but the judge saw no reason to order that any Russian republication should be tried in Russia, which he regarded as "the tail wagging the dog". There was no justification for drawing a distinction between copies of the *Sunday Times* published in Russia and foreseeable repetition of its content by the Russian media.

**Problems over US enforcement of English judgments.** The US Speech Act,    **26.31**
H.R. 2765 Enr, was signed into law by President Obama on August 10, 2010. According to the official summary of the act, it:

> "Prohibits a domestic court from recognizing or enforcing a foreign judgment for defamation whenever the party opposing recognition or enforcement claims that the judgment is inconsistent with the First Amendment to the Constitution, unless the domestic court determines that the judgment is consistent with the First Amendment. Prohibits a domestic court from recognizing a foreign judgment for defamation if the party opposing recognition or enforcement establishes that the exercise of personal jurisdiction by the foreign court that rendered the judgment failed to comport with the due process requirements imposed on domestic courts by the Constitution. Prohibits a domestic court from recognizing or enforcing a foreign judgment for defamation against the provider of an interactive computer service whenever the party opposing recognition or enforcement claims that the judgment is inconsistent with the Communications Act of 1934 regarding protection for private blocking and screening of offensive material, unless the domestic court determines that the judgment is consistent with such provisions. Provides that an appearance by a party in a foreign court rendering a foreign judgment to which this Act applies for the purpose of contesting the foreign court's exercise of jurisdiction, moving the foreign court to abstain from exercising jurisdiction, defending on the merits any claims brought before the foreign court, or for any other purpose, shall not deprive such party of the right to oppose the recognition or enforcement of the judgment under this Act. Allows the award of reasonable attorney fees under certain conditions if the party opposing recognition or enforcement of the judgment prevails."

The Act was hailed in the US as a victory over "libel tourists". However, for a corrective to the somewhat one-sided and self-serving media coverage of the "libel tourism" issue both in the UK and in the US, see Lord Hoffmann's Dame Ann Ebsworth Memorial Lecture, delivered on February 2, 2010 at Inner Temple (new note 123A). Lord Hoffmann observed that

> "Complaints about libel tourism come entirely from the Americans and are based upon a belief that the whole world should share their view about how to strike the balance between freedom of expression and the defence of reputation. Naturally the American view is enthusiastically supported by the media in this country."

He added:

> "It is only if you think, as many Americans do, that an American should only have to say *civis Americanus sum* to cloak himself in the immunity of the First Amendment against liability for injury which he has caused in a foreign country, or, as much of media in this country does, that we ought to become the second country in the world to adopt the *New York Times v Sullivan* rule, that there can be any basis for criticism . . . But before we are stampeded into changing our law, we should bear in mind that the points about which complaint is made are either binding on us as a matter of European law, as in the *Shevill* case, or have been approved by the Strasbourg court as compliant with the right to freedom of speech under the Convention."

*Add new note 123A.* An edited version of the speech is available on the website of Index on Censorship, at *http://www.indexoncensorship.org/2010/02/the-libel-tourism-myth/*.

Section 4. Other Complaints Procedures

**26.35**     **PCC Code of Practice.** *Note 127.* The latest version was ratified in September 2009.

**26.38**     **Privacy.** *Note 136. Murray v Pig Pictures (UK) Ltd* is now also reported at [2009] Ch 481.

*Note 138.* Delete "clause 11" and replace with "clause 10(ii)".

**26.41**     **Ofcom's Broadcasting Code.** *Delete the first sentence, and replace as follows.* The current Broadcasting Code applies to television and radio programmes broadcast on and after December 16, 2009. Its predecessor, the 2005 Broadcasting Code, applied (and continues to apply) to programmes broadcast between that date and July 25, 2005, before which date programmes were regulated under the relevant "legacy" code.

*Delete the second sentence, and replace as follows.* The Code may be found on the Ofcom website (*http://stakeholders.ofcom.org.uk/binaries/broadcast/code09/bcode.pdf*).

**26.44**     **Advertising.** New codes for CAP (non-broadcast) and BCAP (broadcast), as they now wish to be known, come into effect on September 1, 2010. From that date there will be only one broadcast code instead of the four previously in place. The codes may be found on the CAP website at *http://www.cap.org.uk/The-Codes/New-Advertising-Codes.aspx*.

CHAPTER 27

# INTERIM INJUNCTIONS

SECTION 1. GENERAL PRINCIPLES

**Precise words unknown.** *Note 18, after reference to Totalise Plc v Motley* **27.4**
*Fool*. Note that in the rather different context of confidence and private information, a similar order was made against Wikipedia for disclosure of the IP address
of a third party who had disclosed private and confidential information concerning the claimant and her child: *G v Wikimedia Foundation Inc* [2009] EWHC
3148 (QB); [2010] E.M.L.R. 14.

**Evidence of an intention to repeat or publish.** *Note 43*. See also *Martin v* **27.10**
*Channel Four Television Corp* [2009] EWHC 2788 (QB).

**Injunctions based on other causes of action.** *Note 57*. See now the important **27.14**
decision of Tugendhat J. in *Terry (formerly LNS) v Persons Unknown* [2010]
EWHC 119 (QB); [2010] E.M.L.R. 16, in which the judge decided on the
evidence that the nub of the applicant's true complaint (the application was
brought in breach of confidence and misuse of private information) was the
protection of his reputation rather than his private life.

**Section 12(3).** *Note 85*. The flexibility of the pragmatic approach in *Cream v* **27.20**
*Banerjee* has been valuable in the context of applications for interim injunctions
made without notice, where the ring has to be held until the inter partes hearing.
In that context, the question is whether there is a sufficient likelihood that the
claimant will succeed at trial to justify granting an injunction for the short period
until an inter partes hearing: *ASG v GSA* [2009] EWCA Civ 1574 at [5], per
Waller L.J.
The case of *Browne v Associated Newspapers Ltd* is now reported at [2008]
Q.B. 103.

***Add new paragraph.*** *Recent developments*. The courts are increasingly alert to **27.21A**
attempts to circumvent the rule in *Bonnard v Perryman* by means of applications
in confidence or misuse of private information, particularly where the words to
be restrained would arguably be defamatory.

The problem raised its head in *RST v UVW* (new note 90A), where the claimant applied without notice to restrain the publication of confidential information which might well also have been defamatory of him. Tugendhat J. was concerned as to whether the action was brought to protect the claimant's right to protect private information or to protect his reputation. While it was true that a claimant was entitled to choose his cause of action (new note 90B), there were many cases in which statements had been made that a claim purportedly brought to protect confidential or private information was or might be an abuse of process if the real issue at stake was one of reputation (new note 90C). Tugendhat J. regarded the question of whether the case was a genuine claim to protect privacy, and not to protect reputation, as one to be argued at a substantive hearing of the application. He also raised the question of whether the rule in *Bonnard v Perryman* should apply to an application made in confidence or misuse of private information where the material which was the subject of the application was arguably defamatory, suggesting that the question needed to be addressed in the light of authority as to the status of reputation as an art.8 right, and in the light of the balancing test which must be applied between competing Convention rights.

The problem confronted Tugendhat J. again in *Terry (formerly LNS) v Persons Unknown* (new note 90D), where a claim was brought in confidence and misuse of private information to restrain publication of material which appeared to be largely, if not entirely, true, but which was probably defamatory of the applicant. The judge concluded on the evidence that the nub of the applicant's true complaint was the protection of his reputation rather than his private life, and in particular the impact of any adverse publicity on his business of earning sponsorship and similar income, and dismissed the application on the basis (inter alia) of the rule in *Bonnard v Perryman*. The judge held at [88] that it was a matter for the court to decide whether the principle of free speech applied or not, and that did not depend solely on the choice of the claimant as to his cause of action.

The question, raised by Tugendhat J. in *RST v UVW*, of whether the rule in *Bonnard v Perryman* should apply to an application made in confidence or misuse of private information where the material which was the subject of the application was arguably defamatory, in the light of authority as to the extent to which protection of reputation was an art.8 right, and in the light of the balancing test which must be applied between competing Convention rights, was not in the event determined in *Terry*.

However, the status of reputation as an art.8 right was determined by the Supreme Court in *Application by Guardian News & Media Ltd, HM Treasury v Ahmed* (new note 90E). Moreover, the need to apply the "ultimate balancing test" between competing Convention rights, stated by Lord Steyn in *S, Re* (new note 90F) has been re-stated by the House of Lords in *BBC, Re* (new note 90G).

The case of *Terry* shows that where the facts of a case give rise to a claim both in defamation and in confidentiality or privacy, it is for the court to decide whether the free speech principle applies or not, and the claimant's choice of cause of action is not conclusive. But in most cases the applicant's true concerns will not be as easily divined as they were in *Terry*. Since in most cases the court will not be able reliably to determine the applicant's true object in seeking an injunction, some other principled criterion will have to be developed. Even if that difficulty can be overcome, in the light of modern authority at the highest level it will not be easy to justify continued application of a rule (the rule in *Bonnard v Perryman*) which gives at least presumptive priority to one Convention right, that of free speech under art.10, to the detriment of another, namely the right of reputation now established to be protected under art.8 (new note 90H).

*Add new note 90A.* [2009] EWHC 2448 (QB); [2010] E.M.L.R. 13. See also *Ambrosiadou v Coward* [2010] EWHC 1794 (QB) at [56(4)] and *BKM Ltd v BBC* [2009] EWHC 3151 (Ch) at [13], where Mann J, dealing with an application to restrain misuse of private information, observed that he got the impression that the claimant's concern for its reputation was a "significant underlying factor". In both cases, injunctions were refused on other grounds.

*Add new note 90B.* The judge referred to *Joyce v Sengupta* [1993] 1 W.L.R. 337 at [342].

*Add new note 90C.* The judge referred to *Gulf Oil (Great Britain) Ltd v Page* [1987] ch.327 and *McKennitt v Ash* [2006] EWCA Civ 1714; [2008] Q.B. 73 at [79]–[80] per Buxton L.J.

*Add new note 90D.* [2010] EWHC 119 (QB); [2010] E.M.L.R. 16.

*Add new note 90E.* [2010] UKSC 1; [2010] 2 W.L.R. 325.

*Add new note 90F. S (A Child) (Identification: Restrictions on Publication), Re* [2005] 1 AC 593. At [17], Lord Steyn described what he meant by the ultimate balancing test between competing Convention rights (in that case, arts 8 and 10):

> "First, neither article has *as such* precedence over the other. Secondly, where the values under the two articles are in conflict, an intense focus on the comparative importance of the specific rights being claimed in the individual cases is necessary. Thirdly, the justifications for interfering with or restricting each right must be taken into account. Finally, the proportionality test must be applied to each".

*Add new note 90G.* [2009] UKHL 34; [2010] 1 A.C. 145.

*Add new note 90H.* Tugendhat J. has himself spoken (in the context of *Reynolds* privilege, not interim injunction) of the "necessity", consequential on the recognition of reputation as an art.8 right, of applying to defamation cases the "ultimate balancing test" of *S, Re*: see *Flood v Times Newspapers Ltd* [2009] EWHC 2375 (QB); [2010] E.M.L.R. 8. (His decision was overturned in part, but not in that respect, by the Court of Appeal at [2010] EWCA Civ 804; [2010] E.M.L.R. 26).

In *BKM Ltd v BBC* [2009] EWHC 3151 (Ch) at [37], Mann J, after referring to Lord Steyn's speech in *S, Re* and considering the art.8 factors, stated that he "must give special weight to free speech". If he was thereby giving priority to the art.10 right over art.8, it is respectfully submitted that—to that limited extent—he was wrong to do so.

**Section 12(4).** *Replace the last line of this paragraph with:* Relevant privacy **27.22** codes include the Press Complaints Commission Code of Practice and the 2009 Ofcom Broadcasting Code (as to which see para 26.41 above).

SECTION 2. PRACTICE AND PROCEDURE

**27.25** **Urgent applications.** *Note 106.* Where neither requirement is satisfied, it appears that there is no discretion to make an order—the court simply has no jurisdiction to do so: *Martin v Channel Four Television Corp* [2009] EWHC 2788 (QB).

*Note 108.* Notifying intended defendants may be problematic when the real target of the application is a person or persons unknown, but media organisations are interested, and the applicant intends to serve the order upon at least some of them in reliance on the *Spycatcher* principle. It would be a real burden for an applicant, who might be of limited means, to notify and serve evidence on a large number of media non-parties, and the applicant's obligation has now been explained as a duty to serve those media organisations which the applicant has reason to believe have displayed an interest in publishing the story, so that they have an opportunity to be heard: see *WER v REW* [2009] EWHC 1029 (QB); [2009] E.M.L.R. 17, explaining *X v Persons Unknown* [2006] EWHC 2783 (QB), and *TUV v Persons Unknown* [2010] EWHC 853 (QB); [2010] E.M.L.R. 19, where Eady J. stated that applicants should not be required to speculate or guess which media bodies had an interest in the story, but if there were "solid grounds in the light of the available evidence" to believe that a particular media organisation had shown an interest in the material, that organisation should be notified.

In *TUV v Persons Unknown,* Eady J. was prepared to make an order which qualified the obligation on an applicant under CPR 25 PD 9.2 to supply any non-party served with the order, on request, with a copy of the material produced to the judge and a note of the hearing, by ordering that the applicant need only serve documents on a third party on the provision of a written undertaking to use the documents and information served for the purposes of the proceedings in which the application was made. The necessity for that order arose from the fact that CPR 31.22(1), which protects the use to which disclosed documents may be put, applies only to a "party", which a media third party plainly was not, and indeed protects only "disclosed" documents, i.e. documents disclosed through the procedure defined at CPR 31.2.

For a case where an order varying the effect of CPR 25 PD 9.2 would have been refused had an injunction been granted, see *Terry (formerly LNS) v Persons Unknown* [2010] EWHC 119 (QB); [2010] E.M.L.R. 16.

**27.29** *Note 112.* The claimant will usually be required to undertake to serve a note of the hearing (suitably anonymised, if appropriate) and, in some cases, a transcript: see e.g. *RST v UVW* [2009] EWHC 2448 (QB); [2010] E.M.L.R. 13 at [32].

*Note 119.* Orders against persons unknown are now commonplace: see e.g. *TUV v Persons Unknown* [2010] EWHC 853 (QB); [2010] E.M.L.R. 19 and *Terry (formerly LNS) v Persons Unknown* [2010] EWHC 119 (QB); [2010] E.M.L.R. 16. They may give rise to real difficulties for the maintenance of open justice. In *Terry*, for example, it was unlikely that the applicant would ever have served a claim form on a respondent, given the unlikelihood that the source of any leaked information would be identified, and in that event no trial would have been held. The real target of the application was those media third parties whom the applicant chose to notify once an injunction was granted. Nobody else would have known about the order at all, and given that the applicant sought an order that there should be no publication of the existence of the proceedings and no requirement to provide any third party with a copy of the order or any other materials, those media third parties notified of the order would have had to apply to the court, at risk on costs, to find out what the application had been about. The likely effect of the order sought would therefore have been that of a permanent injunction, granted without a trial, binding on anyone on whom the applicant chose to serve the order. Tugendhat J. made it clear that even had he otherwise been prepared to grant an injunction, a return date would have been required and none of the other ancillary orders would have been made.

*Note 120.* The applicant's obligation has now been explained as a duty to serve those media organisations which (so the applicant has solid grounds to believe) have displayed an interest in publishing the story, so that they have an opportunity to be heard: see fn.108 above.

SECTION 3. INJUNCTIONS TO RESTRAIN MISUSE OF PRIVATE INFORMATION

**Evidence.** *Note 124.* The test as to whether the applicant has a reasonable    **27.32**
expectation of privacy or whether the respondent is under an enforceable obligation of confidence in respect of the relevant information is an objective one: *Author of a Blog v Times Newspapers Ltd* [2009] EWHC 1358 (QB); [2009] E.M.L.R. 22. In that case a "blogger", a serving police officer, who wished to restrain a newspaper from identifying him as the author of a particular blog, was taking part in an essentially public activity, analogous to journalism, and in the circumstances he had no reasonable expectation of privacy for his identity. In *Terry (formerly LNS) v Persons Unknown* [2010] EWHC 119 (QB); [2010] E.M.L.R. 16, the paradigm of a disastrous application, an injunction was refused because (inter alia) the evidence of breach of confidence was insufficient to enable the court to be satisfied in accordance with s.12(3), Human Rights Act 1998, that the applicant was likely to establish at trial that there had been a breach of a duty of confidence owed to him. Inevitably, given that the applicant was a well-known footballer, the judgment refusing the injunction was widely publicised.

*Note 127.* Despite the general need for the court to be satisfied that the relevant information is not publicly available, Sir Charles Gray was reluctantly prepared to continue until trial or further order an injunction granted by telephone three days before in a case in which counsel for the applicant declined to place before the court any information about the availability to the public of the information the publication of which he wished to restrain: *WER v REW* [2009] EWHC 1029 (QB); [2009] E.M.L.R. 17. It was no doubt material that the defendant did not oppose continuation of the injunction, but the order was likely to have had some impact on the considerable number of third party media organisations which the applicant intended to serve.

**27.33**    **Balancing competing rights under articles 8 and 10.** *Note 135.* See also *BBC, Re* [2010] UKHL 34; [2010] 1 A.C. 145.

**27.34**    **Truth irrelevant.** *Note 138.* It may also be irrelevant that the applicant declines to tell the court whether the information is true or false, given that truth or falsity is not an issue on an application for an injunction in privacy, although, as Sir Charles Gray suggested, one might speculate as to the reaction of the Court of Appeal in *McKennitt v Ash* had the claimant remained tight-lipped as to whether the information she was seeking to protect was true: see *WER v REW* [2009] EWHC 1029 (QB); [2009] E.M.L.R. 17 at [9]. It is plainly material that the application was not opposed. The difficulty for applicants, as the judge made clear in *WER*, is that if they are candid about the truth or falsity of the allegedly private information, or at least give some detail of the extent to which it may be true, CPR 25 PD para.9.2 requires them to supply a copy of the materials read to the judge and a note of the hearing on any non-party served with the order who requests it, unless the court orders otherwise. If all the media non-parties whom the applicant has served are made aware of the extent to which the relevant information is true, they will make what they can of it; and if the judge makes an order under CPR 25 PD 9.2, those served may well realise that he has done so and "smell a rat", deducing that the information or some of it is true. On that basis, Sir Charles Gray was prepared to accept in *WER* that the decision by counsel for the applicant to limit the information which he placed before the court was a proper exercise of discretion on his part as counsel and not such as to deprive his client of a continued order.

For an order qualifying CPR PD 9.2 by in effect requiring any third party supplied with the relevant documents to give a written undertaking not to use them for any purpose other than that of the proceedings, see *TUV v Persons Unknown* [2010] EWHC 853 (QB); [2010] E.M.L.R. 19, discussed at fn.108 above.

*Note 139.* Such an order is commonplace where the applicant seeks to protect confidential or private information. For a case in which the applicant sought so many ancillary orders in the cause of secrecy that the effect of the injunction, had it been granted, would have been that of a permanent injunction, granted without a trial, binding on anyone on whom the applicant chose to serve the order, see *Terry (formerly LNS) v Persons Unknown* [2010] EWHC 119 (QB); [2010] E.M.L.R. 16, and fn.119 above. It is quite clear that any applicant seeking such wide-ranging derogations from the principle of open justice as were sought in *Terry* will be required to justify them in the most cogent terms.

CHAPTER 28

# PARTICULARS OF CLAIM

SECTION 1. INTRODUCTION

**Generally.** *Note 2.* In *Radu v Houston* [2009] EWHC 398 (QB) Eady J.  **28.1**
said

"There is nothing in Lord Woolf's general observations in *McPhilemy v Times News-papers Ltd* [1999] 3 All E.R. 775 that should be taken to sanction any relaxation of the basic rule that a claimant is entitled to know the case he has to meet; nor would it justify postponing that entitlement to the later stage of proceedings when witness statements are exchanged. For a few years after *McPhilemy* was reported, people from time to time argued that it provided a warrant for keeping their case up their sleeves until exchange. That was long ago, however, recognised to be a misunderstanding. Inevitably, if a new case is revealed when statements are served, the Claimant will have to look into it and respond in a further round of evidence. This is certainly not in accordance with the overriding objective."

SECTION 2. PREFATORY AVERMENTS

**Prefatory averments.** *At end of note 16 before the sentence beginning,* "For  **28.4**
the position in Australia" *add*: A charity claimant should make clear whether or not it is incorporated: see *North London Central Mosque Trust v Policy Exchange* [2009] EWHC 3311 (QB) where Eady J. struck out the claimant's claim because the charity had not been incorporated and stated that the trustees could only sue on behalf of the charity if the charity existed as a legal entity. The Court of

Appeal gave permission to appeal but the action later settled. In *British Chiropractic Association v Singh* [2010] EWCA Civ 350; [2011] E.M.L.R. 1 Lord Judge L.C.J. said at [10],

> "If, like many trade and professional associations, the BCA was not incorporated but consisted simply of the totality of its members, neither individually nor collectively would they have had standing to sue. Some corporations—municipal ones, for example—also lack standing to sue in defamation. The BCA is not subject to either of these disadvantages. If the present claim is well founded in law, the BCA is entitled to pursue it."

*Note 16. Atlantis World Group of Companies NV v Gruppo Editoriale L'Espresso SpA* is now also reported at [2008] E.M.L.R 15.

Section 3. Publication

**28.5**      **Details of publication: libel.** *Note 18. Bray v Deutsche Bank AG* is now reported at [2009] E.M.L.R. 12.

*Note 22.* See *Khader v Aziz* [2010] EWCA Civ 716; [2011] E.M.L.R. 2 at [9] and [24], where a claim was struck out because the pleaded case on publication was no more than assertion. The decision was upheld on appeal.

*Note 23.* When relying upon an inferential case of publication on the internet it is necessary to plead a solid basis for the inference: see *Carrie v Tolkien* [2009] EWHC 29 (QB); [2009] E.M.L.R. 9 where Eady J. said at [17] and [18],

> "It would appear to be established that there is no presumption in law to the effect that placing material on the Internet leads automatically to a substantial publication: see e.g. *Al Amoudi v Brisard* [2001] 1 W.L.R. 113. It is necessary to plead and establish any publication relied upon. There must be some evidence on which an inference can be drawn in relation to that very short period of time. It will not suffice merely to plead that the posting has been accessed 'by a large but unquantifiable number of readers'. There must be some solid basis for the inference. That form of pleading is no more than bare assertion".

See also *Lonzim Plc v Sprague* [2009] EWHC 2838 (QB) at [19]; *Metropolitan International Schools Ltd v Designtechnica Corp* [2009] EWHC 1765 (QB); [2009] E.M.L.R. 27 at [33]; *Hughes v Risbridger* [2009] EWHC 3244 (QB) at [33] and *Baturina v Times Newspapers Ltd* [2010] EWHC 696 (QB); E.M.L.R. 18 at [29] to [32].

**28.6**      **Details of publication: slander.** *Note 26.* For an example of a case where a slander action was struck out as an abuse of process once the investigation into the number of publishees had been completed, see *Lonzim Plc v Sprague* [2009] EWHC 2838 (QB).

**28.7**      **Publication to persons unknown.** *Note 32.* See *Hughes v Risbridger* [2009] EWHC 3244 (QB) at [33].

**Republication.** *Note 35.* See *Palace Films Pty Ltd v Fairfax Media Publica-*  **28.8**
*tions Pty Ltd* [2010] NSWSC 415 at [15]–[23] set out at para.28.10 below.

**Vicarious Liability.** *Note 37. Mosley v News Group Newspapers Ltd* [2008]  **28.9**
EWHC 1777 (QB) is now reported at [2008] E.M.L.R. 20.

**Form of Words.** In *Palace Films Pty Ltd v Fairfax Media Publications Pty*  **28.10**
*Ltd* [2010] NSWSC 415 McCallum J. sitting in the New South Wales Supreme
Court commented on this passage in the following terms:

"15 The pleading alleges that the first, second and third defendants 'wrote and
published or caused to be written and published' the primary article. As to the first and
third defendants (referred to in argument as the Fairfax defendants), the existence of a
proper factual basis for that allegation is uncontroversial. The first defendant is Fairfax
Media Publications Pty Ltd. It was acknowledged on behalf of that company that it is
the proprietor and publisher of the printed newspaper version of the Australian Financial Review. The third defendant is the journalist under whose by-line the primary
article was published, Ms Boland.

16 The Fairfax defendants submit, nonetheless, that the formulation 'wrote and
published or caused to be written and published' is embarrassing and should be struck
out. They submit that the pleading in that form conflates a number of different concepts
and may generate unnecessary complexity in the future conduct of the proceedings.

17 In my view, the formulation 'wrote and published or caused to be written and
published' is problematic. Mr Evatt, who appeared with Mr Rasmussen for the plaintiffs, defended the form of the pleading on the basis that 'it comes from *Gatley*'. He did
not, however, point to any particular part of that text.

18 Since at least its ninth edition, the precedent for pleading publication of a
newspaper article in Appendix 1 of *Gatley on Libel and Slander* has recommended the
following formulation:

'The defendants and each of them published the following words defamatory of the
[plaintiff/claimant]': see A1.12 (9th edn); A1.13 (10th edn); A1.10 (11th edn).

19 It is true that there are other forms of words recommended in other precedents in
*Gatley*, including 'the defendants published and/or caused to be published' (A1.17, 11th
edn). With respect to the learned authors of that text, I think that is an unfortunate
formulation, particularly in the use of the conjunction 'and/or'. Separately, the chapter
in Gatley headed "Particulars of Claim" in the 11th edition notes at [28.10] that it is
usual to describe in the particulars of claim the mode of publication. The examples
offered are "wrote and caused to be published" and "spoke and published". For my
part, I think the repetition of the words "and published" in the particulars is unnecessary.

20 In *Webb v Bloch* it was noted that the text, *Starkey on the Law of Slander and
Liable*, 1st edition (1830) stated (my emphasis):

'The declaration generally avers, that the defendant published and caused to be
published; *but the latter words seem to be perfectly unnecessary* either in a civil or
criminal proceeding; in civil proceedings, the principal is to all purposes identified
with the agent employed by him to do any specific act' (at 364 per Isaacs J).

21 The vice of the form 'spoke and published' (or 'wrote and published' as pleaded
in the present case) is that it combines a purely factual allegation as to the mode of
publication (he spoke the words) and a conclusion (he published the words). A
preferable formulation, in my view, is that set out in the precedents in *Gatley* cited
above, that is, simply to allege that the defendant in question published [the following]
words defamatory of the plaintiff. For the reasons stated above, that in my view would

be a proper pleading of either a publication or a republication. Separately, the pleading should then identify the facts, matters and circumstances relied upon to support that contention, including (where it is not obvious from the premises already pleaded) identification of the mode of publication or the acts by reason of which it is contended that the defendant made the matter available for comprehension by others.

22 In my view, the additional words used in the present case 'or caused to be written and published' are confusing. They may be understood as an attempt to plead direct publication in accordance with the practice described in *Webb v Bloch* at 364, although a similar form of words was there acknowledged to be 'perfectly unnecessary'. Alternatively, they may be understood as an attempt to plead republication (as the same words were understood by the Court of Appeal in *Habib* at [171]).

23 If intended only as an alternative formulation of the allegation of publication, the words add nothing. If intended to allege against any defendant that the primary article was a republication, that should be explicitly pleaded."

## SECTION 5. FOREIGN PUBLICATION

**28.19**     **Foreign publication.** In *Baturina v Times Newspapers Ltd* [2010] EWHC 696 (QB); [2010] E.M.L.R. 18 Eady J. said at [63] that

"The English law relating to liability for an innuendo meaning would be the same irrespective of where publication takes place; that is to say, it is not necessary for a claimant to prove that the defendant knew that the words were capable of bearing such a meaning or foresaw that there were likely to be readers with knowledge of particular facts. The only additional requirement in respect of foreign publication would be that of establishing double actionability."

## SECTION 6. THE MEANING OF THE WORDS

**28.21**     **Pleading the natural and ordinary meaning.** The Court of Appeal held in *Ajinomoto Sweeteners Europe SAS v Asda Stores Ltd* [2010] EWCA Civ 1717; [2010] E.M.L.R. 23 that the single meaning rule did not apply to claims for malicious falsehood. For pleading requirements in malicious falsehood claims see 28.39 below.

**28.22**     **Pleading innuendoes.** In *Baturina v Times Newspapers Ltd* [2010] EWHC 696 (QB); [2010] E.M.L.R. 18 Eady J. declined to strike out re-pleaded innuendo meanings relating to publications in Russia and England. The judge said at [63]:

"The English law relating to liability for an innuendo meaning would be the same irrespective of where publication takes place; that is to say, it is not necessary for a claimant to prove that the defendant knew that the words were capable of bearing such a meaning or foresaw that there were likely to be readers with knowledge of particular facts. The only additional requirement in respect of foreign publication would be that of establishing double actionability."

Section 7. Identification of the Claimant

**Averment of reference to the claimant.** *Add new note 96A after the first*   **28.25**
*sentence of this paragraph.* For an explanation why it is necessary to prove
reference in a libel claim see *Marathon Mutual Ltd v Waters* [2009] EWHC 1931
(QB); [2010] E.M.L.R. 3.

Section 8. Actions for Slander

**Actions for Slander.** *Note 103.* In *Noorani v Calver (No. 2)* [2009] EWHC   **28.26**
561 (QB) Coulson J. accepted at [15]–[17] that an allegation of being an Islamic
terrorist was sufficient to relate to the commission of serious and specific
criminal offences.

Section 9. Damages

**Where damage must be pleaded.** *Note 114.* For guidance on pleading   **28.28**
aggravated damages see *Lait v Evening Standard Ltd* [2010] EWHC 642 (QB),
in which Eady J. struck out an aggravated damages plea which stated a meaning
different from the meaning pleaded in respect of publication of the words
complained of. The judge said at [20]

> "The plea in aggravation of damages should be about the Defendant's conduct, at or
> after the time of publication. It is muddling to rely on a different meaning as aggrava-
> tion in respect of the damage supposedly occasioned by the publication of the words
> themselves."

*Note 117.* However, case management considerations may mean that reliance
upon other articles in support of aggravation of damage may make such a plea
vulnerable to a strike out: *Clarke (t/a Elumina Iberica UK) v Bain* [2008] EWHC
2636 (QB). See also *Baturina v Times Newspapers Ltd* [2010] EWHC 696 (QB);
[2010] E.M.L.R. 18 at [45]–[65].

**Special damage.** *Note 123.* In *Monks v Warwick DC* [2009] EWHC 959 (QB)   **28.29**
Sharp J. addressed the claimant's claim for damages for "general loss of custom
and business" in the context of a (successful) application to strike out the whole
claim. The judge said at [28]–[30] that where a claimant who is a sole director
of a company which is not a party to the action claims for that company's loss
of profit, the loss would not be recoverable by the claimant except to the extent
that he could identify an indirect loss to himself.

**Exemplary damages.** *Note 138. Mosley v News Group Newspapers Ltd*   **28.33**
[2008] EWHC 1777 (QB) is now also reported at [2008] E.M.L.R. 20.

SECTION 12. MALICIOUS FALSEHOOD

**28.39**    **Generally.** In *Marathon Mutual Ltd v Waters* [2009] EWHC 1931 (QB); [2010] E.M.L.R. 3 the court held that the law requires that there is some reference, direct or indirect, in the words complained of to the claimant though it is not necessary to go further and establish identification of the claimant in the minds of publishees.

*The second sentence of this paragraph and note 151 should be deleted and replaced with the following.* The Court of Appeal held in *Ajinomoto Sweeteners Europe SAS v Asda Stores Ltd* [2010] EWCA Civ 1717; [2010] E.M.L.R. 23 that the single meaning rule did not apply to claims for malicious falsehood. Accordingly, there would be no need for a court to determine a single meaning (as Jacob J. did with some reluctance in *Vodafone Group Plc v Orange Personal Communications Services Ltd* [1997] E.M.L.R. 84 when invited by consent to find a single meaning of words sued on in a malicious falsehood claim). A claimant will need to plead (1) the possible reasonable meanings of the publication said to mislead a substantial number of people and (2) that such statements were false and maliciously made: see [14], [33]–[34].

For a case decided before *Ajinomoto Sweeteners* where criticism was made of the natural and ordinary meanings pleaded see *Quinton v Peirce* [2009] EWHC 912 (QB) at [21]–[26].

SECTION 13. MISUSE OF PRIVATE INFORMATION

**28.40**    **Generally.** *Notes 158 and 160. Murray v Big Pictures (UK) Ltd* is now also reported at [2009] Ch 481.

*Notes 168 and 170. Mosley v News Group Newspapers Ltd* [2008] EWHC 1777 (QB) is now also reported at [2008] E.M.L.R. 20.

SECTION 14. AMENDMENT OF PARTICULARS OF CLAIM

**28.42**    **Permission necessary.** *Note 174.* In *Hughes v Risbridger* [2009] EWHC 3244 (QB) Eady J. refused an amendment to the Particulars of Claim which he described at [23] as "too vague to justify . . . at this late stage."

SECTION 16. APPLICATION FOR FURTHER INFORMATION

**28.44**    *Note 189.* See *Dee v Telegraph Media Group Ltd* [2009] EWHC 2546 (QB), where Eady J. ordered the claimant to answer two requests for further information and said at [17]:

"I see no reason why the Claimant should not offer further clarification on these matters. It has not been suggested that he is unable to do so. It is important to place as many cards as possible on the table at this stage. There is nothing to be gained from arguments about whether a request for further information is the right mechanism to adopt. I shall simply direct that the questions are to be answered constructively, rather than merely by way of non-admission, so that the Defendant can know the full extent of the real dispute."

CHAPTER 29

# DEFENCE

SECTION 2. PLEA OF JUSTIFICATION

**29.5** **When to plead this defence.** *Note 20. Adelson v Associated Newspapers Ltd* [2008] EWHC 278 (QB) is now also reported at [2009] E.M.L.R. 10.

**29.7** **Justifying the words in their natural and ordinary meaning.** *Add to the end of note 32 before "Meanwhile":* For examples of recent Australian courts addressing *Polly Peck* and also whether parts of truth and contextual truth defences should be struck out see *West Australian Newspapers Ltd v Elliott* [2008] WASCA 172; *Con Ange v Fairfax Media Publications Pty Ltd* [2010] NSWSC 645 and *Wookey v Quigley* [2009] WASC 284.

*Note 39. Curistan v Times Newspapers Ltd* is now also reported at [2009] Q.B. 231.

**29.10** **Pleading particulars of justification.** For a useful summary of the principles see *Radu v Houston* [2009] EWHC 398 (QB) where Eady J. said:

"9. [Counsel for the Claimant] points to a number of elementary principles which need to be complied with in a plea of justification, not for reasons simply of formality or discipline, but rather because of the need for fairness and transparency.

10. First, it is necessary to set out the facts relied upon clearly and succinctly, although not the evidence by which they are to be proved.

11. Secondly, one should only plead justification if one has reasonable evidence to support the defence or reasonable grounds for supposing that sufficient evidence will be available at trial: *McDonald's Corporation v Steel* [1995] EMLR 527, 535.

12. Thirdly, where dishonesty is pleaded, it is necessary to give particulars of the dishonest state(s) of mind alleged.

13. Fourthly, if a defendant seeks to justify 'grounds to suspect' (sometimes referred to as a *Chase* level two meaning: *Chase v News Group Newspapers Ltd* [2002] EWCA Civ 1772), he must comply with the disciplines identified in *Musa King v Telegraph Corporation* [2004] EMLR 23—not least by (i) identifying the conduct of the particular claimant said to have founded the suspicion, and (ii) not seeking to shift the burden of proof on to the claimant (for fuller discussion see *Gatley on Libel and Slander*, 11th edn, at paras 11.6 and 29.10).

14. Fifthly, it is not permitted to introduce reams of newspaper articles (whether on liability or damages) to show that third parties have made defamatory allegations about the claimant in the past: see *Associated Newspapers Ltd v Dingle* [1964] AC 371.

15. Sixthly, there is nothing in Lord Woolf's general observations in *McPhilemy v Times Newspapers Ltd* [1999] 3 All ER 775 that should be taken to sanction any relaxation of the basic rule that a claimant is entitled to know the case he has to meet; nor would it justify postponing that entitlement to the later stage of proceedings when witness statements are exchanged. For a few years after *McPhilemy* was reported, people from time to time argued that it provided a warrant for keeping their case up their sleeves until exchange. That was long ago, however, recognised to be a mis-understanding. Inevitably, if a new case is revealed when statements are served, the Claimant will have to look into it and respond in a further round of evidence. This is certainly not in accordance with the overriding objective."

*Note 51.* In *Taranissi v BBC* [2008] EWHC 2486 (QB) Eady J. said at [15], in the context of an application for disclosure, "The claimant is entitled to know the charges he has to meet, which should be spelt out with something approximating to the clarity of an indictment."

*Note 54.* In *Radu v Houston* [2009] EWHC 398 (QB) Eady J. dismissed the suggestion by Counsel for the Defendant that the defence of justification was merely "over particularised". The Judge said "Where I would disagree with him is in his assessment that it was merely 'over-particularised'. There is an obvious difference between excessive particulars and material which is simply confusing and irrelevant."

*Note 57.* *Curistan v Times Newspapers Ltd* is now also reported at [2009] Q.B. 231.

*Add new paragraph.* **Similar fact evidence and justification.** Where a defen-　　**29.10A** dant is pleading to a general sting (see para.29.7 above) then he must plead in the defence of justification all the matters upon which he relies. However, where he is seeking to justify a specific sting with reference to matters not directly in issue but by way of similar fact evidence it is not a requirement to plead the evidence relied upon. The general rule is that evidence should not be pleaded. However it would be wise to notify the claimant of the matters upon which there is an intention to rely by way of similar fact evidence.

In *Desmond v Bower* [2008] EWHC 2952 (QB) the defendant sought to defend the specific defamatory sting by pleading matters relating to other incidents than the one referred to in the words complained of. The claimant successfully applied to strike out those particulars of justification on the basis that they did not support the specific sting. Eady J. left open the question whether evidence of those incidents could come back into the case at trial as similar fact evidence under the principles outlined by the House of Lords in *O'Brien v Chief Constable of South*

*Wales Police* [2005] UKHL 26; [2005] 2 A.C. 534. In the course of his judgment the judge said "One does not introduce into the pleading evidence which is intended to support and make out [the] pleaded facts. That is not the purpose of a pleading" and added that a decision could not be made whether or not the material was probative and admissible until the witness statements were served.

Later, the defendant applied for permission to serve a witness summons in respect of one other incident. Eady J. refused permission. That decision was subsequently appealed. See [2009] EWCA Civ 667; [2010] E.M.L.R. 5.

SECTION 3. PLEA OF FAIR COMMENT

**29.12** **Defence must be specially pleaded.** The Court of Appeal in *British Chiropractic Association v Singh* [2010] EWCA Civ 350; [2011] E.M.L.R. 1 said at [36] that the defence should be re-named "honest opinion" because it "better reflects the realities."

*Note 63.* In *British Chiropractic Association v Singh*, above, without making reference to *Associated Newspapers v Burstein* (where a differently constituted Court of Appeal had held that the court must find the single meaning of the words before considering whether the words complained of were fact or comment) the Court of Appeal said at [32]:

"It may be said that the agreed pair of questions which the judge was asked to answer... was based on a premise, inherent in our libel law, that a comment is as capable as an assertion of fact of being defamatory, and that what differ are the available defences; so that the first question has to be whether the words are defamatory even if they amount to no more than comment. This case suggests that this may not always be the best approach, because the answer to the first question may stifle the answer to the second."

A defendant is bound by the requirements of CPR Part 53 PD 2.6(1) and (2) to set out the defamatory meaning he seeks to defend as fair comment on a matter of public interest and to give particulars. It will then be a matter for the court to decide the order to determine the question of the natural and ordinary meaning of the words and whether or not they are fact or comment upon an application by a party.

SECTION 4. PLEA OF PRIVILEGE

**29.20** **Pleading *Reynolds* qualified privilege.** *Note 82. Seaga v Harper* is now also reported at [2009] 1 A.C. 1

*Add at the end of the first sentence:* "and continued to be published" *after* "such that it was in the public interest for it to be published".

*Note 86.* In *Flood v Times Newspapers Ltd* ([2010] EWCA Civ 804; [2010] E.M.L.R. 26, the Master of the Rolls at [59] accepted the submission that whilst the subject-matter of the article, alleged police corruption, was a matter of public interest, it did not follow that there was a public interest in publishing details of the allegations against the claimant, at least not without having taken reasonable care to verify their truth. See also [105]–[106] per Moore-Bick L.J. and [115] per Moses L.J.

*Note 91.* It will not be responsible journalism to leave an article online without some qualification once further information has come to light which qualifies or undermines it: see *Flood v Times Newspapers Ltd* [2009] EWHC 2375 (QB); [2010] E.M.L.R. 8, upheld in that respect on appeal: [2010] EWCA Civ 804; [2010] E.M.L.R. 26. The defendant sought to argue that once the result of an official investigation into the allegations was known, it made reasonable proposals to the claimant for alterations to the internet article which were rejected, and reasonably assumed that the claimant would not require any change unless he said otherwise. However, Lord Neuberger MR rejected that submission, stating at [81] that

" . . . the fact that the claimant's refusal [to agree a form of follow-up publication] is unreasonable will, save perhaps in the most unusual circumstances, not be enough to justify the defendant doing nothing if responsible journalism would require him to retract or modify a website publication if further relevant information comes to light. The essential point is that it is for a defendant to decide on the appropriate course to take."

*Note 93. Bray v Deutsche Bank AG* is now also reported at [2009] E.M.L.R. 12.


SECTION 6. MITIGATION OF DAMAGES


**Mitigation of damages.** *Note 112. Warren v Random House Group Ltd* [2008]   **29.26** EWCA Civ 834 is now also reported at [2009] Q.B. 600.

CHAPTER 30

# REPLY AND DEFENCE TO COUNTERCLAIM

SECTION 3. PLEADING AN AFFIRMATIVE CASE IN REPLY GENERALLY

**30.3**    **Pleading an affirmative case.** *After* "defence of justification or fair comment" *add*: Equally, where a defendant is a public authority and pleads that the publication was privileged, the claimant should, if art.8 is engaged, respond to that plea by taking issue with whether or not the publication was necessary and proportionate.

*After* "proportionate" *add new note 6A*. See *Clift v Slough BC* [2009] EWHC 1550 (QB); [2010] E.M.L.R. 4 at [49]–[76] per Tugendhat J. Judgment is pending from the Court of Appeal. Such a response would not be appropriate where the defendant is not a public authority: see *Underhill v Corser* [2009] EWHC 3058 at [13].

SECTION 4. MALICE

**30.5**    **Malice.** *Note 13.* This statement of the law was endorsed by Eady J. in *Hughes v Risbridger* [2009] EWHC 3244 at [14]. See also *Monks v Warwick DC* [2009] EWHC 959 (QB) at [23] and [24] and *Bray v Deutsche Bank AG* [2008] EWHC 1263 (QB); [2009] E.M.L.R. 12 at [35]–[36].

*Note 15.* See also *Bray v Deutsche Bank AG*, above, at [42]–[43].

*Note 19.* See also *Monks v Warwick DC* [2009] EWHC 959 (QB) at [23] and [24] and *Bray v Deutsche Bank AG*, above, at [16].

CHAPTER 31

## APOLOGY, OFFER OF AMENDS AND COMPROMISE

SECTION 1. APOLOGY

**Apology: mitigation and defence.** The publication of an apology may, in **31.1** certain circumstances, sustain an argument that the commencement or continuation of defamation proceedings is an abuse of process [new note 4A].

*New note 4A*: In *Hays Plc v Hartley* [2010] EWHC 1068 (QB), Tugendhat J. ruled that for the claimant company to pursue its claim for libel after the publication of a statement publicly retracting the allegations complained of—a public statement in terms which had been agreed between the claimant and the originators of the allegations complained of in settlement of Employment Tribunal proceedings between them—was an abuse of process. Following the publication of the statement, Tugendhat J. held at [60], "there is simply nothing of value that [the action] can achieve for the claimant". See further para.32.44 below.

**Nature of an apology.** *Note 5. Adelson v Associated Newspapers Ltd* [2008] **31.2** EWHC 278 (QB) is now also reported at [2009] E.M.L.R. 10.

**Publicising the apology.** *Add new note 13A*. In *Winslet v Associated News-* **31.3** *papers Ltd* [2009] EWHC 2735 (QB); [2010] E.M.L.R. 11 it may be noted that part of Eady J.'s reasoning (at [23]) in deciding to permit the claimant to make a unilateral statement in open court was that, in the absence of agreed wording for an apology, the defendant had chosen to put its own "spin" on the settlement by publishing its apology in a rather dismissive way. In such circumstances, there was no reason why the claimant should not also be allowed to publicise her understanding of the settlement, provided she did so in a fair and proportionate way.

SECTION 2. SETTLEMENT

**Subject-matter of settlement.** *Note 24*. In *Adelson v Associated Newspapers* **31.7** *Ltd* [2008] EWHC 278 (QB); [2009] E.M.L.R. 10 the court held (at [93]) that the part of the defendant's open offer to settle the claim that related to costs, and which envisaged that the costs of the litigation would "be decided by the judge according to ordinary principles", was too uncertain to be capable of binding acceptance by the claimant. See also *McLaughlin v Newall* [2009] EWHC 1925 (QB), where the judge observed obiter that a defamation settlement which left the wording of a proposed apology open was at grave risk of being found unenforceable.

**31.8**    **Methods of settlement.** *Add the following text after the first sentence.* Where a claimant wishes to accept an offer made by the defendant in correspondence to resolve the proceedings between them, he should do so promptly, or run the risk that the offer will be construed by the court as having expired [new note 28A].

*Note 28.* There is now a 7th edition (2010) of Foskett, *The Law and Practice of Compromise.*

*New note 28A. Wakefield (t/a Wills Probate and Trusts of Weybridge) v Ford* [2009] EWHC 122 (QB), Eady J.

**31.10**    **Statements in court.** *Note 39.* In *Winslet v Associated Newspapers Ltd* [2009] EWHC 2735 (QB); [2010] E.M.L.R. 11 the court allowed the claimant's application to read a unilateral statement in open court, the application having been made after the claimant had accepted the defendant's unqualified offer of amends. Eady J. rejected the defendant's arguments that, following acceptance of the offer of amends, the claimant was entitled only to the remedies provided for by ss.2–4, Defamation Act 1996, which did not contemplate the making of a statement in open court by the claimant, and that in applying to read the statement the claimant was "continuing" defamation proceedings in contravention of s.3(2) of the Act. The court held that the wording of CPR 53 PD, para.6.1 was very broad and was intended to provide for the possibility of a statement in open court following any form of settlement in defamation proceedings. Further, to apply to make a unilateral statement in open court was not to "continue" defamation proceedings, but to bring them to an end. S.3(2) of the Act did not therefore prevent an application to make or the making of a unilateral statement by a claimant who had accepted an offer of amends.

*Note 48.* However, the court will not give permission for a bilateral statement in open court to be read if, before the statement is read, it is reliably informed that the defendant is proposing to join in the making of a statement which it believes to be false: *Adelson v Associated Newspapers Ltd* [2008] EWHC 278 (QB); [2009] E.M.L.R. 10 at [70].

**31.14**    **Authority to settle.** *Note 66.* See the amendment to fn.28 above.

SECTION 3. PART 36 OFFERS

**31.16**    **General.** *Add new note 72A at the end of the second sentence in the paragraph.* Part 36 is a self-contained code prescribing the manner in which an offer may be made and the consequences flowing from accepting or failing to accept it. Although basic concepts of offer and acceptance clearly underpin Pt 36, Pt 36 is not to be understood as incorporating all the rules governing the formation of contracts. Certainty is to be commended in a procedural code which has to be understood by ordinary citizens, and it was with that in mind that Part 36 had been drafted. Pt 36 was to be read and understood according to its own terms without importing other rules derived from the general law, save where that was clearly intended: *Gibbon v Manchester City Council* [2010] EWCA Civ 726; [2010] 1 W.L.R. 2081.

**Acceptance of offer.** *Add new note 84A after the sentence* "In other instances **31.19** the court will make an order as to costs unless liability for costs is agreed".

In the absence of any express provision in Pt 36 (such as is contained in CPR r.36.14(3)) there is no presumption that the court would order a late accepting party to pay the other side's costs on an indemnity basis. The usual basis will be the standard basis, unless, for example, a party's conduct is in issue, in which case the position will be governed by the general provisions of CPR r.44.3: *Fitzpatrick Contractors Ltd v Tyco Fire and Integrated Solutions (UK) Ltd* [2009] EWHC 274 (TCC).

*Note 85.* For the latest instalment in this long-running saga, see *Pell v Express Newspapers* [2009] EWHC 118 (QB), per Sir Charles Gray.

**Statement in Open Court.** *Note 89.* Although the case was not concerned **31.23** with a Pt 36 offer (but with the claimant's asserted right to read a unilateral statement in open court following her acceptance of the defendant's offer of amends), see *Winslet v Associated Newspapers Ltd* [2009] EWHC 2735 (QB); [2010] E.M.L.R. 11 (as summarised in para.31.10 above) in relation to CPR 53 PD, para.6.1 in general.

**Verdict or judgment and costs.** *Note 97.* But now see *Gibbon v Manchester* **31.25** *City Council* [2010] EWCA Civ 726; [2010] 1 W.L.R. 2081 in which the Court of Appeal criticised and placed some important qualifications upon its earlier decision in *Carver v BAA Plc* [2008] EWCA Civ 412; [2009] 1 W.L.R. 113. See, for instance, the remarks of Carnwath L.J. at [51]:

" . . . the judgment in *Carver* should not be interpreted as opening the way to a wide ranging investigation of emotional and other factors in every case, even where the financial advantage is significant. I agree with Moore-Bick L.J. that in most cases success in financial terms will be the governing consideration".

**Non-disclosure of offer or payment.** *Note 102.* In this regard, see the order **31.27** that was made by Tugendhat J. in *Adelson v Associated Newspapers Ltd* [2008] EWHC 278 (QB); [2009] E.M.L.R. 10, as recorded at [1] in his judgment, in order to prevent information concerning the defendant's Pt 36 offer coming to the attention of the trial judge.

*Note 106.* For an account of the consequences that may result for a defendant from the making of an open offer of settlement, see generally *Adelson v Associated Newspapers Ltd* [2008] EWHC 278 (QB); [2009] E.M.L.R. 10.

SECTION 4. OFFER OF AMENDS

**31.29**    **The offer.** *Add at end of paragraph*: Nor will a purported offer of amends be treated as an offer falling within the Act if it is accompanied by a reservation to the effect that the offeror does not admit that the words complained of refer to the aggrieved party [new note 115A].

*Add the following text after reference to note 113*: A defendant may make an offer of amends in respect of part of a publication [new note 113A].

*New note 113A. Warren v Random House Group Ltd* [2007] EWHC 2856 (QB); [2008] 2 W.L.R. 1033, [42] per Gray J.; *Club La Costa (UK) Plc v Gebhard* [2008] EWHC 2552 (QB); *The Times*, December 10, 2008, at [16].

*New note 115A: Club La Costa (UK) Plc v Gebhard* [2008] EWHC 2552 (QB).

**31.30**    **Acceptance and non-acceptance.** *Note 117. Tesco Stores Ltd v Guardian News & Media Ltd*, July 29, 2008, is now also reported at [2009] E.M.L.R. 5.

**31.31**    **Consequences of acceptance.** The party accepting the offer may, if needs be, apply to read a unilateral statement in open court [new note 127A].

*Note 123. Warren v Random House Group Ltd* [2008] EWCA Civ 834 is now also reported at [2009] Q.B. 600.

The party accepting an offer of amends does not "continue defamation proceedings" within the meaning of s.3(2) of the Act by applying to make a unilateral statement in open court: *Winslet v Associated Newspapers Ltd* [2009] EWHC 2735 (QB); [2010] E.M.L.R. 11.

*New note 127A.* CPR PD 53, para.6.1, as interpreted in *Winslet v Associated Newspapers Ltd*, above.

**31.33**    **Compensation: general.** *Note 137.* However, it appears that it would be impermissible for a claimant first to accept an offer of amends and then to contend, in support of his claim for compensation, that the words complained of had been published dishonestly: *Bowman v MGN Ltd* [2010] EWHC 895 (QB), at [19].

**31.35**    **Discount on compensation for offer of amends.** *Add new note 144A at end of penultimate paragraph.* In *Bowman v MGN Ltd* [2010] EWHC 895 (QB), Eady J. applied a discount of 50 per cent to a starting figure of £8,500 in respect of a libel adjudged to be "at the less serious end of the scale" (at [14]) "because of the early apology, the willingness to remove the offending words immediately and the very prompt reliance on the offer of amends regime" (see [20]), leaving the claimant with compensation of £4,250.

**31.39**    **Rejection of offer of amends.** *Note 155.* See the amendments to notes 117 and 123 above.

*Note 159.* In *Club La Costa (UK) Plc v Gebhard* [2008] EWHC 2552 (QB), Tugendhat J. observed at [28] that the defendants had "rightly" acknowledged that a denial or non-admission that the statement complained of referred to the claimant was "any other defence" within the meaning of s.4(4) and so could not be relied upon if the defendants chose to rely on an offer of amends as a defence.

CHAPTER 32

## PRE-TRIAL APPLICATIONS

SECTION 2. RULINGS ON MEANING

**32.2**   **Rulings on meaning: CPR PD 53, paragraph 4(1).** *After the phrase* "whether they are capable of being defamatory of the claim", *add a new note 2A.*

For some recent examples of successful applications by defendants for rulings that the words complained of were not capable of being defamatory of the claimant, see *Tiscali UK Ltd v British Telecommunications Plc* [2008] EWHC 3129 (QB); *Freeguard v Martlet Homes Ltd* [2008] EWCA Civ 1577; *The Times*, January 15, 2009; *Ecclestone v Telegraph Media Group Ltd* [2009] EWHC 2779 (QB); and *Thornton v Telegraph Media Group Ltd* [2010] EWHC 1414 (QB); [2010] E.M.L.R. 25. Conversely, for some recent examples of applications advanced on this basis which failed, see *Johnson v MGN Ltd* [2009] EWHC 1481 (QB); *Lait v Evening Standard Ltd* [2010] EWHC 642 (QB); *Baturina v Times Newspapers Ltd* [2010] EWHC 696 (QB); [2010] E.M.L.R. 18; *Miller v Associated Newspapers Ltd* [2010] EWHC 700 (QB); and *Dee v Telegraph Media Group Ltd* [2010] EWHC 924 (QB); [2010] E.M.L.R. 20.

**32.4**   **Conceptual problems.** *Note 8.* For further consideration of the "single meaning" rule, see *Ajinomoto Sweeteners Europe SAS v Asda Stores Ltd* [2010] EWCA Civ 609; [2010] E.M.L.R. 23 in which the Court of Appeal decided that the rule had no role to play in the tort of malicious falsehood.

**32.5**   **Principles to be applied.** *Delete the word* "Finally" *from the last sentence of the paragraph and add the following sentence.* Applications for rulings on meaning may have implications under art.10 of the European Convention on Human Rights [new note 19A]. Finally, so far as meaning is concerned, for words to be defamatory, the allegation they comprise must cross a threshold of seriousness, so as to exclude trivial claims [new note 19B]. As regards the issue of reference, where a defendant applies to strike out a defamation claim on the ground that the words complained of are not capable of referring to the claimant, the governing principles are the same as those to be applied where the issue is whether the words complained of are capable of bearing a defamatory meaning [new note 19C].

*The last sentence of note 9 should read as follows*: It is wrong to suppose that questions of meaning are more suited to a jury where the words complained of represent "demotic literature and popular culture": "In every case, meaning is a matter for the jury unless a judge concludes . . . that the words complained of could not be defamatory" (*Jeynes v News Magazines Ltd* [2008] EWCA Civ 130 at [20]).

*Note 9.* In *John v Guardian News & Media Ltd* [2008] EWHC 3066 (QB) Tugendhat J. stated at [16] that he did not read Sedley L.J.'s observations in *Berezovsky v Forbes* [2001] EWCA Civ 1251; [2001] E.M.L.R. 45 at [16]—to the effect that a judicial ruling on meaning should be an exercise in generosity rather than parsimony—as saying that a judge may more safely err on one side than on the other:

"If a judge does err in holding words to be incapable of bearing a meaning pleaded by a claimant, then he deprives the claimant of his right to vindicate his reputation before a court. If the judge errs in holding words to be capable of a meaning pleaded by a claimant, then the defendant is wrongly burdened with defending libel proceedings. This can be a very onerous burden and one which interferes with the right of freedom of expression".

*Note 18.* See also the account of the principles given by Sir Anthony Clarke M.R. in *Jeynes v News Magazines Ltd* [2008] EWCA Civ 130, at [14].

*Note 19.* In *Dee v Telegraph Media Group Ltd* [2010] EWHC 924 (QB); [2010] E.M.L.R. 20 Sharp J. held, applying *Charleston v News Group Newspapers Ltd* [1995] 2 A.C. 65, that for the purpose of determining meaning, when a single article was under consideration, the ordinary reasonable reader was to be taken to have read the whole article before reaching a conclusion on meaning, even though many readers would not in fact have read the whole article. This was so whether the article appeared on one page of a publication or was spread over several pages. Furthermore, where more than one article was under consideration, the key issue was whether the relevant articles were sufficiently closely connected as to be regarded as a single publication. If this was so, it did not matter that in reality many readers would have read only one of the relevant articles. As regards what might represent "context" when one is considering internet publications, see *Islam Expo Ltd v Spectator (1828) Ltd* [2010] EWHC 2011 (QB).

*New note 19A*: In *John v Guardian News & Media Ltd* [2008] EWHC 3066 (QB) Tugendhat J. observed at [17] that the principle derived from Strasbourg authorities to the effect that an adverse finding for expressing honest value judgements was very likely to involve a violation of art.10 of the Convention "must also apply to rulings on meaning":

" . . . the Strasbourg cases show that a claimant can make an action more difficult to defend by characterising an impugned statement as fact rather than as a value judgment.

A claimant can also do that by attributing to an impugned statement a meaning that is on any view high. There is a real risk of a violation of art.10 if a claimant strains to attribute to words complained of a high factual meaning, which cannot be defended as true, and at the same time claims aggravated damages on the footing that the defendant knew the words to be false in that meaning".

For other recent observations on the relationship between art.10 and issues of meaning, see *Ecclestone v Telegraph Media Group Ltd* [2009] EWHC 2779 (QB) at [10]; *Dee v Telegraph Media Group Ltd* [2010] EWHC 924 (QB); [2010] E.M.L.R. 20 at [29] and *Thornton v Telegraph Media Group Ltd* [2010] EWHC 1414 (QB); [2010] E.M.L.R. 25 at [60]–[62] and [93]–[94].

*New note 19B. Ecclestone v Telegraph Media Group Ltd* [2009] EWHC 2779 (QB); *Thornton v Telegraph Media Group Ltd* [2010] EWHC 1414 (QB); [2010] E.M.L.R. 25 at [50]–[95].

*New note 19C. Islam Expo Ltd v Spectator (1828) Ltd* [2010] EWHC 2011 (QB), at [6].

**32.8**      **Meaning and the repetition rule.** *Notes 36 and 37. Curistan v Times Newspapers Ltd* [2008] EWCA Civ 432 is now also reported at [2009] Q.B. 231.

**32.9**      **Meaning and preliminary issue.** *Note 37*: For recent examples of this jurisdiction being exercised, see *Bond v BBC* [2009] EWHC 539 (QB); *British Chiropractic Association v Singh* [2009] EWHC 1101 (QB) in which Eady J.'s ruling on meaning was found by the Court of Appeal to have been in error: [2010] EWCA Civ 350; [2011] E.M.L.R. 1; and *Horlick v Associated Newspapers Ltd* [2010] EWHC 1544 (QB). In *Horlick v Associated Newspapers Ltd*, having identified the "well settled" principles to be applied when a judge is invited to determine meaning in a defamation case, Eady J. observed at [10] that "[i]t would seem to follow that a judge should be wary of allowing his impression of a newspaper article to be coloured by the detailed submissions of counsel". See also *Bond v BBC*, unreported, February 5, 2009, in which Eady J. considered a contested, and ultimately successful, application that the court should rule on meaning as a preliminary issue.

If the presumption of jury trial in defamation proceedings is reversed (as was contemplated in cll.14 and 15 of the Defamation Bill [HL] 2010–2011), it is quite conceivable that interim judicial rulings on meaning where meaning is in dispute and on issues of fact or opinion (as to which see further below)—given the narrowing of the issues between the parties (with consequent savings in costs) such rulings are apt to produce—will become a standard feature of defamation litigation.

For an example of this jurisdiction being exercised in the tort of malicious falsehood, see *Ajinomoto Sweeteners Europe SAS v Asda Stores Ltd* [2010] EWCA Civ 609; [2010] E.M.L.R. 23.

*Add to note 38 after the phrase* "So far it always has been for a judge". (with the sole exception of *Marks & Spencer Plc v Granada TV*, unreported, February 23, 1998, in which a jury determined the meaning as a preliminary issue, as to which, see further para.32.50 below)

*Add new paragraph.* **Preliminary issue: fact or opinion.** The court also has **32.9A** the power to determine as a preliminary issue whether the words complained of are allegations of fact or opinion [note 39A] and, if opinion, whether or not, for the purposes of the defence of honest opinion [note 39B], they relate to matters of public interest [note 39C]. Where there are applications before the court both for a ruling on meaning and for a ruling on whether the words at issue represent allegations of fact or opinion, it would seem that the court ought to determine the issue of meaning first [note 39D].

*New note 39A.* See e.g. *British Chiropractic Association v Singh* [2010] EWCA Civ 350; [2011] E.M.L.R. 1, in which the Court of Appeal allowed the defendant's appeal against Eady J.'s decision that the words complained of consisted of allegations of fact and substituted its own view that the words were expressions of opinion, and *Horlick v Associated Newspapers Ltd* [2010] EWHC 1544 (QB), at [23], where Eady J. ruled in the defendant's favour on this issue.

*New note 39B.* For this change in nomenclature, see *British Chiropractic Association v Singh*, above, at [36].

*New note 39C.* See *Horlick v Associated Newspapers Ltd*, above, at [23]–[25], where Eady J. ruled in the defendant's favour on this issue.

*New note 39D. Burstein v Associated Newspapers Ltd* [2007] EWCA Civ 600; [2007] E.M.L.R. 21, at [7]–[8] per Keene L.J. (with whom Dyson and Waller L.JJ. agreed), relying upon *Lowe v Associated Newspapers Ltd* [2006] EWHC 320 (QB); [2007] Q.B. 580. In *British Chiropractic Association v Singh*, above, however, the Court of Appeal appears to be suggesting that (in certain cases, at any rate) the question of whether the words at issue are fact or opinion should precede any determination of meaning: see e.g. at [16] and [23].

**Jurisdiction.** *Add to note 40 before the final sentence.* More recently, see *John* **32.10** *v Guardian News & Media Ltd* [2008] EWHC 3066 (QB) in which Tugendhat J. ruled that the words complained of, which consisted of a humorous "peek at the diary of Sir Elton John", could not be understood by a reasonable reader to bear the serious defamatory meanings pleaded in the particulars of claim. As regards the first of these two pleaded meanings, which comprised an imputation to the effect that the claimant hosted a charity ball "knowing that once the costs of the Ball have been covered only the small proportion of the money raised which is left over is available for [his charity, the Elton John Aids Foundation] to distribute to good causes", Tugendhat J. observed at [32] that, "[i]f that was the allegation being made, a reasonable reader would expect so serious an allegation to be made without humour, and explicitly, in a part of the newspaper devoted to news".

**Appeals.** Save in exceptional cases it seems unlikely that the Court of Appeal **32.11** would wish to interfere with judges' rulings on meaning as a preliminary issue [new note 49A].

*New note 49A.* As Eady J. put the matter in *Bond v BBC*, unreported, February 5, 2009, at [14]: "It is fair to say that the likelihood of the Court of Appeal interfering with . . . a ruling on natural and ordinary meaning is relatively remote". Nevertheless, this is what happened in *British Chiropractic Association v Singh*, above.

SECTION 3. SUMMARY DISPOSAL AND SUMMARY JUDGMENT

(a) *Summary disposal under the Defamation Act 1996*

**32.13**     **Introduction.** *Note 53. Substitute the following*: See paras 32.28–32.29 below. So far as our researches have been able to establish, only one judgment (*Hughes v Alan Dick & Co Ltd* [2008] EWHC 2695 (QB)) concerning the statutory summary disposal procedure has been handed down since the Main Text was completed in August 2008. This suggests that ss.8–10 of the Defamation Act 1996 may be on the way to becoming a dead letter.

**32.19**     **Reasons why the claim should be tried.** *Note 84.* Now see the account at para.32.44 below and also the observations in para.32.5 above concerning the new requirement for words, if they are to be recognised as defamatory, to cross a threshold of seriousness, so as to exclude trivial claims.

(b) *Summary judgment under CPR Part 24*

**32.29**     **CPR Part 24 and the right to trial by jury.** *Note 119.* See also the President of the Queen's Bench Division in *Khader v Aziz* [2010] EWCA Civ 716; [2011] E.M.L.R. 2 at [23]:

> "It is of course axiomatic that, in defamation proceedings, questions of law are for the judge, but questions of fact for the jury; so that neither the judge nor this court should presume to make decisions dependant on issues of fact which ought properly to be left to the jury. But that does not mean that a claimant can secure a full jury trial simply by asserting that there are issues of fact".

**32.31**     **Subject-matter of applications under Part 24.** *Substitute the following text.* Defendants' applications have been made on the basis that the claimant has no real prospect of proving publication, reference [new note 125A], that the defendant is responsible in law for an alleged republication [new note 125B], and malice, on the ground that the words complained of are incapable of bearing any meaning defamatory of the claimant [new note 125C], and on the footing that the claimant has no real prospect of resisting defences of qualified privilege, fair comment, absolute privilege, justification and under reg.19 of the Electronic Commerce (EC Directive) Regulations 2002 [new note 130A]. There have been a number of claimants' applications for summary judgment, including several in cases where qualified privilege has been pleaded, and more than one in which the claimant contended that a plea of malice advanced in response to a defence of qualified privilege was bound to be upheld at trial [new note 131A]. Other claimants' applications have sought judgment on defences of justification and fair comment, on the defendants' case that the words complained of did not refer to the claimant [new note 133A], and on an argument (which failed) that there was a presumption of substantial internet publication.

*Note 125. Bray v Deutsche Bank AG* [2008] EWHC 1263 (QB) is now also reported at [2009] E.M.L.R. 12. The defendant's application for summary judgment, advanced on the basis that the claimant had no real prospect of establishing his case of publication, was unsuccessful. The defendant later renewed its application for summary judgment on the publication issue. This application also failed: *Bray v Deutsche Bank AG* [2009] EWHC 1356 (QB). See also *Budu v BBC* [2010] EWHC 616 (QB) in which an application for summary judgment advanced on this footing in respect of one of the articles the subject of proceedings succeeded.

*New note 125A.* See e.g. *Budu v BBC*, above, in which the defendant's application for summary judgment in respect of one of the articles complained of also succeeded on the ground that the claimant had no real prospect of establishing his case of reference.

*New note 125B.* See *Baturina v Times Newspapers Ltd* [2010] EWHC 696 (QB); [2010] E.M.L.R. 18 in which Eady J. entered summary judgment for the defendant on some of the republications sued on having concluded that it did not accord with principle, applying *McManus v Beckham* [2002] EWCA Civ 939; [2002] 1 W.L.R. 2982, that the defendant should be held liable in respect of allegations in publications produced by third party publishers which went beyond the allegations made in the articles the defendant had published itself in the *Sunday Times*. In relation to this point, see also *Budu v BBC* [2010] EWHC 616 (QB) in which Sharp J. held at [70] that,

> "for an original publisher to be liable for a republication (sued on as a separate cause of action) or for damage suffered by the repetition of the original publication, the secondary publication must, as a minimum, repeat the whole, or at least part of the sting of the original libel".

Thus, it would seem, for an alleged republication properly to form the subject of defamation proceedings, the republication in question must (a) repeat at least part of the sting of the original libel sued on and (b) not go beyond the sting of that original libel.

*New note 125C.* See e.g. *Baturina v Times Newspapers Ltd*, above, in which the defendant's application for summary judgment on the whole of the claimant's claim, advanced on this basis, failed.

*Note 126.* The defendant's application succeeded in *Bray v Deutsche Bank AG* [2009] EWHC 1356 (QB) (revised plea of malice struck out as having no real prospect of success), in *Khader v Aziz* [2009] EWHC 2027 (QB) (claims in defamation struck out where there was no real prospect of the defence of qualified privilege being defeated by proof of malice; decision upheld by the Court of Appeal: [2010] EWCA Civ 716; [2011] E.M.L.R. 2), and in *Henderson v London Borough of Hackney* [2010] EWHC 1651 (QB) (libel claim struck out where no real prospect of establishing malice to defeat the defence of qualified privilege). By contrast, the defendant's application failed in *Hughes v Risbridger* [2009] EWHC 3244 (QB) (defendant's application for summary judgment, advanced on the basis that a jury would be perverse to conclude that he had acted maliciously in making an allegation of theft against claimant).

*Note 127. W v JH and A CC* [2008] EWHC 399 (QB) is now also reported as *W v H* [2009] E.M.L.R. 11.

*Note 129. Buckley v Dalziel* [2007] EWHC 1025 (QB) is now also reported at [2007] 1 W.L.R. 2933. *Westcott v Westcott* [2008] EWCA Civ 818 is now also reported at [2009] Q.B. 407.

*Note 130.* See also *H v Tomlinson* [2008] EWCA Civ 1258; [2009] E.L.R. 14 (Court of Appeal upholding Mr Recorder Moloney Q.C.'s decision to enter summary judgment on the defamation claim for the defendant on this basis (while setting aside his order permitting the claimant to bring a claim based on the same facts as the defamation proceedings under s.7 of the Human Rights Act 1998)); *Ali v Associated Newspapers Ltd* [2010] EWHC 100 (QB); *Budu v BBC* [2010] EWHC 616 (QB) (at [98]) and *Dee v Telegraph Newspapers Ltd* [2010] EWHC 924 (QB); [2010] E.M.L.R. 20 in which summary judgment was granted to the defendants on the basis that there was no real prospect of their defences of justification failing.

*New note 130A.* Which confers a defence in certain circumstances on "information society service providers" who do nothing more than store information. See *Kaschke v Gray* [2010] EWHC 690 (QB) in which the defendant's application failed. In libel proceedings arising out of the publication of an article on a website blog, Stadlen J. concluded that it would be inappropriate to grant summary judgment to the defendant information society service provider who controlled and operated the website where there was a real prospect that the provider might not establish at trial that he could avail himself of the defence under reg.19 of the 2002 Regulations because his control over the blog arguably went beyond mere storage of information.

*New note 131A.* In both cases, the claimant's application (ultimately) failed. In *Hayter v Fahie* [2008] EWCA Civ 1336 summary judgment had been granted to the claimant on the footing that a jury would be perverse to conclude that the defendant had *not* acted maliciously in publishing the words complained of. The Court of Appeal set aside this order and directed a trial, observing that an issue concerning the defendant's state of mind should not have been determined summarily. The court reached the same conclusion in *Hughes v Alan Dick & Co Ltd* [2008] EWHC 2695 (QB):

> "[counsel], on behalf of the claimant, makes the bold submission that I should be prepared to hold at this stage that not only would there be a plea of malice available to defeat the defence of qualified privilege but that I am in a position, on the evidence disclosed so far, to rule that a plea of malice is bound to succeed and thus defeat qualified privilege. It would be a very unusual set of circumstances where the court could be satisfied, without the matter being tested by witness statements and cross-

examination, that a plea of malice was bound to succeed and this is not, in my judgment, such a case" (per Eady J., at [16]).

*Note 132.* In *Berezovsky v Russian Television and Radio Broadcasting Co* [2009] EWHC 1733 (QB), Eady J., in acceding to the second defendant's application to set aside a judgment which had been entered against him in default of acknowledgment of service pursuant to CPR r.12.3(1), rejected the claimant's argument that the second defendant's defence of justification had no real prospect of success.

*New note 133A. Club La Costa (UK) Plc v Gebhard* [2008] EWHC 2552 (QB); the claimant's application failed. Tugendhat J. held that he was not in a position to determine whether or not the defendant's pleaded case of "no reference" had or did not have a real prospect of success.

**The approach which the court will take.** *Add new note 135A after the second*    **32.32**
*paragraph of text in the extract from Eady J.'s judgment in Bataille v Newland [2002] EWHC 1692 (QB).* That the approach outlined by Eady J. in the first two paragraphs of this extract from *Bataille v Newland* [2002] EWHC 1692 (QB) is the correct approach for the court to take is supported by the decision of the Court of Appeal in *Campbell v Frisbee* [2002] EWCA Civ 1374; [2003] E.M.L.R. 3 at [11] per Lord Phillips M.R. giving the judgment of the court; see also *Bray v Deutsche Bank AG* [2008] EWHC 1263 (QB); [2009] E.M.L.R. 12 at [38]–[39] per Tugendhat J.

However, for the purpose of an application under CPR Part 24 at any rate, the court is not obliged to assume that pleaded facts will be established at trial if what is contended for is inherently improbable: *Fashion Gossip Ltd v Esprit Telecoms UK Ltd* [2000] EWCA Civ 235. See also the obiter remarks of Carnwath L.J. in *Khader v Aziz* [2010] EWCA Civ 716; [2011] E.M.L.R. 2 at [46]–[48]:

"We were asked, by both parties, to assume that it could be proved at trial that these apparently nonsensical words were indeed spoken by Mr Dowd. This was said to be the correct approach to an application for summary judgment under CPR Part 24 . . . Eady J. proceeded on the same basis. For my part, I am unable to see why the court should be so constrained. This was not an application under the 'striking-out' provisions, which direct attention to whether the statement of case itself discloses reasonable grounds for bringing the claim (rule 3.4(2)(a)). The issue under rule 24.2 is simply whether the claimant has a 'real prospect of succeeding on the claim' (rule 24.2(a)(i)). Under that rule there seems to be no reason why the court should be required to assume proof of allegations, merely because they are pleaded".

**Practice and procedure.** *After* "it is the almost invariable practice to combine    **32.33**
an application for summary judgment under Pt 24 with an application to strike out under CPR 3.4(2)", *add new note 140A.* Since this is so, see also the authorities referred to in paras 32.36 and 32.37 in the Main Text, as supplemented below. The court's powers to strike out under CPR r.3.4(2)(a) and to enter summary judgment under CPR r.24.2 are commonly invoked in tandem and exercised interchangeably.

Section 4. Striking Out Pleadings

*Change title of Section 4 to* Section 4. Striking Out Statements of Case

**32.34**       **Striking out pleadings: CPR, r.3.4(2).** *Change title of paragraph to* **Striking out statements of case: CPR, r.3.4(2).**

*Note 145.* With regard to the common practice of combining an application for summary judgment under Pt 24 with an application to strike out under CPR 3.4(2), see also paras 32.32–32.33 in the Main Text as supplemented above.

**32.36**       **Applications by claimant.** *Add after* "A plea of qualified privilege will not be struck out where it is arguable that the sender and recipient of the allegedly defamatory communication had corresponding interests in its contents": A plea of qualified privilege will however be struck out where, for example, the defendant had no obligation to put the relevant defamatory allegations into the public domain and a wide publication was plainly not fairly warranted by the occasion [new note 168A].

*Add after* "the application failed, because the judge found that there was no such presumption, and that it was for the claimant to prove publication". An application to strike out a defence of compromise succeeded because the agreement relied upon contained conditions precedent to a concluded, binding settlement with which the defendant had not complied. As such the defendant had no real prospect of establishing that the claimants were contractually debarred from pursuing their libel action against him [new note 174A].

*Note 161.* For a recent example of the court striking out the whole of a plea of justification, having found that it was defective in a number of discrete ways, see *Radu v Houston* [2009] EWHC 398 (QB).

*Note 164.* See *JWH Group Pty Ltd v Buckeridge (No.3)* [2009] WASC 271 (Le Miere J.) for a recent example of the Supreme Court of Western Australia exercising the power to strike out certain meanings advanced by the defendant as part of a plea of justification.

*Note 168A. Joseph v Spiller* [2009] EWHC 1152 (QB). (The defendant in *Joseph v Spiller* sought and obtained permission to appeal against the striking out of his defence of fair comment and of justification (in part) (as to which see [2009] EWCA Civ 1075; [2010] E.M.L.R. 7), but did not appeal against the decision to strike out his defence of qualified privilege.) See also the authorities referred to in the footnotes to para.32.31 in the Main Text (as supplemented above), which concern claimants' application for summary judgment where qualified privilege has been pleaded. As indicated in paras 32.33 and 32.34 in the Main Text, the court's powers to strike out under CPR r.3.4(2)(a) and to enter summary judgment under CPR r.24.2 are commonly invoked in tandem and exercised interchangeably.

*Note 173.* In *Joseph v Spiller* [2009] EWCA Civ 1075; [2010] E.M.L.R. 7 the Court of Appeal upheld, on different grounds, the decision of Eady J. ([2009] EWHC 1152 (QB)) to strike out the defence of fair comment. The ground relied upon by the Court of Appeal was that the relevant comment was not capable of being fair since it was not based on facts alleged or referred to in the words complained of which were truly stated. (On February 2, 2010 the Supreme Court of the United Kingdom gave the defendant permission to appeal against this decision. The appeal was heard in late July 2010. Judgment was reserved.) See also *Thornton v Telegraph Media Group Ltd* [2009] EWHC 2863 (QB) in which Sir Charles Gray struck out the defence of fair comment on similar grounds (no real prospect of defence of fair comment succeeding because book review complained of materially misstated a fact upon which the comment being defended was based). (Subsequently in the *Thornton* case, Tugendhat J. entered summary judgment for the defendant on the whole of the claimant's claim for libel on the ground that the words complained of were not capable of being defamatory of the claimant: [2010] EWHC 1414 (QB); [2010] E.M.L.R. 25.)

*New note 174A.* *McLaughlin v Newall* [2009] EWHC 1925 (QB).

*Note 180.* (*Buckley v Dalziel* [2007] EWHC 1025 (QB) is now also reported at [2007] 1 W.L.R. 2933. *Westcott v Westcott* [2008] EWCA Civ 818 is now also reported at [2009] Q.B. 407.) *Karim v Newsquest Media Group Ltd*, unreported, October 27, 2009 (Eady J.) (website article summarising a hearing in the Solicitors Disciplinary Tribunal absolutely privileged under s.14, Defamation Act 1996, as being a fair, accurate and contemporaneous report of legal proceedings).

**Applications by defendant.** *Delete the phrase* "or where the claimant's **32.37** special damage claim is unsound in law" *(and contents of note 182) and substitute.* or where the defendant cannot be regarded as a publisher at common law [new note 182].

*Add at end of paragraph*: If some specific aspect of the particulars of claim or reply fails to disclose a reasonably viable case, a pleaded claim for aggravated or special damages [new note 186A] or a plea of malice in answer to a defence of qualified privilege [new note 186B] for example, the defendant may of course apply to strike out that specific part of the claimant's pleaded case alone.

*New note 182.* See *Metropolitan International Schools Ltd v Designtechnica Corp* [2009] EWHC 1765 (QB); [2009] E.M.L.R. 27 (a decision setting aside an order of the Master permitting the claimant to serve libel proceedings out of the jurisdiction on Google Inc, the operator of Google's search engines, chiefly because Google Inc could not be regarded as a publisher at common law of allegedly defamatory material appearing on an internet search return).

*New note 186A.* CPR r.3.4(1). In relation to pleas of aggravated damages, see e.g. *Collins Stewart Ltd v Financial Times Ltd* [2005] EWHC 262 (QB); [2006] E.M.L.R. 5; *Adelson v Associated Newspapers Ltd* [2007] EWHC 997 (QB), at [89]–[98] (application for permission to amend plea of aggravated damages dismissed principally on proportionality grounds, but in this section of his judgment Tugendhat J. considered the proposed amendments as a matter of substance); *Clarke (t/a Elumina Iberica UK) v Bain* [2008] EWHC 2636 (QB), at [35]–[68] (particulars relied upon in aggravation of damages struck out on various grounds); *Lait v Evening Standard Ltd* [2010] EWHC 642 (QB), at [17]–[30] (particulars in aggravation of damages struck out as being reliant upon defamatory meanings different from the meaning attributed to words complained of). As regards pleas of special damages, see e.g. *Collins Stewart Ltd v Financial Times Ltd* [2004] EWHC 2337 (QB); [2005] E.M.L.R. 5 at [24] (application to strike out part of a special damage plea based on the loss of value in shares of one claimant—the parent company of the other claimant—succeeded on grounds that it represented a measure of damage which was unsound in law, and that the claim was untriable and a waste of the court's resources); *Monks v Warwick DC* [2009] EWHC 959 (QB) (pleaded claim for special damages struck out where the claimant sought to recover losses claimed to have been incurred by his company).

*New note 186B.* See e.g. recently *Monks v Warwick DC* [2009] EWHC 959 (QB). See also, for the reason given in new note 168A above, the authorities referred to in note 126 to para.32.31 in the Main Text, which concerns applications by defendants for summary judgment made on the ground that the claimant has no real prospect of establishing his case of malice.

**32.42**    **The need for finality.** *Note 201.* In *Crossley v Wallace* [2008] EWHC 2846 (QB), Openshaw J. held that a libel action had been properly struck out where the proceedings were a flagrant and obvious attempt to re-litigate issues already determined between the parties in a nuisance action.

*Note 204.* For the approach taken to such matters by the New South Wales Court of Appeal, see *Habib v Radio 2UE Sydney Pty Ltd* [2009] NSWCA 231.

**32.43**    **Impermissible collateral objective.** *Note 210. Ashley v Chief Constable of Sussex* [2008] 2 W.L.R. 975 is now also reported at [2008] 1 A.C. 962.

*Note 215.* In *Desmond v MGN Ltd* [2008] IESC 56, the Supreme Court of Ireland (by a majority; Kearns J. dissenting) dismissed the defendant's appeal against Hanna J.'s decision not to strike out a libel action for want of prosecution. The Court held that, although the plaintiff's delay in prosecuting the action had been both inordinate and inexcusable, the balance of justice favoured the plaintiff being allowed to proceed with his action given the nature of the defence that had been filed (which included a plea of justification).

**32.44**    **Proceedings which are not "worth the candle".** *Note 225.* In *Hughes v Alan Dick & Co Ltd* [2008] EWHC 2695 (QB), Eady J. remarked at [20] that since the decision of the Court of Appeal in *Jameel v Dow Jones & Co Inc* [2005] Q.B. 946 "there have . . . not been many examples of its being implemented". Since then a plethora of applications by defendants to strike out or stay defamation claims on *Jameel* grounds has come before the court. As Tugendhat J. commented in *Thornton v Telegraph Media Group Ltd* [2010] EWHC 1414 (QB);

[2010] E.M.L.R. 25 at [62], "recent cases demonstrate that each of the three judges who are currently hearing most of the defamation cases are applying the principle of *Jameel v Dow Jones* with some frequency, and in a number of different, but related, contexts in defamation actions". These applications (set out below in chronological order) have had mixed results:

(i) In *Hughes v Alan Dick & Co Ltd* [2008] EWHC 2695 (QB) (application failed), a slander action, Eady J. set aside the default judgment that had been entered against the defendant, but dismissed the defendant's application to strike the claim out as an abuse of process. Eady J. observed at [21]

> "This is a complaint potentially of a serious slander, published not technically by way of a website which may or may not have been accessed by readers, but to an immigration officer and arguably also to a police officer. Subject to the defences of privilege and justification, it seems to me that it cannot be said that the claim 'would not be worth the candle'. It is a genuine claim in relation to a serious allegation . . . ".

(ii) In *Mardas v New York Times Co* [2008] EWHC 3135 (QB); [2009] E.M.L.R. 8 (application failed), Eady J. allowed the claimant's appeal against a decision of Master Leslie striking out on *Jameel* grounds his libel claims against two newspapers. Eady J. found that the Master had erred in making findings of fact in both cases on the basis of incomplete evidence which should have been left to trial, and had been too ready to conclude that no real and substantial tort had been committed within the jurisdiction. Eady J. notably remarked at [15] that the question of whether there had been a real and substantial tort "cannot depend upon a numbers game, with the court fixing an arbitrary minimum according to the facts of the case". (The Court of Appeal refused the defendant's application for permission to appeal against Eady J.'s ruling: [2009] EWCA Civ 633.)

(iii) *Carrie v Tolkien* [2009] EWHC 29 (QB); [2009] E.M.L.R. 9 (application succeeded) concerned a libel action brought in respect of comments allegedly posted by the defendant on an internet website operated and controlled by the claimant. The claimant did not dispute that he had had it within his power to remove the offending comments from his website once they came to his attention, but he had not done so (for a period of some 22 months, by the time of the hearing of the defendant's application). Eady J. acceded to the defendant's application to strike the claim out. Regarding the period after the offending comments came to the claimant's notice, the defendant had an unanswerable defence of consent and acquiescence. In relation to the period before the claimant became aware of the posting, there was no evidence of substantial publication and therefore no basis for concluding that a real and substantial tort had been committed such as to justify the deployment of the court's resources.

(iv) In *Haji-Ioannou v Dixon* [2009] EWHC 178 (QB) (application failed), Sharp J. dismissed the defendants' application to strike out on *Jameel* grounds the claimant's claim for libel and slander. Where serious allegations about a well-known businessman—allegations which had previously been held to be capable of imputing dishonesty—had been made by senior directors of a large and successful company to a journalist on a leading financial newspaper with the intention that they be published, it could not be inferred that the journalist was likely to disbelieve or discount what he had been told. In these circumstances, the judge held, the court could not safely conclude that the claimant's reputation had not been damaged.

(v) *Noorani v Calver (No. 1)* [2009] EWHC 561 (QB) (application succeeded), a slander action brought in respect of comments concerning the claimant said to have been made by the defendant to the claimant's wife and daughter was struck out by Coulson J. as an abuse of process in accordance with the principles laid down in *Jameel*. Publication was very limited and there was no good evidence of damage to reputation, the offending words having allegedly been spoken in the course of one brief conversation in the street and only to two people who were wholly "within the claimant's camp". It would be wholly disproportionate, the judge held, to involve a judge and a fully staffed court, let alone a jury, in the detailed consideration of such a claim. There was no need for vindication. There was no basis for concluding that a real and substantial tort had been committed.

(vi) In *Sanders v Percy* [2009] EWHC 1870 (QB) (application succeeded in part), H.H. Judge Moloney Q.C. struck out "on *Jameel* and case-management grounds" that part of a slander claim which was concerned with a publication by the defendant to one individual, the claimant's solicitor, the effect of which was to call into question the claimant's abilities as an "Ali G" impersonator. However, the judge dismissed the application to strike out on *Jameel* grounds other parts of the claim based upon the more serious allegation that to the effect that the claimant might have been involved in benefit fraud.

(vii) *Khader v Aziz* [2009] EWHC 2027 (QB) (application succeeded): see further below.

(viii) In *Lonzim Plc v Sprague* [2009] EWHC 2838 (QB) (application succeeded), Tugendhat J. struck out the whole of a claim based partly upon allegedly slanderous words spoken by the defendant shareholder at a company's general meeting and partly upon an alleged libel by the defendant said to have been published in this jurisdiction via a South African newspaper's website. As regards the former, the judge stated that he was

> "at a loss to understand what vindication the claimants might obtain from the verdict of a court, or why, or on what grounds, this claim in slander is being brought at all . . . [t]he prospect for a shareholder at a company meeting of being sued by claimants such as these, for expressing opinions or views such as those alleged here to be slanders, would inhibit free expression. It would be very much against the public interest. The public interest in relation to company meetings is that there should be a free expression of views, and that differences be resolved by the votes cast".

As for the latter, the court held that the evidence adduced by the claimants suggested at most minimal publication of the offending words in this jurisdiction, which certainly was not evidence of any real or substantial tort having been committed in England and Wales.

(ix) In *Williams v MGN Ltd* [2009] EWHC 3150 (QB) (application succeeded), where the claimant in a libel action had a background of serious criminal convictions, Eady J. held that it would be inappropriate to regard the references to the claimant in the newspaper article sued on (which described him as a "henchman" of another individual identified as a "ruthless crime boss") as constituting a real and substantial tort. Accordingly, the claim was struck out as an abuse of process.

(x) *Budu v BBC* [2010] EWHC 616 (QB) (application succeeded): (per Sharp J., at [128])

> "I am conscious that the abuse jurisdiction is exceptional. But if the Claimant were to succeed at trial in relation to a vestigial case, the cost of the exercise would, in my judgment, have been out of all proportion to what had been achieved. If it were necessary for me to do so, considering the matter 'in the round' I would take the view that the BBC should not have to be put to the cost and trouble of defending these proceedings so many years after the initial publications, taking into account all the factors to which I have referred, including the potential prejudice to it in doing so; and that permitting this action to continue, on the facts of this case, would constitute a disproportionate interference with the BBC's article 10 rights and would be an abuse of the process".

(xi) In *Baturina v Times Newspapers Ltd* [2010] EWHC 696 (QB); [2010] E.M.L.R. 18 (application failed), Eady J. held that, to the extent the claimant's case—which concerned various claims for libel by innuendo in respect of words published in the print edition of the *Sunday Times* and via the internet in this jurisdiction and in Russia, and thereafter allegedly republished by third party publishers in Russia—survived the defendant's applications for rulings on meaning and to strike out the particulars of claim (on grounds that the case was defectively pleaded), the principles set forth in *Jameel* had no application.

(xii) In *Kaschke v Osler* [2010] EWHC 1075 (QB) (application succeeded), Eady J., applying *Jameel*, concluded that a defamation claim brought in respect of an article posted on the defendant's website blog and certain comments posted in response by readers of the blog was an abuse of process. Having regard in particular to the contents of a posting made by the claimant on her own website which covered some of the same ground as the article complained of and which prompted the defendant to write his own article about the claimant, and of a "right to reply" article written by the claimant which the defendant agreed to publish on his website following the claimant's complaint, Eady J. ruled that any award of damages, if the claimant succeeded, could not be "other than very modest". In such circumstances, "any such award would be out of all proportion to the time and money spent on this litigation and, in particular, to the cost of a two-week jury trial" (at [25]).

(xiii) In *Hays Plc v Hartley* [2010] EWHC 1068 (QB) (application succeeded), a libel claim brought against an intermediary news and press agent over the publication by him to a journalist of allegations concerning the claimant company, allegations that were later published in a national newspaper, was struck out by Tugendhat J. as an abuse of process on the ground that there was nothing of value that it could achieve. The claimant had already received vindication by means of a statement made by the originators of the allegations and published on the newspaper's website to the effect that the allegations were unfounded, there was no realistic prospect of the defendant agent republishing the allegations, and the value of the potential damages made them not worth pursuing.

(xiv) (The appeal in respect of case (vii) above) In *Khader v Aziz* [2010] EWCA Civ 716; [2011] E.M.L.R. 2 (application succeeded) the Court of Appeal dismissed the claimant's appeal from the decision of Eady J. to strike out her claims of slander and libel against the former wife of the Sultan of Brunei and her solicitors: [2009] EWHC 2027 (QB). As regards the first of two alleged publications which were the subject of the appeal, the court held that Eady J. had been correct to conclude that the claim was disproportionate and should be struck out as an abuse of process:

> "In my judgment, the principle in *Jameel* applies in the present appeal. The appellant's claim on the first publication is at best fraught with difficulties. But even if it were to succeed at trial, it would not be worth the candle. She would at best recover minimal damages at huge expense to the parties and of court time . . . the parties' expenditure must vastly exceed the minimal amount of damages which the appellant might recover even if she were to succeed in overcoming all the obstacles in the path of such success" (per the President of the Queen's Bench Division (May L.J.) at [32], with whom Carnwath L.J. at [48] and Moore-Bick L.J. at [49] agreed.)

(xv) In *Henderson v London Borough of Hackney* [2010] EWHC 1651 (QB), Eady J. dismissed the claim for libel against the second defendant on the ground that the claimant had no real prospect of establishing malice in order to defeat the defence of qualified privilege. However, at [42] Eady J. added this:

> "This is one of those cases in which one might have expected to see an application founded on abuse of process in light of the Court of Appeal decision in *Jameel* . . . This would be on the basis, as it was put, that 'the game was not worth the candle'. It could have been argued, in view of the very limited publication and the uncontested facts, that the action could hardly be expected to achieve any tangible advantage for [the claimant] by way of vindication. But no such application was made and, in the circumstances, there is no need to say anything further about it".

(xvi) Stadlen J. struck out as an abuse of process the libel action in *Kaschke v Gray* [2010] EWHC 1907 (QB) (application succeeded) on grounds similar to those which Eady J. had relied on in reaching the same conclusion in *Kaschke v Osler* (see case (xii) above) (i.e. on the basis that, on the specific facts of the case, "the game was not worth the candle", but not on the discrete ground that the *Kaschke v Gray* action represented an improper attempt to re-litigate issues which could and should have been resolved in the *Kaschke v Osler* action.

In summary, *Jameel v Dow Jones & Co Inc* has conferred upon the court an important, new, flexible power to put a stop to ostensibly pointless defamation claims at an interim stage in the proceedings where previously such claims, absent settlement, would have had to proceed to trial. The difficult question is knowing exactly when and in what circumstances the court will consider it appropriate to exercise this power in a defendant's favour.

*Note 229. Adelson v Associated Newspapers Ltd* [2008] EWHC 278 (QB) is now also reported at [2009] E.M.L.R. 10.

## Section 5. Stay of Proceedings

**Situations in which stay ordered.** In *Blake v Associated Newspapers Ltd*   **32.48**
[new note 260A], Gray J. ordered a stay of a libel action on the ground that certain key issues which had to be decided in the case (which related to the validity of a consecration of a bishop outside the mainstream churches) were not justiciable in a civil court. Eady J. stayed the libel proceedings the subject of *His Holiness Sant Baba Jeet Singh Ji Maharaj v Eastern Media Group Ltd* [new note 260B] on similar grounds.

*Note 259. Ashley v Chief Constable of Sussex* [2008] 2 W.L.R. 975 is now also reported at [2008] 1 A.C. 962.

*New note 260A.* [2003] EWHC 1960 (QB).

*New note 260B.* [2010] EWHC 1294 (QB).

## Section 6. The Trial of Issues

**Civil Procedure Rules.** *Delete note 271.*   **32.50**

**Other issues.** *Note 282. Curistan v Times Newspapers Ltd* [2008] EWCA Civ   **32.52**
432 is now also reported at [2009] Q.B. 231.

CHAPTER 33

# INTERLOCUTORY MATTERS

SECTION 1. DISCLOSURE

**33.2**   **Disclosure before action.** *Note 3.* For the position in New South Wales, see *Hatfield v TCN Channel Nine Pty Ltd* [2010] NSWCA 69, in which the New South Wales Court of Appeal dismissed the applicant's appeal against a decision of the first instance judge refusing to order preliminary discovery of "any episode of, and the transcript of any episode of, the television series known as '*Underbelly: The Golden Mile*' . . . in which the applicant is named, depicted (by an actor or picture or otherwise) and/or referred to" in order that the applicant might, if so advised, sue the respondent for defamation.

**33.5**   **Internet cases.** *Add new note 21A after the first sentence in this paragraph.* For a recent example of the exercise of this jurisdiction, see *G v Wikimedia Foundation Inc* [2009] EWHC 3148 (QB); [2010] E.M.L.R. 14, which contains some important guidance on the circumstances in which the court will or will not be disposed to make certain orders ancillary to the *Norwich Pharmacal* relief being sought; orders, for example, that the application be heard in private, for the anonymisation of one or other of the parties to the application, and restricting the access of non-parties to information and documents concerning the case from court records.

**33.6**   **Scope of disclosure in defamation.** *Add word to heading of paragraph*: **Justification.**

*Note 29.* In *Taranissi v BBC* [2008] EWHC 2486 (QB) Eady J. observed at [13] that the principle in *Yorkshire Provident Life Assurance Co v Gilbert & Rivington* [1895] Q.B. 148 "is as sound today as it was at that time", the principle being that:

"[t]he defendant's right . . . is to have discovery of all matters relating to the questions in issue as narrowed by the particulars. I do not think in a libel action he is entitled to

[178]

get anything more ... I think it would be a very bad precedent to suggest that a person can simply by libelling another obtain access to all his books and see whether he can justify what he has said or not. I think it would be very lamentable if we should say when a person has libelled another and has justified and given particulars, that he is entitled to more than discovery of that which relates to those particulars" (per Lindley L.J. at 152).

Applying the principle in *Yorkshire Provident*, Eady J. dismissed the defendant's application whereby it sought specific disclosure from the claimant of documents which it believed would support a case of justification that it had not yet pleaded.

For an example of an application by defendants in a libel action for disclosure from a non-party of documents which they contended were likely to support their case on justification (application refused on a number of grounds, including that it was difficult to see what relevance the documents sought have to any matter other than the credit of certain witnesses), see *Briscoe Mitchell v Hodder & Stoughton Ltd* [2008] EWHC 2852 (QB).

*Note 30.* Now subject always, of course, to one or other of the CPR r.31.6 conditions being satisfied.

**Qualified privilege.** *Delete the last sentence of this paragraph.* **33.7**

*Add new paragraph.* **Malice.** Where the claimant has pleaded malice in his **33.7A** reply whether in response to a defence of qualified privilege, fair comment, offer of amends [new note 32A] or otherwise, or put in issue the defendant's motivation or state of mind in publishing the words by the way in which he has pleaded his claim for damages, the parties must give disclosure of all documents which support or undermine the claimant's case on the defendant's state of mind.

*New note 32A.* As to which see further para.33.8 of the Main Work.

*Note 34.* In *Fiddes v Channel 4 Television Corp* [2010] EWCA Civ 516 the Court of Appeal dismissed an appeal by the claimant against a decision of Tugendhat J. whereby he had refused to order the defendant to carry out a search of back-up tapes of computer records in order to retrieve certain deleted emails. The claimant alleged that these emails, if retrieved by the defendant and specifically disclosed, were likely to bear materially on the correctness or otherwise of his case of malice, which was being advanced in response to the defendant's defence of fair comment. The Court of Appeal decided that the judge had correctly considered the various factors that were relevant to a decision on whether to order the defendant to conduct such a search, and that he had been entitled to conclude that there was no sufficient likelihood of the retrieval of emails that were significant and relevant to the issues in the action.

**Offer of amends.** *Note 43. Tesco Stores Ltd v Guardian News & Media Ltd* is **33.8** now also reported at [2009] E.M.L.R. 5.

**Use of disclosed documents.** *Note 45. Westcott v Westcott* [2008] EWCA Civ **33.9** 818 is now also reported at [2009] Q.B. 407.

SECTION 2. FURTHER INFORMATION AND INTERROGATORIES

**33.12**      **Introduction.** *Note 52.* For a recent decision concerning an application governed by Part 22 of the NSW Uniform Civil Procedure Rules 2005 that a defendant in a libel action be ordered to answer certain interrogatories and to give better answers to others, see *Zaetta v Nationwide News Pty Ltd* [2009] NSWSC 508 (Nicholas J.). Meanwhile, for the approach of the Federal Court of Australia to a wide-ranging request for further and better particulars by a defendant to proceedings for, inter alia, libel, see *Metcash Trading Ltd v Bunn (No.4)* [2008] FCA 1607 (the court ordered the plaintiffs to give further and better particulars of their case, for example, as to (a) which part or parts of the publications complained of gave rise to the pleaded imputations, (b) their trading reputation, and (c) in relation that part of their claim which rested upon a true innuendo imputation.)

*Add new note 52A after the phrase* "whether or not the matter is contained in or referred to in a statement of case". *Dee v Telegraph Media Group Ltd* [2009] EWHC 2546 (QB) stands as an example of the court taking a non-technical approach to an application for further information in a defamation case and ordering a party to provide further information concerning a matter which was not, strictly speaking, in issue on the pleadings. Eady J. ordered the claimant to answer two questions posed by the defendant where the purpose of asking the questions was to comprehend the scope of the issues that would be outstanding at trial if the defendant succeeded on its arguments as to the meaning of the words complained of (specifically, on the facts of the case, the question to be resolved was whether or not certain tennis matches played by the claimant in Spanish tournaments were matches on the "international professional tennis circuit"). The court's reasoning at [17] was as follows:

"I see no reason why the claimant should not offer further clarification on these matters. It has not been suggested that he is unable to do so. It is important to place as many cards as possible on the table at this stage. There is nothing to be gained from arguments about whether a request for further information is the right mechanism to adopt. I shall simply direct that the questions are to be answered constructively, rather than merely by way of non-admission, so that the defendant can know the full extent of the real dispute".

(b) *The practical scope of interrogatories and requests for further information by claimants*

**33.28**      **Defendant's state of mind.** *Note 130. Tesco Stores Ltd v Guardian News & Media Ltd* is now also reported at [2009] E.M.L.R. 5.

**33.30**      **Sources.** *Add new note 140A at the end of the paragraph.* For an authoritative statement of the applicable principles concerning protection of journalistic sources in Canada, see the decision of the Supreme Court of Canada in *R v National Post* 2010 SCC 16.

**The newspaper rule.** *Note 143.* Now see also *Bond v Western Australian*    **33.32**
*Newspapers Ltd* [2009] WASCA 127.

**CPR rule 53.3.** *Note 157.* Now see also *Flood v Times Newspapers Ltd* [2010]    **33.33**
EWCA Civ 804; [2010] E.M.L.R. 26.

**Contempt of Court Act 1981, section 10.** *Note 163.* Now see *Financial Times*    **33.34**
*Ltd v UK* [2010] E.M.L.R. 21 in which the European Court of Human Rights
determined that the applicant media organisations' rights under art.10 had been
violated by an order requiring them to disclose documents which might lead to
the identification of a journalistic source (see *Interbrew SA v Financial Times Ltd*
[2002] EWCA Civ 274; [2002] E.M.L.R. 24). The Strasbourg court concluded at
[71] that Interbrew SA's interests in taking proceedings against the source to
prevent damage from further dissemination of confidential information "were,
even if considered cumulatively, insufficient to outweigh the public interest in the
protection of journalists' sources". See also *Sanoma Uitgevers BV v The Nether-
lands* (App. no.38224/03); [2011] E.M.L.R. 4, a Grand Chamber decision of the
European Court of Human Rights.

(c) *The practical scope of interrogatories and requests for further information*
*by defendants*

**Justification.** *Note 174.* It is not unreasonable to view the decision in *Dee v*    **33.38**
*Telegraph Media Group Ltd* [2009] EWHC 2546 (QB) as a modern application
of this principle. See para.33.12 above.

SECTION 3. SECURITY FOR COSTS AND MAINTENANCE

**General.** *Note 187.* For the approach in Scotland to security for costs—or    **33.42**
"caution" as it is referred to in that jurisdiction—in a defamation action, see
*Ewing v Times Newspapers Ltd* [2008] CSOH 169.

**Difficulty of enforcement.** *Note 202. Kahangi v Nourizadeh* [2009] EWHC    **33.45**
2451 (QB), at [10]–[20] (concerning the possibility of enforcement in Iran).

SECTION 4. CONSOLIDATION, JOINDER AND SEVERANCE

**Consolidation: general.** *Add new note 233A at the end of the paragraph.* For    **33.51**
the position in Victoria, where the guiding principle is whether ordering consolidation is likely to expose a plaintiff to a substantial risk of real prejudice, see
*Buckley v Herald and Weekly Times Pty Ltd* [2009] VSCA 118.

**Objections to consolidation.** *Note 231.* This was the basis on which Sharp J.    **33.57**
declined to direct that two libel actions brought by the claimant against two
different newspaper groups (MGN Ltd and Telegraph Media Group Ltd) over
newspaper articles making similar allegations should be tried together: *Ronaldo
v MGN Ltd* [2009] EWHC 2862 (QB). The judge's reasoning at [25]–[26] was
that,

"it would be better if these actions were not tried at the same time, and the trial of the Telegraph action should follow that of the Mirror action. It seems to me that there are significant differences between them, in particular in relation to the meanings that are justified and as to the character of each of the articles complained of; and I think [the Telegraph's advocate] is right when he says that there is a risk, whatever direction is given by the judge, that the jury's view of the meaning of the Telegraph's article will be affected by the view that it takes of the Mirror article . . . [the claimant's counsel] is unable . . . to identify any real prejudice to the claimant if the actions are tried separately, save in respect of costs. It seems to me that when one balances the extra costs . . . against the risk of injustice to the defendant in the Telegraph action if the jury were unable to approach the matter properly, then it seems to me that the balance lies in favour of having these two actions tried separately".

## Section 5. Mode of Trial

**33.62**     **General.** *Note 246.* "the constitutional importance of the right to trial by jury . . . is undoubtedly a factor which has to be borne in mind on the issue of convenience as well as of discretion": *Fiddes v Channel Four Television Corp* [2010] EWCA Civ 730; [2011] E.M.L.R. 3 at [21].

**33.63**     **Prolonged examination of documents.** *Add after the phrase* "and the word 'conveniently' means without substantial difficulty in comparison with carrying out the same process with a judge alone". The inconvenience to be considered is exclusively that arising from "the prolonged examination of documents" [new note 253A].

*Add at the end of paragraph.* Nonetheless, the number of documents is not, of itself, the issue [new note 256A]. The fact that juries in criminal trials sometimes have to consider complex documentation is irrelevant to the questions posed under s.69 [new note 256B].

*Note 249.* See also *Fiddes v Channel Four Television Corp*, above, in which the Court of Appeal reviewed and refined the applicable principles (upholding Tugendhat J.'s decision to dispense with a jury).

*Note 251. W v Westminster City Council* [2004] EWHC 2866 (QB) is also reported at (2005) 1 F.L.R. 816.

*Note 253.* But note the caveat in *Fiddes v Channel Four Television Corp*, above, at [18]:

"We would like to emphasise the need for caution when invoking the additional length, and (even more) the additional cost, of a jury trial as factors to be taken into account on the second, convenience, section 69 question. Jury trial will almost always take longer, and cost more, than trial by judge alone. The extra time taken, and the extra costs involved, in a jury trial may often be a useful sort of quantitative cross-check of what might otherwise be a purely qualitative assessment of the extra inconvenience of a jury trial (as was done in *Beta Construction* [1991] 1 W.L.R. 1042). However, it would be dangerous if those two factors were given much independent weight, as it would risk undermining the important right to a jury trial which section 69(2) gives—to defendants as well as to claimants—in libel actions".

*New note 253A. Fiddes v Channel Four Television Corp*, above, at [20]:

"it is important to appreciate that the inconvenience to be considered in the second [convenience] section 69 question is that arising from 'the prolonged examination of documents': the court should not, at that stage, look at any other inconvenience which may arise as a result of a jury trial, although it could well be relevant when considering the third [residual discretion to order jury trial] question".

*New note 256A. Fiddes v Channel Four Television Corp*, above, at [19], per Lord Neuberger M.R.:

"The number of documents is not the issue when it comes to the first [prolonged examination of documents] and second [convenience] section 69 questions. As Slade L.J. said [in *Goldsmith v Pressdram Ltd* [1988] 1 W.L.R. 65, 74–75] in a passage cited by the Judge, '[t]here may be many cases where numerous documents will be required to be looked at, but no substantial practical difficulties are likely to arise in their examination being made with a jury', and, by contrast, there can be cases where 'relatively few documents will require examination, but nevertheless long and minute examination of them is likely to be required'."

*New note 256B.*

"The fact that juries in criminal trials (especially those trials involving allegations of complex financial fraud and the like) sometimes have to consider complex documentation does not really bear on the three section 69 questions. It may well be that, in some such criminal trials, the section 69 questions would result in the conclusion that the trial should be by judge alone, but the questions do not arise in the criminal field even in relation to such cases: there is an absolute right to a jury trial, save in circumstances which are very different from those covered by section 69": *Fiddes v Channel Four Television Corp*, above, per Lord Neuberger M.R. at [22].

**Residual discretion.** *Note 260.*     **33.65**

"the fact that one party is a public figure may often be a reason for favouring a jury trial, but that does not mean that the fact that neither party is a public figure is a reason against a jury trial": *Fiddes v Channel Four Television Corp*, above, per Lord Neuberger M.R. at [20].

*Note 263.* See also *Fiddes v Channel Four Television Corp*, above.

CHAPTER 34

# THE TRIAL: THE CLAIMANT'S CASE

SECTION 3. PROOF OF PUBLICATION

**34.9**    **Internet publication.** *Note 33.* Unsurprisingly, this has been a growth area for applications to strike out. To similar effect see also *Budu v BBC* [2010] EWHC 616 (QB); *Carrie v Tolkien* [2009] EWHC 29 (QB); *Hays Plc v Hartley* [2010] EWHC 1068 (QB); *Henderson v London Borough of Hackney* [2010] EWHC 1651 (QB) at [42]; *Hughes v Alan Dick & Co Ltd* [2008] EWHC 2695 (QB); *Kaschke v Osler* [2010] EWHC 1075 (QB); *Kaschke v Gray* [2010] EWHC 1907 (QB); *Khader v Aziz* [2010] EWCA Civ 716; [2011] E.M.L.R. 2; *Lonzim Plc v Sprague* [2009] EWHC 2838 (QB); *Noorani v Calver (No. 1)* [2009] EWHC 561 (QB); *Sanders v Percy* [2009] EWHC 1870 (QB); *Williams v MGN Ltd* [2009] EWHC 3150 (QB). See also para.32.44 of Supplement, above.

But—given that the right of reputation is now established to be protected by art.8—care must be taken not to deprive a litigant too readily of his art.6 right of unimpeded access to the courts in pursuit of his remedies: *Mardas v New York Times* [2008] EWHC 3135; [2009] E.M.L.R. 8 (the converse argument, of course, is that failure to strike out may be a disproportionate interference with the defendant's art.10 rights: see e.g. *Hays Plc v Hartley*, above). As Eady J. said in *Mardas* at [15], the question of whether there has been a real and substantial tort within the jurisdiction cannot depend on a numbers game. Similarly, even where publication is limited, if the allegation is serious and the damage potentially substantial, a claim will not be struck out: *Haji-Ioannou v Dixon* [2009] EWHC 178 (QB); *Sanders v Percy* (above) at [15].

On the lack of any presumption of internet publication, see also *Baturina v Times Newspapers Ltd* [2010] EWHC 696 (QB); [2010] E.M.L.R. 18 at [38] and *Brady v Norman* [2008] EWHC 2481 (QB) [23]–[26].

**Action for slander.** *Note 48.* For a recent slander trial in which the judge was   **34.13**
unable to rely on the claimant's own evidence and publication was not proved,
see *Hussein v Farooq* [2008] EWHC 2487 (QB).

SECTION 4. IDENTIFICATION OF CLAIMANT

**Claimant not expressly named.** *Note 69.* It is enough in malicious falsehood   **34.19**
that there should be a reference, direct or indirect, to the claimant's business,
even if publishees did not identify the claimant himself: *Marathon Mutual v
Waters* [2009] EWHC 1931 (QB); [2010] E.M.L.R. 3. For a failure to establish
reference in libel, see *Budu v BBC* [2010] EWHC 616 (QB), where the claimant
failed to adduce any evidence that readers of an article archived on the BBC
website, which contained no express reference to him, would have understood
that he was referred to. Instead, he unsuccessfully attempted to rely on an
inference (as to which, see fn.33 above).

*Add to note 74:* Reliance on an inference of internet publication should be
treated warily: see for instance *Budu v BBC* [2009] EWHC 616 (QB), and cases
cited at fn.33 above.

SECTION 5. DEFAMATORY MEANINGS

**Context.** *Note 95.* Where either party relies for meaning on more than one   **34.26**
article in the same newspaper, the key issue is whether the articles are sufficiently
closely connected to be regarded as a single publication, and it makes no
difference of principle whether the articles are on continuation pages or a
different part (here, a sports supplement) of the same newspaper: *Dee v Telegraph Media Group Ltd* [2010] EWHC 924 (QB); [2010] E.M.L.R. 20.

SECTION 6. EVIDENCE OF MALICE

**Introduction.** *Note 118.* See also *Hughes v Risbridger* [2010] EWHC 491   **34.32**
(QB) at [31]

**Definition.** *Note 122.* In *Crossley v Newsquest* [2008] EWHC 3054 (QB) at   **34.33**
[48] Eady J. thought it

> "important to note . . . that the significance of malice in (the context of fair comment)
> has been significantly reduced in recent years by the recognition that motive is largely
> irrelevant in the context of the expression of honest opinions and that, essentially, the
> important question for the purposes of fair comment is whether or not the commentator
> honestly held the opinion expressed: see eg the observations of Lord Nicholls in
> *Cheng* . . . "

**No honest belief.** *Note 134.* Hence Tugendhat J. was prepared to determine   **34.34**
whether words relied on not as being defamatory of the claimant but as being

relevant to the issue of malice were capable of bearing the meaning attributed to them: *Bray v Deutsche Bank* [2009] EWHC 1356 (QB). It does not appear that CPR Pt 53 PD para.4(1) has been used for this purpose before.

**34.35**      **Recklessness.** *Note 137.* There must be a "genuine indifference" to the truth or falsity of the words: *Hughes v Risbridger* [2010] EWHC 491 (QB) at [24].

*Note 138.* Carelessness, impulsiveness or irrationality plainly could not suffice, because a finding of malice is akin to a finding of dishonesty or fraud (*Hughes v Risbridger* [2010] EWHC 491 (QB) at [24]; *Monks v Warwick DC* [2009] EWHC 959 (QB) at [27], citing *Three Rivers DC v Bank of England* [2003] 2 A.C. 1 at [161], per Lord Hobhouse: "Dishonesty is not to be inferred from evidence which is equally consistent with mere negligence"). For that reason, findings of malice are rare, whether at trial or (a fortiori) on summary application, where it has been said that although such a finding might in theory be possible, "It could scarcely be so where a real issue turns on the defendant's state of mind and a credibility judgment is required": *Hayter v Fahie* [2008] EWCA Civ 1336 at [23], per Sir Anthony May P. See also *Hughes v Alan Dick & Co Ltd* [2008] EWHC 2695 (QB) at [16].

*Note 141.* There must be "genuine indifference" to the truth or falsity of the words: *Hughes v Risbridger*, fn.137 above.

Section 7. Evidence Directed at Defendant's Case of Privilege

**34.48**      *Reynolds* **privilege cases.** *Correction.* The final word of the passage quoted from the judgment of Simon Brown L.J. In *Jameel v Wall Street Journal* [2003] EWCA Civ 1694; [2004] E.M.L.R. 6 at [31] is wrongly printed in the Main Work as "unjustifiable". The final sentence of that passage should of course read: "The former purpose would, as *GKR Karate* makes plain, be impermissible; the latter, however, seems to me entirely justifiable".

*Add a new note 199A at the end of the second sentence following the passage from the judgment of Simon Brown L.J. referred to in the correction above, ending with the words* "the gist of his side of the story". In *Flood v Times Newspapers Ltd* [2009] EWHC 2375 (QB); [2010] E.M.L.R. 8, the claimant was permitted to lead evidence relevant to the context in which the issues relevant to *Reynolds* privilege arose, although much of it was not only unchallenged but common ground. In the event, however, Tugendhat J. drew on his evidence only in so far as it was uncontroversial, save in one respect. He held at [197] that it was relevant to the assessment that had to be made as to whether the interference with the Claimant's right to reputation under art.8 was proportionate. The test was whether the interference was proportionate, not whether the journalists believed it to be so. (The decision was overturned in part on appeal: see [2010] EWCA Civ 804; [2010] E.M.L.R. 26.)

**34.49**      **Necessity of evidence.** *Note 206.* See also *Flood v Times Newspapers Ltd* [2009] EWHC 2375 (QB); [2010] E.M.L.R. 8, where the claimant was allowed to lead evidence, even though it was almost entirely uncontroversial. However, it was relevant to the assessment as to whether the interference with his art.8 right to reputation was proportionate (see [197]).

SECTION 8. EVIDENCE TO SUPPORT CLAIM FOR DAMAGES

**Extent of publication.** *Note 211.* Indeed, if there is very limited publication **34.51** the action will run the risk of being struck out: see fn.33 above.

*Note 214.* See also *Baturina v Times Newspapers Ltd* [2010] EWHC 696 (QB); [2010] E.M.L.R. 18, where the claimant relied on republication in Russia of *Sunday Times* allegations in two categories, one of which replicated the defendant's words and the other of which went beyond them.

**Actual damages.** *Note 226.* It is trite where there is a loss to a company owned **34.54** or controlled by the claimant, that loss will not be recoverable by the claimant unless and to the extent that he is able to show an indirect loss to himself: see e.g. *Monks v Warwick DC* [2009] EWHC 959 (QB) at [28]–[30].

**Aggravated damages.** *Note 237.* For the position where there is more than **34.56** one defendant and their culpability is different, see para.34.59 below and fnn.265 and 266.

**Exemplary damages.** *Note 265.* See now *Berezovsky v Russian Television and* **34.59** *Radio Broadcasting Co* [2010] EWHC 476 (QB) where (in the context of a claim for aggravated damages) Eady J. adopted the lowest common denominator approach, which he regarded as more compatible than the alternative with art.10.

*Note 266.* But see *Berezovsky v Russian Television* [fn.265 above], where the rule was applied in the case of a claim for aggravated damages.

SECTION 11. EVIDENCE IN CLAIM OF MISUSE OF PRIVATE INFORMATION

**General.** *Note 291.* For an example of a case where (at least when applying for **34.64** interim relief) the claimant did not know the identity of the prospective defendants, see *Terry (formerly LNS) v Persons Unknown* [2010] EWHC 119 (QB); [2010] E.M.L.R. 16. For discussion of an ISP's knowledge, albeit in a defamation context, see *Metropolitan International Schools v Designtechnica Corp* [2009] EWHC 1765 (QB); [2009] E.M.L.R. 27.

**"Intense focus".** *Note 295.* See also *BBC, Re* [2009] UKHL 34; [2010] 1 AC **34.66** 145.

*Note 297. Mosley v News Group Newspapers Ltd* is now also reported at [2008] E.M.L.R. 20.

**34.68**     **Damages.** *Note 300. Mosley v News Group Newspapers Ltd* is now also reported at [2008] E.M.L.R. 20.

*Note 301. Mosley v News Group Newspapers Ltd* is now also reported at [2008] E.M.L.R. 20.

CHAPTER 35

# THE TRIAL: THE DEFENDANT'S CASE

SECTION 3. EVIDENCE FOR THE DEFENDANT: GENERAL

**Context of alleged libel or slander.** *Note 24.* The key question when more than one article in a publication is under consideration is whether the relevant items (whether printed on continuation pages or different sections of the publication) are sufficiently closely connected to be regarded as a single publication: *Dee v Telegraph Media Group Ltd* [2010] EWHC 924 (QB); [2010] E.M.L.R. 20, where an article on the front page of the newspaper was complained of, but for the purposes of ascertaining its meaning it had to be read together with an associated article on the back page of the sports section, which was referred to in the front page article.   **35.4**

SECTION 4. PROOF OF JUSTIFICATION

**Evidence confined to particulars.** *Note 34.* However, the defendant may seek to justify a specific sting by reference to similar fact evidence. The general rule is that facts, not evidence, are pleaded, but to avoid ambush the claimant should be notified in advance of trial of the intention to rely on similar fact evidence. Usually that will be achieved by service of witness statements. In *Desmond v Bower* [2008] EWHC 2952 (QB), the defendant's attempt to plead matters relating to other incidents apart from the one referred to in his book failed when the particulars were struck out as not going to the specific sting. However, Eady   **35.9**

J. left open the question of whether evidence of those incidents could come back into the case as similar fact evidence (on the principles set out in *O'Brien v Chief Constable of South Wales Police* [2005] UKHL 26; [2005] 2 A.C. 534), deferring a decision on admissibility until witness statements were served. In the event, the defendant was refused permission by Eady J. a few days before trial to issue a witness summons with a view to leading evidence about another such incident: that decision was successfully appealed ([2009] EWCA Civ 667; [2010] E.M.L.R. 5).

**35.10     Exclusion of evidence.** *Note 40.* So in *Desmond v Bower* [2009] EWCA Civ 857 the trial judge excluded evidence which the defendant sought to adduce, on account of the unfairness which would result to the claimant, the material not having been put to the claimant in cross-examination and his case having closed. However, the Court of Appeal regarded the judge's decision as "plainly wrong", since (in its view) the question to be asked was whether it was manifestly unjust to exclude the evidence, the timing issue being less important than the trial judge had thought.

**35.12     Repetition rule and level 2 and 3 meanings.** *Note 47.* For a full discussion (and endorsement) of the principles stated in *Musa King* by the New Zealand Supreme Court, see *APN New Zealand Ltd v Simunovich Fisheries Ltd* [2010] 1 N.Z.L.R. 315. See also the brief restatement of those principles in *Radu v Houston* [2009] EWHC 398 (QB).

Section 5. Proof of Fair Comment (or Honest Opinion)

*Add new note 71A.* In the view of the Court of Appeal the defence should be re-named "honest opinion", because recent legislation in other common law jurisdictions (New Zealand, Australia and Ireland) now describes the defence as "honest opinion", and because "to describe the defence for what it is would lend greater emphasis to its importance as an essential ingredient of the right to free expression", and "better reflects the realities": *British Chiropractic Association v Singh* [2010] EWCA Civ 350; [2011] E.M.L.R. 1 at [35]–[36].

**35.19     Supporting facts.** *Note 72.* For a recent decision that comment was not capable of being fair because it was not based on truly stated facts alleged or referred to in the words complained of, see *Joseph v Spiller* [2009] EWCA Civ 1075; [2010] E.M.L.R. 7. (The case went to the Supreme Court in July 2010 and judgment is expected in October 2010.)

**35.20     Fact or comment.** *Note 77.* It is instructive to observe the approach taken to this issue by the Court of Appeal in *British Chiropractic Association v Singh* [2010] EWCA Civ 350; [2011] E.M.L.R. 1, where the allegations complained of concerned the lack of reliable scientific evidence for treatments promoted by the claimant.

SECTION 6. PROOF OF PRIVILEGE

**Facts creating privilege must be proved.** *Note 85.* Privilege (*Reynolds*) was    **35.23**
determined as a preliminary issue in *Flood v Times Newspapers Ltd* [2009]
EWHC 2375 (QB); [2010] E.M.L.R. 8, and on appeal at [2010] EWCA Civ 804;
[2010] E.M.L.R. 26.

**"*Reynolds*" type privilege.** *Note 93.* Lord Nicholls' list was most recently    **35.25**
considered and applied in *Flood v Times Newspapers Ltd* [2010] EWCA Civ 804;
[2010] E.M.L.R. 26, and in *Radu v Houston* [2008] EWCA Civ 921; [2009]
E.M.L.R. 13.

*Note 107.* But where the meanings pleaded by the parties are not far apart, no
decision on meaning will be required for the purposes of considering the defence
of qualified privilege: *Flood v Times Newspapers Ltd* [2009] EWHC 2375 (QB);
[2010] E.M.L.R. 8. (The case went to appeal—[2010] EWCA Civ 804; [2010]
E.M.L.R. 26—but not on that issue).

**Reportage.** *Note 109. Roberts v Gable* is now also reported at [2008] Q.B.    **35.26**
502.

SECTION 7. REBUTTAL OF MALICE

**Allegation of express malice.** *Note 114. Warren v Random House* is now also    **35.28**
reported at [2009] Q.B. 600

SECTION 8. EVIDENCE IN MITIGATION OF DAMAGES

**Categories of evidence.** *Note 116. Gur v Avrupa* is now also reported at [2009]    **35.29**
E.M.L.R. 4.

(a) *Claimant's bad reputation*

**Other publications.** *Note 138.* To the same effect see also *French v Triple M*    **35.36**
*Melbourne Pty Ltd* [2008] VSC 550, Forrest J.

(b) *Facts relevant to the contextual background in which the defamatory*
*publication was made*

**What evidence is admissible.** *Note 183. Warren v Random House* is now also    **35.46**
reported at [2009] Q.B. 600.

*Note 185. Warren v Random House* is now reported at [2009] Q.B. 600.

(d) *Facts which tend to disprove malice*

**Defendant not the original author.** *Note 197.* It may be worth observing that    **35.50**
the fact that a defendant was not the originator of the words complained of was

one of the factors which led Tugendhat J. to strike out a claim as an abuse of the process: *Hays Plc v Hartley* [2010] EWHC 1068 (QB). The judge was considering the value of any vindication which the claimant might obtain, in the particular context of the likely size of an award of damages.

### (f) *Apology or other amends*

**35.55**      **Effect of apology.** *Note 226. Adelson v Associated Newspapers Ltd* is now also reported at [2009] E.M.L.R. 10.

### (g) *Damages already recovered for same libel*

**35.58**      **General rule.** *Note 230.* See also *French v Triple M Melbourne Pty Ltd* [2008] VSC 550, Forrest J.

### Section 9. Evidence in a Claim of Misuse of Private Information

**35.63**      **Reasonable expectation of privacy.** *Note 243. Murray v Big Pictures (UK) Ltd* is now also reported at [2009] Ch. 481.

*Note 245. Mosley v News Group Newspapers Ltd* is now also reported at [2008] E.M.L.R. 20.

CHAPTER 36

## THE TRIAL: FUNCTIONS OF JUDGE AND JURY

**Preliminary observations.** *Note 2A after* "there will be a consequential   **36.1**
saving of costs". However, in *Fiddes v Channel Four Television Corp* [2010]
EWCA Civ 730; [2011] E.M.L.R. 3, the Court of Appeal warned that giving too
much independent weight to the additional length and cost of jury trial would risk
undermining the important right to jury trial: "Jury trial will almost always take
longer, and cost more, than trial by judge alone", per Lord Neuberger M.R. at [18].
Nonetheless, Tugendhat J.'s decision to order trial by judge alone was upheld.

**Capable of defamatory meaning.** *Note 16.* Hence the tendency to refer to the   **36.4**
question of whether the defamatory meaning alleged by the claimant is within the
range of possible meanings as one "regarded" as a question of law: see *British
Chiropractic Association v Singh* [2010] EWCA Civ 350; [2011] E.M.L.R. 1 at
[13].

**Two or more meanings reasonably possible.** *Note 22.* The single meaning   **36.5**
rule no longer applies in malicious falsehood: *Ajinomoto Sweeteners Europe SAS
v Asda Stores Ltd* [2010] EWCA Civ 609; [2010] E.M.L.R. 23.

**Meanings in the statements of case.** *Note 31.* The judge may even rule as to   **36.6**
whether words relied on not as being defamatory of the claimant but as being
relevant to the issue of malice are capable of bearing the meaning attributed to
them: *Bray v Deutsche Bank* [2009] EWHC 1356 (QB). It does not appear that
CPR Pt 53 PD para.4(1) has been used for this purpose before.

**Fair comment.** *Note 70.* The practice of determining first whether words are   **36.15**
defamatory, and then whether they are comment, has been criticised by the Court
of Appeal in *British Chiropractic Association v Singh* [2010] EWCA Civ 350;
[2011] E.M.L.R. 1 at [32]: "This case suggests that this may not always be the
best approach, because the answer to the first question may stifle the answer to
the second".

***Reynolds* privilege.** *Note 83. Roberts v Gable* is now also reported at [2008]   **36.17**
Q.B. 502.

**Absolute privilege.** *Note 84. Westcott v Westcott* is now also reported at   **36.18**
[2009] Q.B. 407.

**Qualified privilege under statute.** *Note 94.* In *Crossley v Newsquest* [2008]   **36.20**
EWHC 3054 (QB) at [23] Eady J. observed that the apparent requirement of
s.15(3) that a defendant must show, even in the case of a court report untainted
by malice, that the report was of public concern *and* for the public benefit, was
an onerous burden, although the court's construction of the provision would have
to take into account the requirements of art.10.

CHAPTER 37

# THE TRIAL: THE FINAL STAGES

SECTION 2. SUMMING-UP

**37.3** **Guidance on damages.** *Note 16. The Gleaner Co v Abrahams* is reported at [2004] 1 A.C. 628; *Mosley v News Group Newspapers Ltd* is reported at [2008] E.M.L.R. 20.

*Note 18. Purnell v Business F1 Magazine Ltd* is reported at [2008] 1 WLR 1.

SECTION 3. VERDICT

**37.5** **Questions for the jury.** *Amend note 21 to read as follows.* In *Loutchansky v Times Newspapers Ltd* Gray J. left 15 questions of primary fact to the jury. That decision was not challenged, but his ruling on qualified privilege, founded on the jury answers ([2001] E.M.L.R. 38) was overturned by the Court of Appeal: [2001] EWCA Civ 1805; [2002] Q.B. 783.

**37.8** **Verdicts.** *Note 37.* But in principle it must be for the judge to rule first as to the basis on which aggravated or exemplary damages should be awarded, and in particular as to the lowest basis of common liability where there is more than one defendant and their culpability differs: see paras.34.56 and 34.59 both in the Main Work and in this supplement, and fnn.265 and 266 in Ch.34 above.

SECTION 4. JUDGMENT

**37.10** **Generally.** *Note 44.* See amended note 21 above.

SECTION 5. COSTS

**37.11** **Introduction.** Lord Justice Jackson's Review of Civil Litigation Costs, published in December 2009, recommended that success fees and ATE (After The

Event) insurance premiums should no longer be recoverable from defendants, so that claimants would have to pay their lawyers' success fees on the basis of a percentage of their base costs, capped at an agreed percentage of damages. The quid pro quo is the proposal that general damages for defamation and misuse of private information should rise by 10 per cent. Moreover, the claimant would be able to enhance his recovery substantially by means of a realistic claimant's offer which, if not accepted (but ultimately proves sufficient) would result in an order (unless unjust) for indemnity costs and additional damages. In addition there would be a regime of what is called "qualified one way costs shifting", by which the costs ordered against a claimant should not exceed a reasonable amount, having regard to the financial resources of all the parties and their conduct in connection with the dispute.

Brief mention should be made of the Defamation Proceedings Costs Pilot Scheme (see CPR 51 DPD), which ran from October 1, 2009 to September 30, 2010 at the Royal Courts of Justice and in Manchester District Registry, and applied to all proceedings in libel, slander or malicious falsehood started in either centre after October 1, 2009. It provided for the court to manage the costs of the litigation as well as the case itself, and for each party to produce a costs budget in a standard form in advance of any case management or costs management conference. At any case or costs management conference or pre-trial review, the court was to have before it the detailed costs budgets of both parties to the litigation, and was obliged to take into account the costs involved in each proposed procedural step: armed with that information, it was to record approval or disapproval of each side's budget. Any judge conducting a detailed or summary assessment of costs would have regard to the budget estimates of the receiving party and to any view previously expressed by the court, and (unless there had been a significant change in circumstances) would approve any costs as reasonable and proportionate any costs claimed which fell within the last approved budget, but would not (save in exceptional circumstances) approve as reasonable or proportionate any costs claimed which did not fall within the last approved budget.

**Amount of costs.** *Note 80.* In *Wakefield v Ford* [2009] EWHC 122 (QB), Eady   **37.17**
J. ordered indemnity costs against a claimant on discontinuance where he had acted completely unreasonably in launching and persisting in litigation in which he sought vindication which was clearly unwarranted, in that he sued on an allegation of negligence which he must have known was justified. In *Noorani v Calver (No. 2)* [2009] EWHC 592 (QB) Coulson J. made a similar order against a discontinuing claimant whom he found to have brought what the claimant well knew to have been a hopeless claim.

**Payment on account.** *Note 98.* In *Noorani v Calver (No. 2)* [2009] EWHC   **37.21**
592 (QB) Coulson J. ordered an interim payment of £50,000 where the defendant's likely total costs were £100,000, a proportion in accordance with authority, but was unsympathetic to the claimant's submission that a lower sum should be awarded because of his financial difficulties:

> "Those who start High Court libel proceedings must realise that, if those proceedings fail, and if, as here, the court concludes that those proceedings should never have been

started, then they will be held responsible for the consequences, whatever their personal circumstances" [35].

*Add new note 98A at the end of the paragraph.* Orders for payment on account of costs are now becoming the standard practice (see e.g. per Eady J. in *Wakefield v Ford* [2009] EWHC 122 (QB) at [31]).

**37.26**     **Conditional Fee Agreements.** *Note 108.* In *Noorani v Calver (No. 2)* [2009] EWHC 592 (QB) at [36] Coulson J. observed that

> "The existence of a CFA can inure a party like the claimant to the chilly winds of reality; it can make him oblivious to the significant financial risk that he is running, and the potentially ruinous costs liability that he may be incurring. In my judgment, the conduct of libel proceedings on credit is a thoroughly bad idea . . . ".

**37.27**     **Costs capping orders.** The real difficulty with making costs capping orders is that para.23A.1 of the Costs Practice Direction stipulates that the courts should make such an order only in exceptional circumstances, and if certain criteria have been fulfilled which are consistent with the underlying exceptionality principle. CPR 44.18 provides, inter alia, that the court may make a costs capping order if there is a substantial risk that without such an order costs will be disproportionately incurred, and it is not satisfied that that risk can be adequately controlled by case management directions and by detailed assessment of costs. Eady J. in *Peacock v MGN Ltd* [2009] EWHC 769 (QB) was inhibited from making an order in a case which otherwise would have been ideally suited to it both by the exceptionality principle and by the fact that he was satisfied that the risk of disproportionality could be adequately controlled by the costs judge at detailed assessment. (As a footnote, it is interesting to record that on July 30, 2010 Master Campbell, the Costs Judge, who—unlike Eady J.—saw the without prejudice save as to costs correspondence, upheld the claimant's solicitors' 100 per cent success fee, and ruled that the solicitors' costs were reasonably and proportionately incurred because they had made an early offer which had been rejected by the defendant).

CHAPTER 38

## APPEAL

SECTION 1. GENERAL PRINCIPLES

**Application for permission to appeal.** *Note 3.* For an example of a libel case **38.1** where permission to appeal was granted on the basis that there was some other compelling reason why the appeal should be heard see *North London Mosque Trust v Policy Exchange* [2010] EWCA Civ 526. The case has now settled.

SECTION 2. IMPROPER ADMISSION OR REJECTION OF EVIDENCE

**Discretion of the trial judge.** *Note 51.* For an example of a case where a **38.6** judge's exercise of discretion was overturned, see *Desmond v Bower* [2009] EWCA Civ 857. In this interlocutory appeal (involving the admissibility of a taped telephone conversation) Hooper L.J. said at [57] "In my view this is not a case of interfering with a case management decision or interfering with some discretionary decision of the judge. It is taking steps to ensure a possible miscarriage of justice does not occur." See also Pill L.J. at [31]–[32].

**Admission of evidence.** *Note 56.* See *Desmond v Bower* at [2009] EWCA Civ **38.7** 667; [2010] E.M.L.R. 5 and [2009] EWCA Civ 857.

SECTION 4. MISDIRECTION

**Misdirection as to defamatory meaning.** *Note 80.* See *British Chiropractic* **38.12** *Association v Singh* [2010] EWCA Civ 350; [2011] E.M.L.R. 1, where the Court of Appeal overturned Eady J.'s conclusions on meaning and as to whether the words were fact or comment at a trial of preliminary issues.

**38.17**      **Miscellaneous misdirections.** *B (Children) (FC), Re* [2008] UKHL 35 is now
reported as *B (Children) (Care Proceedings: Standard of Proof) (CAFCASS
intervening), Re* [2009] A.C. 11.


SECTION 5. UNREASONABLE VERDICT

**38.22**      **Substituting an alternative verdict.** *Note 129.* Similarly, in *Flood v Times
Newspapers Ltd* [2010] EWCA Civ 804; [2010] E.M.L.R. 26, the Court of
Appeal substituted its own view for that of the judge on the issue of *Reynolds*
privilege. Their Lordships disagreed with the view taken by a different constitution of the court in *Galloway v Telegraph Group Ltd* [2006] EWCA Civ 17;
[2006] E.M.L.R. 11 at [68], namely that whether or not *Reynolds* privilege
applied was in effect an exercise of discretion. They considered that although the
issue involved a value judgment or balancing exercise, it raised a question of law
to which as a matter of principle there was only one answer: see Lord Neuberger
M.R. at [45]–[49] and Moore-Bick L.J. at [107].

*Note 130.* See fn.129 above for *Flood v Times Newspapers Ltd*, in particular
at [48].

**38.24**      **Verdict by judge alone.** *Note 136.* See *Flood v Times Newspapers Ltd* [2010]
EWCA Civ 804; [2010] E.M.L.R. 26. Their Lordships disagreed with the view
of the Court of Appeal in *Galloway v Telegraph Group Ltd* [2006] EWCA Civ
17; [2006] E.M.L.R. 11 at [68], namely that whether or not *Reynolds* privilege
applied was in effect an exercise of discretion. They considered that the issue was
one of law: see Lord Neuberger M.R. at [45]–[49] and Moore-Bick L.J. at
[107].

*Note 137.* See also *British Chiropractic Association v Singh* [2010] EWCA
Civ 350; [2011] E.M.L.R. 1 at [13]–[15] and [31], overturning Eady J.'s conclusions at a trial of the preliminary issues as to the meaning of the words
complained of and whether they were fact or comment. In *Fiddes v Channel
Four Television Corp* [2010] EWCA Civ 730; [2011] E.M.L.R. 3 the Court of
Appeal considered a decision by Tugendhat J., shortly before trial, to dispense
with a jury pursuant to section 69(1) of the Senior Court Act 1981. The Court
acknowledged the experience of the judge and his close familiarity with the case
at [11] but went on to say at [12], "Nonetheless, this does not mean that this court
should rubber stamp his decision. That would be fundamentally inconsistent with
the existence of a right to appeal . . . ." In the event, the appeal was dismissed,
since there was no error of law: [44]. In *Hayter v Fahie* [2008] EWCA Civ 1336
the Court of Appeal overturned an order granting summary judgment in a libel
action where the judge found malice even though he had not heard evidence from
the defendant. Sir Anthony May P. said at [24]

> "I consider that summary judgment should not have been given where there was, as I
> have explained, an issue of credibility as to Mr Fahie's state of mind both as to his
> understanding of the material meaning of what he wrote and as to his belief as to
> whether the statement was true in that meaning".

He reserved the question of whether a contested issue of malice could properly be determined in summary judgment proceedings, accepting that it might in theory be possible, but not where a real issue turned on the defendant's state of mind and a credibility judgment was required [23].

APPENDIX 1

## Forms and Precedents

Add:
**A1.6 to A1.9:** These forms should not be used without a careful prior reading of *Terry (formerly LNS) v Persons Unknown* **[2010] EWHC 119 (QB); [2010] E.M.L.R. 16.** It may be thought unlikely that an injunction in the form proposed at A1.9 (see in particular the privacy provision at para.2 of the body of the model order) would now be granted. For a discussion of *Terry*, see ch.27 above and in particular fn.139. There is no doubt that any applicant seeking wide-ranging derogations from the principle of open justice will in future be required to justify them in the most cogent terms.

APPENDIX 3

## Damages Awards

## Part 2: Non-jury Damages awards from 2000

Add:
A3.36A Gregg v O'Gara [2008] EWHC 658 (QB)
A3.36B Coad v Cruze [2009] EWHC 3782 (QB)
A3.36C Levi v Bates [2009] EWHC 1495 (QB)
A3.36D Emlick v Gulf News, unreported, July 23, 2009
A3.36E Warren v Madugqu, unreported, July 27, 2009
A3.36F Bloom v Robinson-Millar, unreported, October 7, 2009
A3.36G Supreme Events Ltd v Anderson, unreported, December 17, 2009
A3.36H Berezovsky v Russian State Television [2010] EWHC 476 (QB)
A3.36I Bryce v Barber, unreported, July 26, 2010
A3.36J Metropolitan International Schools Ltd v Designtechnica Corp [2010] EWHC 2411 (QB)
A3.36K Phillips v Kordowski, unreported, October 12, 2010

## Part 3: Compensation awards under the Offer of Amends Scheme (ss.2–4 Defamation Act 1996)

Add:
A3.42A Bowman v MGN Ltd [2010] EWHC 895 (QB)

## Part 2: Non-jury Damages awards (from 2000)

Add A3.36A
**Gregg v O'Gara [2008] EWHC 658 (QB)**
The claimant was head of the West Yorkshire Police Homicide and Major Enquiry team which was involved in the 2006 investigation into the Yorkshire Ripper hoax letters. This

was a case review of the hoaxes which had misled the police investigation of the 1978 and 1979 murders, and led to the conviction of John Humble for perverting the course of justice in March 2006. The defendant published a series of allegations in an email and on websites, which suggested that the claimant had knowingly brought about the conviction of an innocent man (i.e. Humble), and had been party to tampering with DNA evidence and mistreating the accused during the investigation. The defence relied upon was justification. The claimant applied for summary judgment on the basis that there was no real prospect of the defence succeeding. The claimant showed that the defamatory allegations complained of were indisputably false. He relied upon the fact that John Humble had admitted to the 1970s hoaxes and pleaded guilty, and had continued to assert his responsibility for the hoaxes after he was convicted. The defendant had posted a letter on his own website from John Humble in which Humble had admitted responsibility. The claimant had played no part in the forensic process leading to the conviction of Humble and his only involvement in the police station interviewing process had been to monitor it remotely. The evidence that there had been substantial internet publication in the jurisdiction was uncontradicted. There was no credible evidence to support the plea of justification and no other viable defence. The judge awarded the claimant £50,000.

Add A3.36B

**Coad v Cruze** [2009] EWHC 3782 (QB)

The claimant was a Conservative councillor. She brought claims against two members of a local political organisation over libels contained in an election leaflet distributed in 2007 and a non-election political leaflet published in 2008. The first defendant compromised the action. The second defendant made an unsuccessful application to adjourn the trial of damages, judgment having been entered in default. The judge found that the pleaded meanings contended for by the claimant were unsustainable. He assessed damages on the basis of the meanings that he had determined, namely that there were reasonable grounds to suspect that the Electoral Commission was investigating the claimant for suspected election expense irregularities and that there were strong grounds to suspect voting fraud on the part of the claimant. Although the defence of justification had been struck out, the second defendant had persisted in his allegations. Evidence of publication was lacking, but the judge accepted that the leaflets had been distributed in the claimant's ward and must at least have been read by a few hundred constituents. The admissible evidence as to distress was extremely limited. However, the second defendant had never apologised or offered a retraction. The judge awarded £15,000.

Add A3.36C

**Levi v Bates** [2009] EWHC 1495 (QB)

The claimant, a former director of Leeds United Football Club, brought a claim in relation to comments published in three match programmes for club home fixtures and in a letter to club members by the defendant chairman of the club, Ken Bates. The defendant had referred to the claimant's behaviour as devious and dishonourable. The defendant relied on defences of meaning, fair comment, qualified privilege and justification. The judge determined that the allegations in their actual meanings could not be justified and that whilst the allegations were in the nature of comment, the substratum of fact which underlay them was insufficient for the defence to succeed. Qualified privilege protected the defendant's letter but the match programmes were distributed to those with no immediate interest in club affairs, such as corporate guests, PR people and visiting fans. The defendant had sought to justify the allegations at a public trial lasting many days. The gratuitous inclusion of personal address details in one of the match programmes was an aggravating factor. The judge awarded £50,000 in respect of the three match programmes where the defences had failed, and subdivided that award publication by publication.

Add A3.36D
**Emlick v Gulf News**, unreported, July 23, 2009
The claimant was a property developer in the United Arab Emirates. He brought a claim
in relation to an article published in a newspaper based in the UAE in April 2008 but sued
only in relation to the damage caused by the publication in England and Wales. He
pleaded that the article meant that he was an unscrupulous property developer who had
defrauded investors and evaded those pursuing him. The publisher did not take part in the
proceedings but asserted in writing to the court that UAE was the correct jurisdiction and
that publication data suggested that there were only 100 readers of the publication in
England and Wales. The claimant's case on the extent of publication was that he had been
contacted by dozens of people based within the jurisdiction who had read the article and
relied on its reproduction on fourteen third party websites—republications for which the
judge held the defendant responsible. The judge accepted that the claimant had been
subject to a serious and damaging libel and awarded £25,000 damages. If the whole
publication had been within the jurisdiction he would have awarded £100,000.

Add A3.36E
**Warren v Madugqu**, unreported, July 27, 2009
The defendant, otherwise known as Herbie Hyde, made a series of claims in a television
interview that the claimant, a boxing promoter, had manipulated boxers and bribed them
to give up titles. The specific allegation that the claimant complained of was that he had
dishonestly persuaded one boxer to retire and give up his title so that a younger boxer
promoted by the claimant would gain the title from him. The defendant took no part in the
proceedings and judgment in default was entered against him. The claimant contended
that the publication, particularly the allegation of bribery, had been a serious attack on his
integrity, as his promoter role required that he behaved fairly and honestly. The judge
awarded £35,000.

Add A3.36F
**Bloom v Robinson-Millar**, unreported, October 7, 2009
The claimant, an accountant, sued his neighbour over seven different publications which
alleged that he had committed serious criminal offences including fraud, perjury and
criminal damage in his role as director of the management company of the block of flats
in which both parties lived. The claimant and others had told the defendant that the
allegations were unfounded but she persisted in making them over many years. The
defendant's substantive defences were struck out prior to trial. The number and gravity of
the allegations, over a considerable period, justified a global damages award of £30,000.
The claimant was entitled to the law's protection from behaviour which was obsessive and
irrational and which reasonable people would have realised amounted to harassment.

Add A3.36G
**Supreme Events Ltd v Anderson**, unreported, December 17, 2009
The claimant was a wedding planning company which brought a claim in respect of an
internet publication which stated that it had been taken to court on numerous occasions
and that readers of the posting should therefore avoid dealing with it. The defendant
denied responsibility for publication but admitted that she had been aware of the statements in question. Under s.8 of the Defamation Act 1996 the Master summarily disposed
of the claim, awarding the maximum figure of £10,000 permitted under the statutory
scheme.

Add A3.36H
**Berezovsky v Russian State Television** [2010] EWHC 476 (QB)
The defendant broadcast a television programme which was available to satellite viewers
without subscription within the jurisdiction. The programme alleged that the claimant was

responsible for the murder of Alexander Litvinenko, who had died from polonium poisoning in London in November 2006. The claimant was awarded £150,000.

Add A3.36I

**Bryce v Barber**, unreported, July 26, 2010

The defendant, a chef, had fallen out with the claimant, a certified bailiff who was studying law at Stafford University. The defendant had posted an indecent image of a child on an internet social network site alongside a statement which suggested that the claimant was a paedophile. Judgment was entered against the defendant. The claimant adduced evidence on the assessment of damages that the posting had caused him great distress and would have been visible to more than 800 people. The judge found the posting to have been malicious. There was no apology or expression of remorse, and damages were assessed at £10,000.

Add A3.36J

**Metropolitan International Schools Ltd v Designtechnica Corp** [2010] EWHC 2411 (QB)

The claimant was a distance learning company based in the United Kingdom. It brought claims in respect of two separate internet forum threads, each of which discussed one of the claimant's products. The defendant was a US-based IT industry consumer affairs website operator. The forum threads alleged that there were reasonable grounds to suspect that the claimant offered courses which infringed copyright, were sold in a cavalier manner with improper and fraudulent credit checking procedures and were, in sum, a fraud. The forum threads were extensive, running to hundreds of webpages. The defendant took no part in the proceedings and judgment in default was entered against it, the claims against two other internet intermediaries having been either settled or resolved. On the assessment of damages the claimant chose not to rely on the presumption of falsity in its favour but adduced positive evidence refuting the allegations. The claim was only made in relation to damage sustained within the jurisdiction. There was evidence that the threads were accessed by readers within the jurisdiction, the claimant's business was over-whelmingly UK-based, and its courses were marketed there. The award was £50,000.

Add A3.36K

**Phillips v Kordowski**, unreported, October 12, 2010

The defendant ran a website which encouraged internet users to post statements anony-mously naming and shaming UK solicitors for shoddy work or disreputable conduct. The defendant did not attempt to verify the material which was uploaded to the website, but offered to remove postings if aggrieved subjects paid a £299 administration fee. The specific post on the website to which the claimant objected had received 50,000 hits. It alleged that the claimant was of dubious professional competence. In the absence of any substantive defence the claimant applied for summary judgment. The demand for payment to ensure that the libel was taken down was an aggravating factor. Damages were assessed at £17,500.

## Part 3: Compensation awards under the Offer of Amends Scheme (ss.2-4 Defamation Act 1996)

Add A3.42A

**Bowman v MGN Ltd** [2010] EWHC 895 (QB)

The claimant sued on articles published on the newspaper's website which suggested that he had had a romantic relationship with a fellow actor. Because the claimant was in a serious, committed relationship with another woman, the article would have been under-stood in a defamatory sense by those who knew of his relationship. The article was removed from the internet after 27 hours. The defendant offered an immediate apology and a correction was promptly published on the website. Compensation could not be agreed and an application was made for the court to determine compensation under s.3(5) of the Defamation Act 1996. It was part of the claimant's case that the journalist had been given the correct information before the article went live online. The court awarded the relatively modest sum of £4,250, a sum lower than without prejudice offers made to the claimant, for several reasons. Firstly, in the absence of concrete evidence as to the number of readers who would have understood the defamatory innuendo, a conservative approach to damages was appropriate. Secondly, the allegation was essentially celebrity gossip and there was no strong evidence of an adverse effect on the claimant's relationship. Thirdly, he had not proved that the pre-publication conversation alleged between the agent and the journalist had actually taken place. Fourthly, the mitigating effect of the newspaper's conduct was worth a 50% discount on the notional starting figure for damages, £8,500. However, the defendant was criticised by the judge for adopting a "take it or leave it" approach to its offers, rather than facilitating negotiation by answering enquiries from the claimant.